invisible
harmony

invisible harmony

Essays on Contemplation and Responsibility

Raimon Panikkar

Edited by Harry James Cargas

Fortress Press   Minneapolis

INVISIBLE HARMONY
Essays on Contemplation and Responsibility

Citations of sacred texts from Indian religious traditions are given in the form used in *The Vedic Experience,* trans. and ed. Raimundo Panikkar (Berkeley: University of California Press, 1977).

Interior design: ediType
Cover design: Cheryl Watson, Graphiculture

Library of Congress Cataloging-in-Publication Data

Panikkar, Raimundo, 1918-
    Invisible harmony : essays on contemplation and responsibility /
by Raimon Panikkar ; edited by Harry James Cargas.
        p.   cm.
    Includes bibliographical references.
    IBSN 0-8006-2609-5 (alk. paper)
    1. Theology.   2. Contemplation.   3. Christianity and other
religions.   4. Religions—Relations.   5. Religious pluralism.
I. Cargas, Harry J.   II. Title.
BR85.P25   1995
230–dc20   95-10456
                                                                CIP

The paper used in this publication meets the minimum requirements of American National Standard for Information Sciences—Permanence of Paper for Printed Library Materials, ANSI Z329.48-1984

Manufactured in the U.S.A.   AF 1-2609

99   98   97   96   95   1   2   3   4   5   6   7   8   9   10

Contents

Introduction

Harry James Cargas

It is important to recognize the tone of urgency with which Raimon Panikkar sets forth his ideas. As he writes in his most comprehensive volume, "I am convinced that we live in a state of human emergency that does not allow us to entertain ourselves with bagatelles of no relevance whatsoever. But I am equally convinced that precisely because of the seriousness of the human situation, more short-term solutions and technical stopgaps will not do."[1] His approach is perhaps best exemplified in his own description of the ideal style of the monk in his quest for perfection: "All that is not a ladder is ignored; all that is not the way falls apart."[2]

Panikkar is a Catholic priest who is also a Hindu, a Buddhist and a secularist. He was born in Barcelona, Spain (1918), of a Roman Catholic mother and a father who had come from India, a leader in the movement for India's independence, who very humbly left his native land because he saw that Mohandas Gandhi's efforts for freeing his nation from colonial bonds might be fragmented if Mr. Panikkar continued to be politically active.[3] Thus Raimon grew up in a double tradition—Catholic and Hindu—and later was absorbed by Buddhism and secularism as well. This places him in a unique position to put into practice his own golden rule of hermeneutics: that we describe the other in such a manner as he[4] is able to recognize himself in that description.[5] Panikkar, the man of many cultures, is capable of such descriptions to a remarkable degree. He is a man comfortable communicating in eleven languages. He types in six languages! This is said to illustrate his familiarity with many cultures from the inside. He is a citizen of India where he now spends half a year, the other half in Spain, since his retirement from the University of California in Santa Barbara (1987), where he was professor of Religious Studies. Panikkar earned the first of three doctorates when he received a Ph.D. in philosophy from the University of Madrid (1946) after having also studied at the Universities of Bonn and Barcelona.

Twelve years later he achieved a D.Sc. from the University of Madrid and in 1961 was awarded a Th.D. from the Lateran University in Rome. He has lectured in over a hundred universities worldwide and been on the faculty at Harvard, Union Theological Seminary, the International University of Social Studies (Rome), United Theological College (Bangalore), Theological Seminar (Madrid), and elsewhere including the University of California (Santa Barbara) from 1971 to 1987. Panikkar has produced 30 books, some 300 major articles and serves on numerous editorial boards for journals and encyclopedias in many nations.

A number of themes reappear in the books and articles published by Panikkar. Among these are mutual understanding, mythology, freedom, pain, creativity, sacrifice, faith, relationship, time and space, prayer, work, doing and being, and responsibility. At the risk of appearing simplistic, it might be useful to observe that all of these are discussed from the broad perspective of a trinitarian reality. This does not imply a limited Christian worldview—that would be a false understanding of Panikkar's vision of ultimate meaning which he labors to explore. Rather it is more accurate to say that he sees a trinitarian basis of which the Christian vision is a part.

(One brief personal note: the bases for this Introduction include not only books and articles by Panikkar in several languages, and a number of his lectures which I have been able to attend in various parts of the United States, but also six intensive days of audio-taped interviews with him that I conducted in his home in Santa Barbara, California.)[6]

The cornerstone of Panikkar's vision is integrative. His technique for resolving apparent conflicts is to find new concepts which bring unity to seemingly opposing or exclusive ideas. Consequently neologisms necessarily abound in his work. It might be best to begin with what he calls his cosmotheandric view of reality, a term which unites cosmic, divine and human dimensions on a level not of equality but of identity: "These three are one,"[7] he insists. However, as Panikkar warned in regard to another interviewer's question, "The very nature of reality is not monolithic. Not even Ultimate Reality."[8]

This has enormous implications and is nowhere more impressively stated than in his insights under the general heading of religious pluralism. The real world, concludes Panikkar, is a world of variety and complexity. In his words, "Pluralism penetrates into the very heart of the ultimate reality."[9] His application of this principle to religions is stated thus: "Each religion has unique features and presents mutually incommensurable insights. Each statement of a basic experience is to be evaluated on its proper terrain and merits, because the very nature of truth is pluralistic."[10] If truth is pluralistic, we rightly ask, how do we communicate with others who stand on another truth which is not ours? We must dialogue, Panikkar tells us, but not in a usual, dialectical way. Dialectical dialogue, which exists to convert another or to know the other,[11] must be superseded by what Panikkar labels dialogical dialogue which is "opening myself to another so that he might speak and reveal my myth that I cannot know by myself because it is transparent to me, self-evident."[12] The other person, therefore, in revealing to me my myth assists me in a most paradoxical manner. Panikkar reminds us that "A myth is something in which you believe, without believing that you believe in it."[13] One who aids us in demythicizing our myth actually forces us to establish new myths. People cannot live without myths nor without changing myths[14] and in dialogical dialogue we are able to experience this truth.

It is crucial, Panikkar observes, that we acquire a global awareness in the cosmotheandric dimension of our destiny.[15] And it is "Only dialogue (which) makes pluralism, co-existence, democracy, even justice and peace possible."[16] But how to dialogue? We read that "Formulating the rules for a meeting of cultures is an urgent need of our times."[17] Perhaps a key to approaching such a formulation is Panikkar's insistence on the necessity of the relational, whether we refer to the cosmos, the theos or the anthropos. He writes that "To speak of man as an individual is, in my opinion, totally insufficient and eventually wrong."[18] Several times he repeats the distinction between the individual and the person.[19] The perfection of the human individual is not the fullness of human nature; it is not nature, but personhood; it is not the essence of humanity, but the incommunicable and unique existence of the person."[20] And again: "Everything in the world is interrelated and . . . beings themselves are nothing but relations."[21] Among his most beautiful instructions, Panikkar tells us several times that unlike the King James translation of Luke which says that the kingdom of God is *within* you, or the New English Bible which has God's kingdom *among* you, he finds it more correct to know that the kingdom of God is *between* you, which is what the Greek preposition *entos* means and which clearly emphasized the relational nature of both person and God.[22]

However, there is not much more that Panikkar says firmly about God. He makes certain observations about the trinitarian nature of the Deity, but more in a general sense than specifically about what might be labeled the orthodox Christian God.[23] His approach to this subject is closer to that of the Buddha than it is to most theologians. In an essay titled "Nirvana and the Nature of the Absolute"[24] Panikkar explains the deep rooted theism behind the Buddha's lack of reference to God. Buddha perceived that God is beyond all possible naming. "He tells us that any speaking of the name of God, that any talk about God, and even all thought, are just so many blasphemies."[25] But Panikkar observes, the silence of the Buddha regarding God is not by way of answer to any question. By not responding, the Buddha "puts the question in question."[26] There is no doubt of Panikkar's admiration for the Buddha here: "If there is a transcendence, it will take care of itself; that is the Buddha's message in summary."[27] For Panikkar, God is not a substance, has no name, "but he is a question, he is a simple pronoun and even an interrogative pronoun: *Who?*"[28] One page later we read what may be regarded as Panikkar's fullest intuition about God: He writes that "God is immanent and transcendent, existent and non-existent, and at the same time he is not. There is nothing more to be said. God is that about which there can be no talk."

However Panikkar will talk about the trinitarian structure of all creation, a structure the monopoly of which belongs not to Christianity nor to the divinity. He writes of every bit of reality having the trinitarian imprint.[29] Hence his cosmotheandric principle of Gods, Men and Cosmos. He indicates that "I know of no culture where heaven-earth-hell, past-present-future, Gods-Men-World, and pronouns I-you-it, and even the intellectual triad of yes, no, and their embrace, are not found in one form or another."[30]

It may be helpful at this point to refer to Panikkar's book *The Trinity and World Religion* wherein the author extrapolates three forms of spirituality: action, love, knowledge. These may also be identified as iconolatry ("idolatry has a place in every true religion"),[31] personalism (it is our relationships with God that are important—but it is a refinement of iconolatry)[32] and *advaita* (the experience that God is neither one nor many, that monism and dualism are equally false).[33] This Indian solution to one of the oldest of philosophic problems, that of the One and the Many, is perhaps best expressed in one of Panikkar's footnotes in his major work, *Myth, Faith and Hermeneutics,* where he explains that Advaita Vedanta "understands itself as the culmination of all religions and philosophies insofar as it leads to and interprets the 'ultimate experience' of non-duality, i.e., the essential non-separability of the Self (*atman*) and God (*brahman*)."[34]

This has significant import for the development of Panikkar's thought on pluralism and the relational aspects of persons, nations, cultures, religions. As he notes in a speech the title of which includes a reference to the Tower of Babel, he shows us how "man becomes aware of *both* the need for diversity and the need for unity."[35] In this talk he says that the question of the One and the Many may be the central question in the human mind. Some resolve it in favor of monism, others prefer dualism but Panikkar suggests the more accurate reflection is in *advaita*, neither one nor two but a non-dualism in which a tensile polarity is maintained.[36] Here he goes beyond what we know as Process Theology because those committed to that view "want to be universal from a perspective which is seen as universal only from within the system."[37] The standpoint must not be from the perspective of my Christianity, your Judaism or her Islamic tradition. "To elaborate a Philosophy of Religion we need to take religions seriously and, further, to experience them from within, to believe, in one way or another, in what these religions say."[38] The discrepancies which appear in world religions are fundamental and felt so acutely because they are ultimate. Then "if we take religious pluralism seriously we cannot avoid asserting that truth itself is pluralistic—at least for the time being, which is our being in time, and one on which we need to rely on for our very thinking."[39]

These last words may require some comments on Panikkar's conception of time, one of the most crucial insights to his understanding of reality and meaning. He elaborates his thesis best in an essay titled "The End of History: The Threefold Structure of Human Time-Consciousness."[40] A necessarily inadequate summary of his fifty-eight page article will have to suffice. Time is to be measured not only horizontally, but vertically as well, not only in duration but in depth. He notes three modes of consciousness which are neither mutually exclusive nor dialectically opposed. They are kairologically related. He is willing, for the sake of discussion, to distinguish three moments in history: the nonhistorical, the historical, and the trans-historical. Briefly, "When the past is the paradigm through which we experience time, we have the nonhistorical moment (memory and faith are central); when it is the future, historical consciousness prevails (the will and hope are predominant); and when past and future are lived in terms of the present, we share in the trans-historical experience of reality (the intellect and love become fundamental)."[41]

Before the invention of writing, humans had no way to project all of their creations into the future. The past had them in its grip; tradition was paramount. Time comes from the beginning: *Mythos*. With writing, progress becomes key. Time is seen to march forward. The future belongs to God as God belongs to the future: *History*.

But when Man split the atom, the apparently indestructible elements of reality became vulnerable, the past broke, the future collapsed. Only the present is left: *Mystical*.[42] Time must then be seen not as the construct of culture but as the rhythm of nature. Time is not there for us to build a society but rather to "enjoy." The ideal, mystical life might be the one lived in, to put it awkwardly, a succession of what Elie Wiesel would call "eternal moments."[43] An example that Panikkar gives us of what we might call "other-worldly time" is seen in the life of certain monks for whom all hurry loses its meaning. Efficiency and purpose fade away.[44] The person who lives in this way *is,* not *does* or *has.* Being can be unified. Doing and Having entail multiplicity.[45]

Being is "a kind of total spontaneity" in the Hindu formulation, spontaneity having an ultimate value for Panikkar.[46] The Indian effort is not thinking and being but being and wording: "being and letting being be; being and letting being escape. It is being and letting being express itself, without the reflection of self-consciousness, without going back to the being from which you have departed. It is a kind of total spontaneity. Being explodes itself into being, into word, into the expression of that being...Being is just...explosion!"[47]

Panikkar nowhere specifically links such explosion with creativity but the implication is clearly there. And creation is absolutely related to sacrifice in Panikkar's vision. Since God had not primal matter from which to create, God had to create from the Self. "Creation then is a sacrifice, a giving of oneself, a creative immolation."[48] A few pages later we read that "By sacrifice the world is made and maintains itself in existence; by sacrifice the entire cosmos returns to its source."[49] In the Vedic tradition, the creator was exhausted by his creative act and it is through the sacrifice which is offered by his creatures that he is able to regain his strength. Panikkar stresses the import of this in his book on worship when he writes that "sacrifice is by its nature a theandric act, an act in which God and man have to work together in order that the world be maintained; it is a cosmic act, for the subsistence of the world depends upon it. God alone cannot perform the sacrifice, he requires human cooperation; man alone is impotent to sacrifice, let alone to make the sacrifice acceptable, he requires divine help, divine grace."[50] Elsewhere he reminds us of the Vedic "general understanding of life itself as a kind of sacrifice."[51]

Spontaneous worship for Panikkar, then, is really a part of Being rather than of Doing. Spontaneous worship must be seen as the explosion of Being. Panikkar gives a theological basis for Viktor Frankl's psychological observation that yearning for God is natural in every human person.[52] And the very notion of person insists on the correlative term: responsibility. Obviously this is no cliché idea. We opened with an acknowledgment of Panikkar's sense of urgency. We return to that in his words about the duty we have to each other as fully human beings. Nor should we overlook the echoes of others which Panikkar's thoughts on this recall: Teilhard's encouragement that my vocation is nothing less than to complete the universe;[53] Kazantzakis' recognition that I am a watershed of history, the culmination of all of the past and the beginning of all of the future[54] and Par Lagerkvist's question, which suggests so much regarding both question and responsibility, "Lord over all heavens, all worlds, all fates, what have you meant by me?"[55] Panikkar, at one point, recalls a Vedic perspective when he tells us that "every human birth modified the universal *status quo*. Man must thus re-establish the equilibrium his existence has disrupted."[56] The obligations we have are "constitutive of human life, the debt to the gods,...to the ancestors and to humanity."[57] His most emphatic words on this subject are these: "I feel a cosmic responsibility because the entire universe depends on the positive handling of the *karma* at my disposal. I am the connecting link between the past and future between myself and others, and this on a cosmic and universal level from which not a single being is excluded."[58] In a later publication, Panikkar brings into harmony several of his melodies which we have seen thus far. "To be engaged in the perfection of the cosmos is not vanity, but the fullest realization of the person. The crisis of our contemporary human period, and at the same moment its great opportunity and vocation, is to realize that the human microcosm and the material microcosm are not two separate worlds, but one and the same cosmotheandric reality, in which precisely the third 'divine' dimension is the unifying link between the other two dimensions of reality. Otherwise, to withdraw into the business of saving one's soul becomes sheer egoism or cowardice, and to fling oneself into the task of saving the world sheer vanity or presumption."[59]

We cannot help but reflect on the "restored" importance of the human being. This "restored" refers to the steady psychological shrinking of Man in his own view of himself, since Copernicus and Galileo and Darwin and our astronauts ever reducing us in comparative stature, ever reminding us that materially we are not the center of the cosmos. But as Process Philosophy, Process Theology, the scholarship of Mircea Eliade, the fiction of Elie Wiesel, to name but a few highlights, teach, each of us is a primary value, an ultimate being because each of us participates in being and Being. And this is celebrated by Panikkar, if you will, in his commentary on freedom. As he writes, "in one way or another freedom is always deemed man's goal."[60] He follows this up several paragraphs later by saying that the goal of Man is liberation and "If religion claims to save man, it can do so only by putting him on the path to realizing his destiny."[61] And later: "Non-free beings have no future, they have only a fate."[62]

But how are we free? Strictly speaking, the fullest freedom is only found outside of time[63] (perhaps we can speculate on another occasion how the subject of our dream life may enter here). In our waking world Panikkar maintains, with his emphasis on freedom *for* as well as freedom *from,* that the truer the freedom, the fewer the options. "Freedom is an absence of choices," he told me in our extended interview. "It is a freedom to follow our destinies. We can say yea or nay as we discover our places in the cosmotheandric structure as we live to fulfill Pindar's almost overwhelming admonition: Become what you are."

The freest act for Panikkar is the act of prayer, contemplation, worship. It is fully creative and sacrificial. "Now what saves is by definition *sacrifice,* that is, participation in the cosmos and primordial act through which the world .is 're-made,' comes to its final destruction, remedies in inverse the act that gave birth to the universe. . . ."[64] For Raimon Panikkar, Catholic priest, Hindu, Buddhist, and secularist, the fully free act of worship is the fully necessary act by which each of us fulfills our part in preserving a cosmotheandric harmony.

invisible
harmony

Chapter 1

The Contemplative Mood
A Challenge to Modernity

What is the use of the study of the Vedas
for one who has seen the self?
—Paingala Upanishad, 9

Be still and know
—Psalm 46:10

The Contemplative Mood radically challenges some of the basic assumptions of modern Western society. Its stress on spontaneity, desirelessness, delight in the momentary, indifference to wealth, prestige, success, sets it at odds with the modern labor pathos. Truly, to be a contemplative in this day and age is to be "a rebours," against the grain. Even so, there has been a resurgence of interest in recent years in contemplative life, which has even reached the curricula of modern universities. In the West, probably through the influence of the East, contemplation seems to be regaining a positive value. The return of the Sacred in Western society has been analyzed and predicted since the First World War and has again come to the fore after the second one. Yet Contemplative Studies is dangerous. It represents a Trojan Horse whose belly hides at least five powerful enemies of present-day academia and modern life in general. Whether these enemies are mere antidotes to or possibly the saviors of modern culture will not be our concern here. The question whether Contemplative Studies may help the University to again become real Academia will remain an open one. The *study* of Contemplation is a risky adventure, as the masters of traditional spiritualities have affirmed. Perhaps

This chapter is a revised version of an article that first appeared in *Cross Currents* 31 (Fall 1981): 261–72, under the same title. It was originally written for the Merton-Maritain Symposium, "Spirituality in a Secularized Society," held in Louisville, Kentucky, September 1980.

3

those who most resist Contemplative Studies have instinctively a better grasp of what it actually entails than those who are drawn to it for its novelty alone. Contemplation is an ambivalent word. It spans the opposites: its meaning embraces the highest and noblest of human activities as well as other not so exalted attitudes, including that which may be plainly called a vice of the human spirit.

Without attempting to say what contemplation is or how it may be defined, one trait emerges as constant: contemplation is something definitive, something which has to do with the very end of life and is not a means to anything else. A contemplative act is done for its own sake. It rests on itself. Contemplation cannot be manipulated in order to gain something else. It is not a stage in this sense. It has no further intentionality. It requires that innocence in which the very will to achieve contemplation becomes an obstacle to it. The contemplative act is a free act, unconditioned except by its own impulse or *svadhā*, as the Ṛg Veda would say.[1] The contemplative simply "sits," simply "is."

The Contemplative Mood calls forth certain images: Socrates eagerly learning a new tune on his flute the night before he was to die; Luther deciding to plant an apple tree in the morning of the day on which the world would come to an end; St. Louis Gonzaga continuing to play during recreation time even if he learned his death would come that very night; the delight of the Zen Master in watching the struggle of an ant in spite of the fact that he's hanging over an abyss, tied by a rope that is soon to be cut. These are examples of the contemplative attitude, whether it is called mindfulness, awareness, enlightenment, concentration, or contemplation.

This attitude runs counter to the trends of modern civilization, be they "religious" or "secular," although I would not use these two words in this sense, for the secular as well as the religious can be sacred and both can also be profane.

It seems in fact that there are five great incentives in contemporary society: (1) the Heavens above for the believers, (2) the History ahead for the progressivists, (3) the Labor to be performed for the realists, (4) the Conquest of the Big for the intelligent and (5) the Ambition of Success for almost everyone. These five incentives are radically questioned by the Contemplative Mood. For contemplation stresses the *hic*, the *nunc*, the *actus,* the hidden *centrum* and the inner *pax;* not the elsewhere, the later, the result, the greatness of external actions or the confirmation of the majority. "It is today," said the Rabbi of Nazareth on the Cross, "that you shall be with me in Paradise."[2]

I will attempt in this chapter to give a cross-cultural picture of the problem, outlining with these five points the crucial ways in which contemplation challenges and threatens modern Man's basic assumptions.[3]

The first of these five threats challenges traditional religiousness, which is all too often satisfied with postponing to another world the real values of life.

The second contests the cardinal dogma of a certain secularism which has simply transposed on to a temporal future the ideals of the first mentality.

The third is a praxis directly upsetting the pivotal values of the modern, mainly pan-economic society.

The fourth appears as an extraneous and unwelcome interference with the inner exigencies of the technological world.

The fifth directly questions the prevalent anthropological idea that human fulfillment entails the victory of one over others so that victims are the necessary condition for one's sense of achievement.

The Heavens Above (The Here versus the Elsewhere)

If you act for the sake of a reward in a heaven, you may get what you desire, but this is not a contemplative act—i.e., a loving act, the whole concern of which is for the thing being done, with no preoccupation with acquiring perfection or attaining reward. When contemplatives eat, they eat; when they sleep, they sleep; when they pray, they pray, as the masters remind us. They act *sunder warumbe,* "without a why," as Meister Eckhart would say.[4] The contemplative cannot conceive of what is meant by an *after*-life, as if the life now witnessed were not life, the Life, the thing itself. According to most traditions, the contemplative experiences reality, God, heaven, Brahman, *mokṣa, nirvāṇa, satori,* realization, the truth, being, or nothingness here below, in the very act that is being performed, in the very situation that is being experienced. Contemplative life is already a heavenly status, a final life, as the mystics will say. St. Isaac of Syria, a desert monk in the eastern Christian hesychast tradition, will speak of the inner chamber of the heart that is the chamber of heaven: "For the two are the same and one entrance leads to both."[5] And if this is not the case, if there still remains something to desire, you have not yet reached contemplation.

"Master, three years have I followed you: what have I found?" "Have you lost something?" was the reply of the Hindu guru.[6] "Philip, he who sees me sees the Father," says the Christian Gospel.[7]

Nothing else is needed. You do not need to go anywhere. *Nirvāṇa* is *saṃsāra* and *saṃsāra* is *nirvāṇa*, affirms Mahāyāna Buddhism.[8] "And if I have to go to hell, it does not matter; heaven is this, it is you, it is here," sings that great Muslim woman, a flute player converted into a hermit, Rabi'a al-'Adawiyya.[9]

A desire for anything, even if it be the desire not to desire, is already a sign that you lack the contemplative spirit, that you have not attained that holy indifference so much stressed by the Ignatian and Vedantic spiritualities, which transcends all differences to the point that the contemplative is seen to go "beyond good and evil," as the Upanishad says.[10] This last phrase should be correctly understood.[11] If you do something which you think is wrong, then of course you are not beyond good and evil. One may question that it is possible to go beyond good and evil but, granted this possibility, the concepts of good and evil are no longer adequate to describe an act which has supposedly transcended both. "These two thoughts do not occur (to the realized): I have done evil, I have done good," clarifies the same Upanishadic text.[12] The New Innocence is not something that can be claimed at will.[13]

Contemplatives do not need the Heavens above because to contemplatives everything is sacred: they treat "sacred" things as profane. They eat the forbidden bread, burn holy images, put their feet on the linga and do not keep the detailed precepts of the sabbath. Why? Because they treat all profane things as sacred. The contemplative's heart is a "heart burning for every creature, for Men, birds, animals, for demons and all creation," as the Christian desert fathers will affirm.[14] "So in heaven as it is on earth" is an ancient prayer.[15] And he who discovered this truth "has grasped the secrets of the spiritual path," affirms Ibn Al-'Arabī, the great Ṣūfī mystic.[16] "If you see the Buddha, kill him!" says the Mahāyāna tradition.[17] *If you meet the Christ, eat him!* could be a Christian *mahāvākya,* or "great utterance."

Contemplation is not worried about the morrow; it does not concern itself with reaching *nirvāṇa* or conquering heaven. This is why the contemplative does not quarrel about doctrines. The mystic will accept the given doctrines, but his faith will not entirely depend upon them. The faith of the mystic goes deeper than the demands of a belief-system. Doctrines are crutches, or at best channels or glasses, but do not encompass walking, the water or the sight implied in these traditional metaphors. Dogma is hypothesis, "opinion" (in the original sense of this word), not true seeing, *theoria.*[18] "Truth can only be apprehended by itself," as Nicholas of Cusa said,[19] echoing Meister

Eckhart; this was repeated by Ramana Maharshi and so many others before and after—by each independently because in each case it is an immediate discovery. Any affirmation which is based on something other than itself cannot be absolutely true. The contemplative knows that *"no me mueve, mi Dios, para quererte / el cielo que me tienes prometido"* (I am not moved to love you, my God, / for the heaven you have promised me), as the Spanish contemplative of the Golden Age used to say, struggling to show the positive side of "quietism," re-enacting what the *Gītā* and Buddhist texts had said centuries before: you should neither be careless nor careful because you are neither "less" nor "full," but free and thus carefree.[20] *Svarga kāmo yajeta,*[21] sacrifice for the sake of going to heaven, is a great thing, says the *Mīmāṁsā,* but it is not this way that you will attain *mokṣa* (liberation), adds the Vedānta.

Modern Men may not believe in a God who rewards and punishes, and not care much about a Heaven above, but most modern actions are done with an attentive eye on the moods of Mammon, who punishes and rewards, and who is not above but "behind." Contemplatives are impervious to such incentives. They have discovered in their hearts that *makarioi,* happy, are the poor in spirit.[22] Money is simply not an allurement to contemplatives. It is not that they despise money; they are simply not at all attached to it. They do not *need it* in the same way as does the modern Man. And for this reason a civilization that requires money in order to live is anti-contemplative.

The History Ahead (The Now versus the Later)

Secular Man has to build the City on Earth. But this takes time. That is to say, if temporality is all there is, the City of Man is always the City of the Future, because the present city is far from being what it should be.[23] Modern life is preparation for *later,* for the time to come. Credit, growth, education, children, savings, insurance, business—all is geared for later, oriented toward the possibilities of a future which will forever remain uncertain. We are always on the go, and the quicker the better, in order to gain "time." Without planning, strategy, preparation and purpose for the future, our lives are inconceivable. Temporality haunts Modernity; the time factor is the aspect of nature to be overcome. Acceleration is the great discovery of modern science. Individually and collectively, our lives are all bent forward, straining ahead, running toward the goal, the prize, in unrelenting competition. We must (for we are forced to) keep abreast of all that is new, and be able to foresee what will come next. We must make ourselves, our fellow people, our nation, even our world by marching toward the Future. We are speeding toward the "Great Event." Soteriology has become eschatology, sacred as well as profane.

The contemplative stops this rush of time in the world. Temporality stops for the contemplative—or, rather, it turns toward itself, and thus the tempiternal reality emerges. *Tempiternity* is neither an everlasting time nor a timeless eternity, but the very soul or core of time, as it were. It is not experience of a past regained or a future suddenly grasped in prophetic ecstasis; on the contrary, it is the discovery of the *irreducibility of the present,* the fullness of time in the now. Tempiternity is timefullness.[24] Contemplation is not interested in the later but in this irreducible *now.* And even when the contemplative is actively engaged in something which concerns the future, the act is performed with such absorbing interest in the present that the action which follows is truly unpredictable. The contemplative act is creative, a new beginning, not a conclusion. If you are a contemplative, you may become a Samaritan on the way and come late to the meeting, or just remain playing with some trifle which happened to catch your fancy. Ultimately you have no way to go, no place to reach. All pilgrimage (*yātrā, tīrtha*) is renounced. As Kabīr sang, "Going on endless pilgrimages, the world died, / exhausted from so much bathing!"[25] To the mystic only the tempiternal present counts and is experienced as real. The meaning of your life does not rest only in its final achievement, just as the sense of a symphony is not merely in the finale. Each moment is decisive. Your life will not be unfulfilled even if you do not reach your golden age but meet with an accident along the road. Every day is a life and each day is enough in itself.[26]

Contemplation reveals the fullness of everything that is, in the very fact of its being what is really *is.* "Man has to be happy because he is," says Ramón Llull at the beginning of his bulky *Book of Contemplation.*[27] Happiness seems to be the contemplative's lot because the true contemplative expects nothing for the morrow. Time has been redeemed, overcome or denied. *Tolle tempus,* says Eckhart in his Latin commentary on the Gospel of John, *occidens est oriens.* Take away time, and evening is morning—or in more pregnant terms, "west is east."[28] Here the world is what the "visionary shoemaker" Jacob Boehme would describe as *das Freudenspiel der ewigen Gebärung,* "the joyful play of eternal generation."[29] The Kingdom, *nirvāṇa* (which is already here) is also now—though not in a Newtonian sense. If you are a realized person, realization has brought you nothing. Only (before) you did not know it. You were already there, or rather, you were already *that*.[30] The costly perfume could have been sold and the money given to the poor, but the lover was justified because she performed "a beautiful act" with pure spontaneity, as Jesus implied when he defended her.[31] "Rejoice with me," sings the blind Baul singer: "I cannot see darkness." Nor can we see the light—only the illumined world.

A dangerous and risky doctrine indeed. Contemplatives are "above" or "outside" society, as so many texts affirm, but they can lose their bearings. They can also be abused by people, who take advantage of contemplative indifference and unconcern, for exploitation and injustice. In the end, however, their "perfect joy" seems to be untarnished by any event, as the Franciscan tradition describes.[32]

Modern Man is always in a hurry to get to the "next thing," whereas for the contemplative there is no fundamental difference between heaven above or a history ahead. They are both postponements: you "ingress" into heaven or "progress" into history. Whether it be individualistic capitalism or State capitalism, the traditional belief in heaven or the Marxist belief in history, the difference between a profit which is above and one that lies ahead is one of degree and direction only. The attitudes they encourage are distressingly similar. If Marxism in the West is seen as a (Christian) apostasy, in the East it appears as a (Christian) heresy. If Christianity in the West is seen as alienation, in the East it appears as the first step towards a perfect socialization. Marxism and Christianity are truly cousins.

The contemplative attitude does not follow such a pattern. When you have to play the secular game, you do it honestly but without worshipping the rules. Each moment is full in itself and at most begets the next: *"Caminante no hay camino, se hace camino al andar"* ("Wayfarer there is no way, the way is made in the going"), sings Antonio Machado.[33] Each moment contains the whole universe. Continuity is not a solid thing, not a substance: *anātmavāda,* as a certain Buddhist tradition will say. "Leben geht hin mit Verwandlung," sang Rainer Maria Rilke in the *Elegies:* "Our lives are lived in transformation."[34] There is no sense of frustration if you do not accumulate merits, power, knowledge, or money because every moment is a unique gift and complete in itself. *Khano ve mā upaccagā* ("Do not let the instant escape").[35] It is obvious that this tempiternal *now* that the contemplative experiences is not just the crossing of a hurried past and an accelerated future. It is rather a cross that has in itself all the past because, having died, it has risen, and all the future because, although not yet dawned, it conserves all the luminosity of a hidden sun that can appear in any corner of the horizon.

It is not by escaping from time—even if that were possible—that the contemplative discovers the tempiternal. It is rather by integrating it completely with the vertical dimension which constantly intrudes on the horizontal temporal line. Tempiternity is not the absence but the fullness of time, but this fullness is certainly not just the future.

The Labor Pathos (The Act versus the Product)

It looks as if the modern addiction to labor is becoming an epidemic for humankind. You have to labor because apparently your naked existence has no value; therefore you must justify your life by its usefulness. You have to be useful by contributing to the welfare of a society that has ceased to be a community. You cannot afford to be an ornament; you have to become an asset. It is not just that you have a role to perform; it is not your *svadharma* that is expected of you;[36] it is not that you fit into a more or less dynamic pattern, as is the case in most traditional societies. You are expected to produce, to make something which is not you, something which can be objectified, and through money made available and interchangeable. You have to earn what you consume, in addition to your reputation and privileges, or you will be looked down upon as a worthless parasite. So you must try and try harder and compete again. "He who does not want to work should also not eat...."[37] The mendicant is a criminal liable to prosecution. Nothing is gratuitous, comes as a gift, gratuities are taxable income! Everything has a price and you must earn enough to pay that price. Works may be of many types, but all are here homogenized inasmuch as they are all convertible into money. Everything is monetizable. The realm of quantity required by science has become the reign of money for human life. Money is that which allows for the quantification of all human values and thus makes their transactions possible.

You are real in as much as you are a worker and a producer. There are no other criteria for the authenticity of your work than its results. You will be judged by the results of your works. Grace is an empty word. Justice is what is needed. Your discipline and asceticism must be channeled into better production and more work. You may relax and even entertain yourself but only in order that you may be able to work better and produce more. It is this very work that will entitle you to the reward, the relaxation, and peace which you may, in rare moments of reflection, sometimes long for.

You may be able to choose your type of work, because if you work with pleasure you will produce more and with less attrition. Even cows are given music. "Work is worship." Efficiency is a sacred name and life is subordinated to production. Even food is a military weapon—euphemistically called "political." The situation is complex. We may also recall here the process from production to consumerism and from discipline to permissiveness analyzed by contemporary sociology.

To be sure, traditional societies are not free from a certain compulsion to work and even work for others. We should idealize neither the past nor other cultures. But there is something specific in the work-duty of Modernity. A capital sin in Christian morality used to be sadness, disgust, *acedia*. Nowadays it has been translated into laziness, idleness. *Otium,* real leisure, has become a vice and *negotium,* business, a virtue. In a hierarchial society, once you have reached adulthood, you have your own place which may give you a sense of fulfillment. In an egalitarian society the highest posts are supposedly open to everyone. If you do not reach them, especially since you have theoretically been given equal opportunities with everyone else, you have proved yourself stupid. You have to work better and harder!

The modern technological world has become so complex and demanding that in order to "enjoy its blessings" one must obey its laws. And the first law (your foremost duty) is that you offer a total working dedication to society. Work becomes an end and this end is not the fulfillment of the human being but the satisfaction of its "needs." The anthropological assumption that Man is a bundle of needs whose satisfaction will automatically bring fulfillment is the underlying myth of the "American Way of Life," now collapsing in the country of its origin but spreading all over the world as the necessary condition for a "successful" technology.

Be all this as it may, the contemplative is at loggerheads with such a discourse. First of all the contemplative will have a totally different attitude to work. The primacy will not be given to the work but to working, i.e., to the act itself (the *finis operationis* of the Scholastics) so that every work will have to yield its own justification, or rather its own meaning. If an act is not meaningful in itself, it will simply not be done. Respect for each being and its constitution is characteristic of the contemplative attitude. "The tree gives glory to God by being a tree," as the modern contemplative, Thomas Merton, expressed it.[38] "Who is your master?" the people ask the lover in Ramón Llull's *Book of the Lover and the Beloved:* "The symbols of my Beloved which I see in all creatures," answers the passionate thirteenth-century mystic.[39] A plant will be cultivated because the act of cultivating is meaningful in itself—a collaboration between Man and the vital forces of Nature, an enhancement of both nature and culture, an ennobling inherent in the act itself. It is neither the act of a slave nor that of a lord—but that of an artist.

The second intentionality (the Scholastic *finis operantis*) or the intention of the agent, will be a harmonious prolongation of the very nature of the act. You cultivate the plant not only because it enhances beauty and increases life but also because you may want to eat it. Eating belongs to the cosmic order which stands for the dynamism, mutual influence, growth, and transformation of the whole universe. To eat is not a selfish act. It is a dynamic communion with the whole world. It is in this way that we must understand the famous Upanishadic utterance *annam brahma* (Brahman—the highest Reality—is food).[40] You may even gather for the winter or produce food for those who cannot do it, but not in order to speculate about it or to become rich (rich in what? in money, of course!). Food, like life itself, is non-negotiable.

Thirdly, your intentionality will tend to coalesce with the very end of the act itself (*finis operis*) so that your private intentions are reduced practically to nil. The contemplative renounces the very results of the work, performing every kind of activity, as we have already remarked, for the sake of the act itself and not for what may come of it (the *naiṣkarmyakarma* of the *Gītā*).[41] The act is not treated as a mere means to something else. The kiss will be a kiss; the dance a dance; the poem a poem. Learning will be for the beauty and truth of it, not for the possible benefits it might yield. There is place for art because each and every one of the intermediate steps is discovered to be meaningful in itself, just as the tentative sketch or the torso may be as beautiful and inspiring in its own way as the finished composition. This does not exclude the consciousness of performing partial acts in view of a whole; but, as in a Japanese tea ceremony, each act is an organic part of the entire operation. The contemplative eye is the eye attentive to the radiance of each moment, to the holiness, that is, the transparence, of the most simple, everyday things. There is still place for activity toward the future because the final cause is present from the beginning, and the act itself is the totality of all its different aspects.

The present-day work-obsession, even when it is not geared to productivity and is proudly called creativity, is not able to make of each of us a true *homo faber,* a maker, because what you *make* is neither your life nor your own happiness, nor even that of a collectivity.

You travail—i.e., you are chained to the *tri-palium,* the instrument of torture—in order to somehow justify your existence in the eyes of others and, alas, for many people today, justify it in their own eyes and in the sight of their God. You are worth what your work is worth. Modern civilization may be likened to a colony of ants, incessantly working, driven by some barely conscious instinct—but soon it will be more like a swarm of termites who work far from the brightness of the sun, protected by concrete, neon lights, and oppressed by the heavy atmosphere of polluted air.

The contemplative is not merely the acosmic *muni* or *arhat* who sets to "work" on himself or on others, leaving the joys of the world and of nature behind. This radical asceticism certainly may have its place in the spiritual life—but to the true contemplative asceticism is not only denial of the world, the thirst *(tṛṣṇā)* for the other shore at the expense of this one; rather, it is a cultivation of the wisdom and discrimination which pierces the appearances only to discover at their core the shining forth of the divine. The contemplative enjoys life because life *is* joy and *brahman ānanda,* and sees the whole garden poised in a single flower. He is able to see the beauty of the wild lilies even if the fields are idle. The contemplative has the power to spontaneously transform a situation by the sheer joy of having discerned the bright spot in the otherwise dark canvas of human transactions.

The contemplative does not only work for a salary; he is not a mercenary. His actions, as we have said, are not selfish, but neither are they utilitarian. Work is neither punishment, compulsion nor obligation. It is an expression of Man's creativity. We are here miles away from the attitude prevalent in the technological paneconomic ideology.[42]

The Power of the Big (Intimacy versus Exteriority)

A fundamental praxis in the contemplative life is concentration, i.e., the attempt to reach the center. This center is within; it has no dimensions and is equidistant from all activities, though the "heart," from the early Christian desert fathers of Egypt and Syria to the Kashmir śaivite poet-saints and the Ṣūfis of Spain and Iran, has always been its supreme symbol. When established in the center you acquire contentedness, *Gelassenheit, sosiego, śama, aequanimitas, sōphrosyne*—none of which is to be confused with self-satisfaction. This inner poise is such that it does not draw you to where "the action is" (supposed to be), lead you to the great city, tempt you with greater and greater success, or entice you with the power of the

Big just for the sake of it alone. A concentrated substance has more density but less volume.

The very way in which words like "big" and especially "great" denote quality and goodness betrays the modern temperament in its adulation of empires, corporations, and superpowers. When we speak of the "great religions" we mean the "important" ones. The so-called power of the majority is another example of this. Even though a tiny technocracy can manipulate the masses through the power of technology, the "majority" has the theoretical power. What counts here, what gives value, are numbers. If it happens that you are different from "the rest," you may easily be threatened or at least feel insecure about yourself. In this situation your center is not within you, the "mind" not established in the "heart." You are displaced.

Yet another example of this attitude is linguistic imperialism. Dialects, if not despised outright, are certainly not taken seriously. You have to at least speak a "world language." This makes you important, "global," "universal." The villagers are simply provincial. Their very accent betrays them, and to in some way make up for this "handicap" they try to imitate the pronunciation of those of the great capitals. Idioms, if they do not follow the fashion shaped by mass media, are either unintelligible or considered queer by the majority. Today modern Western Man can hardly imagine that language has always been a creation of the living—speaking—group. The poetry of most languages has its humble birth in the colorful specificity of the spoken dialect. A dialect may encompass everything from Dante's Italian, Llull's Catalán, the Tamil of the Ālvārs, Sanskrit of the court or of the pandits, to even the modern Western academic language subtly imposed by so-called scholarly standards. Academicians, like any other human group, speak a jargon. There is no such thing as a universal language.[43]

Nowadays it is those who have power who send their idiosyncratic language into the air, who propagate their particular way of viewing the world, or saying things, before the eyes and ears of millions of passive spectators. The storytellers and singers of the Indian villages are quickly disappearing. People only listen now to the few successful ones who manage to perform on the All-India Radio. The others are called "beggars." Language has become something that is passively heard or read, a commodity you receive rather than a living way by which you express yourself creatively and also shape the meaning of the words of your partner. We have far more monologues than dialogues. We are unable to answer the person on the radio, in the cinema, or on television—these very influential and widespread modes of modern communication remain outside of dialogue. No wonder we find that our language has deteriorated and that the art of conversation has become elitist, for they are products of those whom we see on the television or hear on the radio, or of those who write the watered-down simplistic prose we are subjected to in our newspapers. Journalism is no longer literature, but has sunk to the lowest common denominator of propaganda. The *idiotès* (one who has one's own proper nature) has become an "idiot" and idiosyncrasy almost an insult. We have to be conformists in order to survive and put on a cultural uniform to be tolerated and accepted.

The very symbol of civilization is the Big City, where the mass media is paramount. The pressure is to move even higher up the ladder of importance, power and success; you have to be promoted in order to feel real to yourself, gain self-confidence and inspire confidence in others. Mobility becomes the very sign of your status. "Stability" and even marriage and the raising of a family are obstacles to the upwardly mobile person of the great cities. If you do not move up you are a failure. Growth has become a quantitative concept. The maximum is the ideal.[44]

The contemplative will not only understand the theoretical need for the decongestion of modern society, but will put it into practice. Who else will go to the villages to practice medicine? Who will prefer to settle in the small town to practice law? Who will welcome a smaller job so as to have more time for leisure, civic activities, and family? Today most of the "educated" Africans and Indians want to emigrate to the West....

If I am not able to find the center of reality in my own self—or at least concentric with my own center—I will not be able to overcome the schizophrenic feeling of being a displaced person if I do not live in the capital or work in the biggest university, industry, corporation, or firm, or earn the highest possible salary. I will be nervous, restless, or at least tense until I have reached the top—not the center.

Contemplatives do not play that game. Not because of selfishness or the kind of hedonism expressed in the Spanish proverb *"ande yo caliente / y ríase la gente"* ("May I go warm / and let the others sneer at me"). Not because they do not care for efficacy or enjoy what is small more than other things, but because the real meaning of life is seen to be elsewhere. Although many statesmen and secular thinkers like Aldous Huxley and Arnold Toynbee have written in their mature age about the "illusion" that politics will change the world, this illusion continues to tempt truly religious people to become *mere* politicians. There is a deeper dimension in life, however, a more profound arena where we can work for true change. Here is where we discover the often neglected monastic dimension of Man.[45]

The contemplative is happy, like a healthy child passionately playing with a toy. Seeing her contentment, some may snatch the toy away, but she will return to her play with another toy, which may in its turn be snatched away from her by the same people who mistakenly believe that joy comes from the toy itself. It sometimes takes an entire lifetime to discover that happiness is not merely in the gadget.

We warned earlier, however, that contemplation is a risky thing, for this "holy indifference" can be exploited by others who will eventually overstep the limits of the tolerable. Often a religion fostering contemplation becomes the opium administered not only, for instance, by the British Empire to the Chinese, but also by missionaries, brahmans, and priests to the people. In this light, the masters have always spoken of *viveka, discretio,* i.e., discernment or discrimination, as an indispensable element in the true contemplative life.

The Ambition of Success (Contentment versus Triumph)

Ambition is a key word for Modernity, but an ambivalent one. On the one hand, every human being wants and needs to achieve something. There is an innate ambition which spurs on the human being towards perfection in a kind of self-transcendence. We want to unfold all our dormant possibilities, actualize our potentialities. It is part of our thirst to discover the core of ourselves and of the world, the "heart" and "center" of the mystic. On the other hand, this urge *to be* is clothed in a very special way with the need for success on a societal level. Thus the almost irresistible thrust for fame, prestige, power. Modern Man is frantically concerned with gaining the acceptance of his fellow beings. Moreover, he not only needs to be respected and admired but in a subtle way also feared, otherwise he will not achieve the desired success. In a so-called democratic society our power is, among other things, directly proportional to the reputation we hold. We are told we must fashion our own image and then skillfully project it outward to others so that our words and actions will carry weight. Propaganda, good advertisements, and at least a properly selected amount of information (often called "education.") are all ways that help us build our "personality."

Modern Man aspires to be at the center of decision-making. He has to be involved in the concerns of society and have his say in all levels because it is merely *society* (a more or less ordered group of individuals) and not part of an acknowledged *dharma,* right, order, way of life, or God which is sovereign and decisive in our lives.

No individual can live without a certain recognition of personal value and societal reputation. But in traditional societies such value is prevalently inherent in the place you occupy in the hierarchical structure of the community and in the value of your subjectivity. Your prestige and thus the sense of self-fulfillment does not lie in your power.

Success in a technological society has become an objectified value, easily measurable in terms of financial power or supposed economic freedom. We need to triumph. Success in a competitive society is measured by the number of people (victims) we have left behind. Success is not personal contentment, or the awakening to a responsibility for others and sense of interdependence, but objectified achievement.

To be sure, many traditional religions have often had the same objectified model, so that only victors and heroes (the "brahmans" or the "chosen ones") reach heaven or *nirvāṇa,* while the others are annihilated, go to hell, or the inferior way of the ancestors, or are condemned to return endlessly to the earth. In such a framework, you can easily fall into the trap of despising earthly ambitions simply because you have projected the same type of desires onto the heavenly realm. Monasteries for both men and women could easily be replenished by people who, realizing they were not likely to succeed in the affairs of this world, were seeking a last chance to succeed by working and toiling for a reward in heaven. A certain anthropomorphic image of God is equally a transfer, if in a somewhat more refined way, of the same attitude. You will do anything to please a personal God, even neglect human recognition, provided you are sure that God is satisfied with you, sees you, and will give you recompense in due time.

This attitude should not be confused with that of the motivation of love for the beloved, human or divine, whereby you do everything to please and for the sake of the beloved. The beloved person, human or divine, is the very end and driving force of your life, of your every action. The *bhakti* spirituality of ardent devotion and surrender to God seems to be a human invariant, found in all times, cultures and places; it will always attract a certain type of person. But even with the necessary corrections, and despite important variations, neither attitude is that of the contemplative.

Contemplation, of course, is not without love, but there can be love without contemplation. Further, to the contemplative, love is not the ultimate motive. Or rather, it is the last *motive,* but the motive is not the thing. In the final instance, the contemplative acts without motive. There is no further external or alien motive that could be separated from the act done solely for its own sake. Jacopone da Todi has expressed this by saying, *"La rosa non ha perchène"* ("The rose has no 'why' "). It is because it is. It is simply there, if only, like the lilies of the field, for a short while. Or rather, no "while" is short, but each while is and is unique. Contemplatives burn their own lives every day. Every day exhausts all the aeons and universes. Each moment is a "new" creation. The authentic contemplative attitude should not, however, be confused with any of its pitfalls, such as narcissism, purely aesthetic pleasure of self-complacency. *"La vertu non è perchène, ca'l perchène è for de tene"* ("Virtue has no why, for the why is out of place"), says the same Franciscan.[46] To contemplatives there is no such thing as above, behind or below; they will never quarrel as to whether there is or is not a "God" in the sense understood by most of the traditional religions.[47]

It is for this reason that contemplatives are startling. You cannot pin them down to anything. There is no predicting what they will do next, what their next move will be. The "fools" of Russia, India, and elsewhere, Platonic madness and the shaman's enthusiasm could provide us with examples of this apparently anarchic phenomenon. They are led by the Spirit. The Spirit is Freedom and is irreducible to the Logos. The mind and reason give way to silence, the womb from which every true word emerges.[48] Yet contemplatives may also learn to act like everybody else, though with another kind of "motivation." You will discover a ray of mirth in their actions; often also a seemingly ironic smile. They do not confront you with another power, an anti-power, but somehow render your power powerless by simply not giving a thought to your might.

"Contemplative *Studies*" will, in the same way, challenge our idea of what it means to "study," or rather will recover its original meaning. You cannot teach contemplation or even "study" it as a subject matter. *Studium* itself may become dedication to contemplation— that thirst for understanding what it is all about for no other motive than to know it—i.e., to practice and become "it." *Study*, then, is contemplation itself, an end in itself and not a means to master a certain discipline or to acquire some information on what so-called contemplatives have been talking about.

The concept of "study" implies something further when applied to contemplation. Contemplative *studium* suggests that the contemplative act is not yet completed and so not yet perfect. It indicates that the act, contemplative itself, is still in the making. *Studium* implies the effort or rather the tension of the soul which, having in some way reached the goal, is still not fully there and so is stretched, as it were, between our common condition and its (relative) fullness. *Studium* is the way. A single brush-stroke in Japanese calligraphy may not yet be the whole phrase or convey the entire meaning. Yet each stroke is a world in itself and contains, in a special way, the final cause or finished phrase. The step already contains the goal, even if you change direction along the way. Way and goal are fused in the process.[49] This means that the contemplative act is a holistic act and cannot be atomized at will. The *study* of contemplation means the *practice* of contemplation and practice means that the contemplative activity is still "on the way."

In the final analysis, contemplative study has no real subject matter of inquiry; it has no object of investigation. It is much more an attitude, a special approach, or rather *the* authentic *ap-propriation,* the real assimilation of the goal. Because all is "near" (*ad-propius:* nearer), contemplative study treats everything as sacred, as an end in itself and not as a means. Your study becomes your life—your love: *amor meus pondus meum!*[50]

Contemplative study is never satisfied with merely knowing *how* things run, how mechanisms function or laws are applicable. It pierces the modern scientific outlook and attempts an insight into reality, even if it often has to renounce it.

When scientists say, for instance, and Nobel laureates comment, that one of the fundamental truths of biology is that "a hen is merely an egg's way of making another egg,"[51] they are far from the Contemplative Mood, which sees the hen as a hen and not as a mechanism for something else. No wonder that for a modern dairy farmer a hen is no longer a hen or a cow a cow, but the egg's and milk's way of generating capital. The consequence of this is that soon there will be neither egg nor milk. And this is only one step from saying that Man is merely Man's way of making another Man. The paradox is that the next step is to say that a Man is merely Man's way of destroying another Man.

Some may say that contemplative life is not fully possible here and now—to which the contemplative might answer by calling into question the "here" and the "now," or by discovering a more universal *here* and a more embracing *now.* Indeed, the challenge is real.

Chapter 2

Action and Contemplation as Categories of Religious Understanding

> *avijñātaṁ vijānataṁ vijñātam avijānatām*
> It is not understood by those who understand;
> it is understood by those who do not understand.
> —Ken U II, 3

> *apolō tēn sophian tōn sophōn,*
> *kai tēn súnesin tōn sunetōn athetēsō*
> I shall destroy the wisdom of the wise,
> and nullify the understanding of the understander.
> —1 Cor. 1:19[1]

Action and Contemplation have, since time immemorial and under one name or another, been invariant religious categories. Lest we become lost in the jungle of meanings and interpretations of the various religious traditions of the world, it may suffice for our purpose to use these words in designating two fundamental human attitudes: the centrifugal and the centripetal. The first is predominantly material, exterior, "realistic," historical, and temporal; the second, predominantly spiritual, internal, "idealistic," archetypal, and atemporal. *Poiesis* and *theoria* or *karman* and *jñāna* could perhaps be equivalent words, whereas *praxis* and *bhakti* would have a role of mediating between them. The active mood checks, interferes, experiments, reasons; it is mostly pragmatic, and tests an idea by its fruits. The contemplative mood observes, sees, experiences, intuits;

This chapter is a revised version of articles that appeared in *Main Currents of Modern Thought* 30 (1973):75–81, and in *Contemplation and Action in World Religions,* ed. Yusuf Ibish and Ileana Marculescu (selected papers from the Rothko Chapel Colloquium "Traditional Modes of Contemplation and Action"; Seattle and London: University of Washington Press, 1978), 85–104, under the same title.

it is mostly theoretical, and accepts an idea by its own radiance and power. The active is existential; truth is conquered (in making it). The contemplative is essential; truth is discovered (in the *simplex intuitus*).

Our purpose here will be threefold: (1) To uncover the paradoxical fact that although contemplation, by and large, has been considered within the respective traditions to be a superior form of religious life, it has hardly played its incumbent role in the interreligious dialogue; (2) To demonstrate the valuable and indispensable use of the contemplative "approach" in the religious encounter, by means of two examples from the Hindu and Christian traditions; (3) To suggest that both approaches are necessary but insufficient if taken in isolation; complementary if rightly understood, leading to a cross-religious fertilization which may be one of the major hopes for Mankind today.

The Primacy of Action

yathākārī yathācārī tathā bhavati

As one acts, as one behaves, so does one become.

—BU IV, 5

ean mē perimēthēte... ou dynasthe sōthēnai

Except you be circumcised... you cannot be saved.

—Acts 15:1[2]

The Active Approach and Recent History. Men today have come much closer to each other, not only externally but also regarding a deeper understanding of the different cultures and religions of the world. This results from modern events such as the spread of the "scientific" mentality along with the rise of technology (which makes mass communication possible) and the end of a certain colonial period in history, i.e., as fruit of historical and cultural actions generally. Every Man lives in and from a human environment, which we may call tradition, culture or religion.[3]

Gone, by and large, are those attitudes of radical arrogance and pride which used to make almost impossible any religious dialogue and cultural understanding. Ill-will and even antipathies are also on the wane in the world of intercultural and interreligious relations. Sincere respect and a genuine thirst for tolerance, on the other hand, are waxing. All this has been brought about by the historical fact of the unavoidable contacts among the diverse peoples of the world, who can no longer afford to live in isolation. The present-day geographical and, to a great extent, historical unity of humankind is a positive factor in bridging the gulf among cultures and religious traditions. We are almost forced to reckon, in some way or another, with the problems of our neighbors: men and women, black and white, rich and poor; Hindus, Buddhists, Christians, Marxists, and associations of ancient and modern types are interacting and, in point of fact, living together within the same national, economic, linguistic, and even cultural framework. The problem of understanding the other has become a burning issue in contemporary societies, East and West.

This opening up on a global scale has also brought its attendant sufferings, conflicts and confusions. But one of the most positive features of our tortured and fecund present is the felt need for a truly human culture which would also make room for an almost indefinite number of subcultures with their respective variations. There is a hunger, not for mere ideologies, but for the emergence of the *humanum*. We breathe in everywhere a desire for tolerance, mutual respect, sympathy and freedom. We can no longer easily justify excommunications, holy wars, wholesale condemnations, and blatantly elitist positions. To be sure, we differ in understanding what respect of freedom may mean, where they are to be found, and even more, on the proper means leading to these values; nevertheless, the thirst for a common language is emerging.

Yet most of these results are the fruit of the almost compulsory situation in which Man finds himself due to a certain historical dynamism, whatever the theory we may cherish in order to explain the fact that the world seeks to become one. Scholars, thinkers, writers, Men of letters, as well as Men of religion, in the wake of the politicians and businessmen, simply follow the times. The scholars are busy explaining the astonishing changes taking place (sociology has become the queen of the sciences) and hardly have time for anything else, let alone to steer the course of events and much less to bring a contemplative and creative view to bear upon them. Most of the prophets in all fields are Men of action.

In a word, action and the active mood dominate the modern scene. It is certainly true that within particular groups or "New Religions," and even in the world at large, many are prepared to accept the contemplative attitude or intuition as the superior one; but contemplation as such, generally reserved for the elect few, will hardly make a noticeable impression on the decision-making agencies which seem to steer the events of the world on many different levels. One is not likely to find many theoreticians, "saints," monks, or contemplatives in these agencies; they will prefer calm and solitude, and disdain or even despise the strains and stresses of the active person. In the encounter of cultures and religions, the events themselves and the Men who direct them play the primary role. But although humankind has come a long way and may be marching in the right direction, there is still an enormous and fundamental task to perform. It may be reserved for a more contemplative approach.

Limitations of the Active Approach. In spite of the hope that human relations are improving, we cannot overlook the fact that we are far from a lasting and real understanding of each other. No amount of good will and sympathy, important as these ingredients are, will suffice. There is an underlying and unavoidable theoretical factor still to be considered. A change of mind has to follow an incipient change of heart.

For example, Christians feel outraged when Hitler and Stalin are characterized as baptized Christians; Hindus are uneasy when reminded that Gandhi was killed by an orthodox Hindu; Indians become weary when faced with the fact that Hindu and Muslim are at each other's throats the moment they are free to do so. The problems of Ireland, Israel, Lebanon, South Africa, Vietnam, El Salvador, Guatemala, Uganda, and many more are far from being explained merely by saying that some people want to dominate others. Are we prepared to accept the statement that over one hundred million American citizens are all criminals because they supported the Vietnam War and continue (at least implicitly) to support the repressive governments of El Salvador and Guatemala or covert actions against Nicaragua? Are all white South Africans inhuman because they put up with apartheid? Are all the Jews and Arabs, Irish and Russians, Chinese and Spaniards responsible for the respective situations they tolerate? Which human group, whether religious, cultural, or historical, has only "white pages" in its records? Not all is a question of personal animosity or individual greed.

There seems to be a built-in double standard for judging one's self and other. First, we judge the situation of our group (of whatever kind) from *within*—from an attitude of participation and concern, having an insight (a contemplative vision) into the inspiring sources of the particular community to which we belong. But we judge others from *without,* from their mixed fruits and without discrimination. We deduce what they are from what they do (according, of course, to our own criteria of judgement), attributing their actions to their particular group, culture or religion. In judging our own group or tradition, we consider its positive values as the decisive criterion for interpretation; we judge what we are not from what we do, but from what we are supposed to be. Are those who speak of the dignity of Christianity and the indignity of Christians ready to accept the dignity of Marxism and the indignity of Marxists? When Christians persecute, they are bad Christians, but when Marxists persecute they are characterized (by Christians) as behaving in ways consistent with their beliefs. When a Christian is tolerant or broadminded, this is thought to be (by the Hindu) because of some Indian or Asian influence. And if a Christian has a burning concern for social justice a Marxist will feel that this must be due to Marxist influence. Can we compare the *Dhammapada* with the Crusades or the Sermon on the Mount with Turkish conquests?

But the misunderstanding goes even deeper, to the very doctrines. Can a Muslim be convinced that the Christian Trinity is not tritheism? Can a Christian agree that Hindu *advaita* is not monism? Can a humanist accept the fact that Islam is more than a theocracy, or a Buddhist acknowledge that the Jewish idea of the "elect" is more than religious caste-ism? Is the Hindu ready to recognize that his idea of tolerance may be a very intolerant one?

These random examples signal the enormous task ahead. The problem transcends the realm of good will, desire to understand, mutual respect, and sympathy. As important and necessary as these factors are, they are not sufficient.

Commitment to truth as one sees it, irrespective of the consequences; loyalty to one's community; fidelity to one's own destiny, *karman,* duty, *svadharma,* historical mission; fear of anarchic eclecticism and of barren syncretisms; mistrust of generalizations, abhorrence of abstract and lifeless statements; avoidance of the deleterious effects of indiscriminate permissiveness, etc.—all this represents the other side of the issue which in no way should be minimized. Not all problems are solved, indeed.

Features of the Active Mood. It would, however, be a distortion of the true perspective if we were only to underline the deficiencies of the active approach, for without its thrust, the world would still be living in compartmentalized and narcissistically self-satisfied little boxes, each thinking itself to be the whole universe and in possession of the whole truth. Were it not for the pressures of history and Man's active spirit, brahmins, pandits, scribes, priests, and professors of all kinds would still be convinced that they held the keys to every human problem and the property rights over any lasting and transcendent value. Only the incursions of one group into another have brought about eclectic and syncretistic attitudes, which were the starting points for more permanent symbioses and syntheses among different cultural worlds and religions. Were it not for the active spirit in Man we would still be in our tribal state. Indeed the tribe is a microcosm just as the human person is the image and mirror of the entire universe, but the one thing should not obliterate the other; nor should the internal dimension of Man cause us to forget his external constitution.

In the encounter of religions, the active approach seeks completion not by going deeper into oneself (with the consequent danger of finding only what one has previously projected) but by looking for fulfillment outside, or rather beyond, ourselves. We will look to our neighbors before we look into our own hearts. The assumption is our own radical insufficiency; in point of fact, the active person is more inclined towards dialogue and learning from others than is the contemplative spirit, which instinctively mistrusts such methods, and looks for truth inwardly. This implies that the active mood is often inclined towards a humble recognition that the other may also have something important to contribute: I do not assume that I have access to the universal range of human experience.

This is precisely what prompts the active spirit to its excursions, and spurs its curiosity into unknown realms. The active spirit certainly wants to dominate, but for this it has both to understand and to compromise. The history of Man, and especially the History of Religions, offers ample testimony of this fact, and exonerates us from pursuing the argument further.

The Primacy of Contemplation

tam yathā yathopaste tadeva bhavati

One becomes that which one meditates upon.
—SB X, 5, 2, 20[4]

ti dōsei anthrōpos antallagma tēs psychēs autoū

What shall a Man give in exchange for his self?
—Matt. 16:26[5]

The Contemplative Approach. Assuming I succeed in understanding the other as other, this is insufficient, for the other does not understand himself as "other" but as "self." Therefore, I shall not really understand the other until I am able to perform on the intellectual-spiritual plane a feat similar to the moral injunction: Love your neighbor as your self (not *as* your neighbor but as your *self*). Is this possible? Traditional Christian morality used to say that this is only possible under the influence of divine grace, for Man's "natural" disposition is incapable of such a transcendence. We may add, similarly, that on the intellectual plane this is possible only if we transcend the field of reason and, without denying it, reach the realm of true contemplation.

In order to understand the other as he/she understands him/herself I have to become the other, viz., share in their experience, participate in their particular world, be converted to their way of life. How can a Christian understand a Hindu if he does not become a Hindu? A Christian may perhaps understand a kind of objectified "Hinduism," but this need not tally with what the Hindu accepts and believes as his Hinduism. Living Hinduism is constitutively linked with the Hindu understanding of it, which includes the Hindu's self-understanding.

And conversely, how can a Hindu enter into the world of Christian belief if he does not somehow hold as true that same belief? Can I possibly understand you if I think that what you hold to be true is wrong? I may perhaps understand you *better* than yourself, but certainly not *as* yourself, if I do not share your self-understanding. Or, to put it more philosophically, the belief of the believer belongs essentially to the religious phenomenon; the *noema* of religion is not an objectified *creditum* or a hypothetical *credendum,* but entails an unbreakable link with the *credens.* The belief of the believer remains opaque for the observer until in one way or another it also becomes the belief of the observer.[6]

Within the categories of action, this enterprise is impossible. I cannot be in your place, just as my body cannot occupy the place your body occupies. If I am an active member of a particular religious group and that community embodies for me the concrete way towards my own ultimate fulfillment, I cannot belong to a parallel group. We may meet, like parallel lines, in the infinite, we may share in the same mystical body, but we should not blur the distinctions and commitments of concrete human groups and sociological bodies. You can be a member of two different clubs, but you cannot belong to two different "churches"—or so it would seem from an active point of view.

Now, contemplation means precisely the overcoming of the

spacio-temporal categories as the only possible way of being consciously in the world and of participating in the ongoing process
of existence. Contemplation does not seek to understand rationally,
nor is it an act of the imagination or a product of fantasy; it is actual participation in the reality one contemplates, real sharing in the
things one "sees," dynamic identification with the truth one realizes.
Contemplation is not merely an act of mind, but is "touch," real
existential contact, to use a metaphor not only precious to Plotinus
in the Western tradition but also to the early Tamil *bhakti* poet-saints
of South India. Contemplation, to further trace this line of thought,
implies an "eating" of the object and also a "being eaten"; it discloses the absolute mutual transparency of subject and object. Seen
in another way, contemplation is the actual building of the temple
of reality, wherein the onlooker is equally part and parcel of the
whole construction. This may be the reason why "concentration,"
i.e., the ontic crystallization of what is, the condensation of reality
in the self above and beyond the mere psychological state, is in all
traditions one of the most important features of the contemplative
mood. It is a vision of totality through the discovery of the center
within: as above, so below, as the ancient hermetic formula put it.
Nothing is then more obvious than that contemplation does not exclusively depend on the will of Man or the "nature of things." It
requires a higher harmony as an integrating force. Contemplation is
an ontological phenomenon.[7]

True contemplation is thus an experience, not an experiment. We
may deny the truth-content of such an act, refuse to accept it or even
refer to it as pathological (a product of shamanic "madness" or the
magical hallucinations of a bygone age), but if we speak of contemplation at all we have to take this claim seriously and deal with it
accordingly. If there is any possible bridge between the different religious traditions (by which we understand ultimate forms or styles
of life), only the contemplative can be in two or more traditions, and
thus perform a mediatorial and integrating role.[8] The fact that not
all Men have access to such an experience does not deny the possibility or even the plausibility of such an experience, since there is
hardly anyone who has not been called upon to transcend his own
limitations by an experience of conversion into "something"—or
rather "somebody"—else which will maintain alive his constitutive
human openness.[9] Assimilation, to return to the metaphor of food,
is essential to life.

Contemplation is not, properly speaking, an approach; neither can
it be used as a tool for anything else or manipulated in favor of any

cause, however good. Contemplation is an end in itself—that superior life of the spirit which certainly does not ignore or despise the life of matter, of the senses and of reason (for it is based on them), but which transcends them. It is irreducible to anything else, like any primary reality.

This thesis may be expounded by means of two religious traditions which form the background of these reflections: Hinduism and Christianity.

The Nature of Karman. No word is more central, more universal and more expressive of indic religious traditions than *karman;* all forms of Hinduism, Buddhism, Jainism, Sikhism, and also many forms of Parsi and animistic religions, in one way or another, recognize its law and its power.

A certain idea of *karman* links it with reincarnation, and thus seems to deny the irrepeatable dignity of the individual, and the uniqueness of Man's personal life on earth. As such, it seems radically opposed to any Christian interpretation of Man and reality. Scores of popular writings have propagated this notion, now widespread in the East as well as in the West. Does it not seem to be today, more than the "personal" character of God, the main stumbling block between a real Hindu-Christian dialogue?

One of the reasons for this impasse is the predominantly active approach which is taken to the question. Given the perspective of the active mood, it would seem that one cannot owe allegiance both to the "immortality of the soul" and to the "reincarnation of the individual."[10] A contemplative approach, on the other hand, may yield unexpected possibilities for a cross-religious understanding, and even for a mutual fecundation.[11]

To begin, the contemplative approach will have no difficulty in disentangling *karman* from its different expressions; it will not identify that mysterious force or reality with any one particular doctrine. If one has had insight into what *karman* stands for and what its law expresses, one will not be satisfied with any given explanation, being aware that concepts are meaningful only within the particular context that has given them birth. This being so, in our discussion about *karman* we may think our partner's explanation is wrong or his integration of the concept into a coherent worldview is weak, but the discussion is possible at all only because, excluding merely dialectical consistencies or inconsistencies, both sides claim access to an insight into that reality, *karman.* This insight gives us the right to discuss, and the strength of our convictions. We know what we are talking about, because our talk is about "something" which has been disclosed to us prior to our talking about it. This attitude does not imply that there is a mysterious "thing in itself" independent of our access to it, but neither does it imply that a mere subjective opinion is all there is. It implies that my conception of a "thing" belongs to reality and even to the "thing" itself. But because the same is true for you, it also implies that neither my vision nor yours is the total Reality.

Thus a contemplative insight into the nature of *karman* will immediately separate it from the idea of reincarnation, which may be one way of exemplifying *karman,* but is by no means the same thing. Just as the Christian idea of the beatific vision is not necessarily connected with a material idea of heaven as a beautiful garden or hall on some celestial planet where God, bearded and enthroned on high, entertains his loyal servants, the Hindu idea of *karman* need not be linked up with an imaginary lingering of the past personality in the new bearer of the past *karman.* If there is anything that *karman* excludes, it is the attitude that "my" life is somehow "private property"; to consider the "next" life as still "my own" amounts to the very negation of *karman.*

The central idea of *karman* relates to the cosmic solidarity of the whole creation, to the irrepeatable and unique value of each act, which never falls in the void or remains barren and without effect. It relates to the ultimate community of all beings, and it expresses also the idea of finiteness and contingency, for no being can escape the law of *karman,* i.e., the interrelatedness with and responsibility for the whole universe.

The contemplative mood is not satisfied with mere exegesis or with simple interpretation of texts. It certainly has a high regard for what others have thought, and especially seen, but does not denigrate itself to the role of a mere scribe or a simple translator. It may eventually prove that they all refer to the same reality, but will, nevertheless, be very conscious of the fact that reality itself has something to do with the vision one has of it. The contemplative insight is more than just a discovery; it is also a creation.

In contemporary terms, we might say that *karman* stands for the vision of the *unity* as well as the *contingency* of all empirical (or created) reality.

Karman is the link that connects us to every speck of reality and restores our sense of unity with the whole universe, for all beings are, without exception, governed (and nurtured) by the same cosmic law. This law is not a mere causal chain, for there are forms of dependence which belong to *karman* and are not necessarily causal, unless we expand the concept of cause to any process of interdependence. Essential in this view is the universality of such a law, All that is, precisely because it *is*, has a relatedness to everything else. The "chain" of being is not truly a chain, for it also liberates; the "communion of all existence" is not exactly communion, for there is also strife; the unity of the universe is not precisely unity, for it is also disunity, as the first of the Buddha's Four Noble Truths will tell us. All are *karman*. To discover how *karman* acts is the acme of wisdom; it is realization.

Karman is also the expression of the *contingency* of all beings. It expresses their interrelatedness and thus their unity precisely because no individual being—nor even the entire universe—is complete, full, perfect, achieved. The world is unfinished and, in this sense, in-finite. It is this "infinitude" which accounts for freedom, and the unforeseeable movement of all that is. Existence is open, ongoing, a spontaneous unfolding of possibility. Thus *karman* stands, paradoxically, both for the unity and the freedom of the contingent creature. This freedom is ultimate, for there is nothing beyond, behind, or more fundamental than *karman,* which is the very coefficient of creatureliness. *Karman* is not a physical law, which has to follow an intellectual or mathematical pattern (thus making the universe a logical or mathematical prison); it is the ultimate law of the universe, governed by the very behavior of the universe itself. *Karman* vouches for and makes possible a real freedom which allows us to jump "outside" the realm of "Being" (of the universe) and reach the other shore, which, strictly speaking, is neither other nor a shore. Here the freedom is so absolute that it is a liberation from being itself (*nirvāṇa*, the Buddhists would say), for when *karman* is "burnt," being is volatilized in the jump outside existence; only nothing reaches Nothingness. *Karman* is coextensive with existence.[12]

Everything that is submits to *karman,* because the karmic structure of the universe is the ultimate pattern. The "Lord of *karman,*" in as much as it is the Lord *of* karman, is also within the embrace of *karman*. If it were outside *karman* it would no longer be its Lord, for there must be a link between the Lord and his world. This link, by definition, cannot but be *karman*. What could it be otherwise? If it were something else, this else would then be the real *karman*.

Significantly, it is in speaking about *karman* that the otherwise sober and concise Upanishads seem to open up not only to esoteric meanings but also to a more cordial and holistic approach to the mystery of life and death.[13] This is in point of fact the subject of the public dialogue wherein Jāratkārava Ārtabhāga puts five questions to the famous sage Yājñavalkya: (1) What are the different organs of reality and how is reality modified by them? (2) What is the death of death, if all is mortal? (3) What is the destiny of *prāna,* the vital breath, when a Man dies? (4) What is the only thing which does not abandon a Man when he dies? (5) What becomes of the person, i.e., what is the mystery of life? It was at this moment, when speaking about the cosmic law connecting all the elements of the universe, that they went away hand in hand and in secret began to discuss and praise *karman.* The whole context helps us to realize that what is involved is not a philosophical subtlety but a fundamental query concerning the nature of the entire universe. The nature of *karman* is not open to mere dialectics; it is revealed in the ultimate dialogue with the Master, in personal meditation, in the contemplation of the mystery of temporal existence. Many doctrinal problems remain to be articulated, but the primacy belongs to a certain intuition of this ultimate mystery.

The Western contemplative will perhaps not speak the same language as the Indian of the East; he may not have access to the same symbols, but once he gets wind of the mystery spoken through the language he will be in tune with it. *Le mystère est commun,* says the poet St. John Perse. It is up to the contemplative, then, in collaboration with the philosopher, theologian or poet, to propound a language which will more reveal that aspect of the mystery of life and Reality.

Seen under this perspective, the nature of *karman* may even help to explain as fundamental a Christian insight as the connection of Adam and Adam's sin, as well as the relation of Christ and Christ's death and resurrection, with the whole of humanity.[14]

The Identity of Jesus. A major stumbling block for the other side is the claim Christians lay upon Jesus as the unique savior, the only name, the single way.

Much ink has been spilled in the attempt either to explain or to explain away such claims.[15] It is here again that a contemplative mood might allow us to overcome the dilemma of either diluting the Christian message, and thereby emasculating the self-identity of one-fifth of the world's population, or making it a tool of domination over all the other religious traditions.[16] With contemplative insight, we may begin to trace the emergence of a middle way.

If we put the question (as Jesus did) of who is this Jesus about whom such claims are made, we discover that the active approach, based mainly on spatio-temporal and thus logical categories, has tried to answer the query by means of a geographical and historical *identification* of Jesus: He was that young Jew, born of Mary, who lived in Palestine twenty centuries ago, died under Pontius Pilate, and still has historical and sociological significance. How to attribute to that man all that Christian belief affirms of Jesus has been one of the crucial problems of Christian theology: how is that man one of the Trinity, how was he before Abraham, how was he the Messiah, the Redeemer of the whole world, the *Alpha* and *Omega,* and thus the only Savior, Way, and Name?

The contemplative approach will not minimize these problems, but will stress another starting point: not the *identification* of *what* Jesus did or is, but the *identity* of *who* he is. Now the *who* of Jesus may or may not be separable from his *what,* but it is certainly not identifiable with it. The *who* of Jesus is only disclosed in the personal encounter of faith, in the interpersonal relationship of finding a *thou* answering to the call (prayer) of the *I;* it will be found when the *metanoia,* the change of perspective and roles, takes place so that Jesus becomes the *I* and the seeker the *thou,* so that the Master's "I am" becomes something more than a metaphysical or psychological statement. Then the Christian will utter: "I live no more but Christ lives in me."[17] He will have become transparent, entirely transformed, and will know that neither flesh nor will has conferred upon him the glory of being God's offspring.[18]

The *who* whom the Christian discovers may have been revealed to him in and through the *what* that tradition has handed down to him, but he will not confuse the two. For example, in the central Christian mystery, the Eucharist, he will recognize Christ's *real presence,* yet he will not believe he is eating the proteins or drinking the hemoglobin of Jesus of Nazareth, for he knows that communion is with the real *who,* not with the *what.* Furthermore, in this light, we will not say that *what* the Buddhist believes in is *what* the Christian worships; but we can admit that the *who* beneath the Buddhist's compassion or behind the Muslim's surrender is not other than the *who* of the Christian's agape.

If we apply the contemplative mood to the first question posed about Jesus, which concerns the trinitarian and the non-trinitarian basic understanding of the Christian and the Muslim, we may begin by emphasizing the traditional *perichōrēsis* or *circuminsessio* that puts in theological terms the staggering affirmation of Jesus: "Philip, he who sees me sees the Father."[19] Our main point refers to the disclosure of the *who* in an actual personal relationship, not to the crystallized concept or even to the intelligibility of the personal name. The personal relationship cannot be objectified without ceasing to be that personal relation. The *who* of the Muslim, assuming he is directing his prayer to Allah, is not the *what* of his theology, but the

living reality with which he believes himself to be connected in a special way, and with which he enters into a very specific relationship.
It is the ultimate "I" of his thou-consciousness unveiled to him in
and through the Qu'rān. We have no criterion whatsoever outside
his personal world to affirm or deny its identity with the *who* of the
Christian. Moreover the question has no meaning and is a contradiction in terms. We say *who* but we mean *what*. Here language fails
us; at this point what is needed is the contemplative leap that would
allow us to experience whether the living I with which a thou is entering into relation is the same or not the same as the living I of the
believer of another tradition.

In the dialogue with the Hindu or Buddhist, the question of the
who also needs an immediate qualification. Obviously, the *what* of
Jesus is not the *what* of Kṛṣṇa, in spite of the many resemblances
which we may find in favor of a merely psychological or archetypal theory regarding the origins of religious cults. But neither do we
need to entertain an anthropomorphic view. A personal relationship
is any free and conscious mutual relationship which wholly or partially constitutes the existence of the persons who emerge by this
act. We have used the personal pronouns—which happen to be the
most universal linguistic symbols—but we do not necessarily assume
a particular conception of a person. The I-Thou relationship does
not need to be seen under the angle of two separate beings exchanging the overflow of their lives. We could easily consider the personal
relationship in a more radical way, so that nothing of the I would be
there if the thou were not also there, and vice versa.[20]

To show the possibilities of the contemplative approach in the encounter of religions, just as we have quoted Yājñavalkya on *karman*,
let us quote the Evangelist's witness about Jesus: "He is not here, for
he is risen," said the angel,[21] explaining with real insight what the
Resurrection is all about to the courageous women, bewildered at the
sight of the empty tomb. Avoiding the theology of the Resurrection, a
contemplative insight into one of its dimensions might be: It is good
and necessary that I go, that I disappear, otherwise the Spirit will not
come;[22] otherwise you will make of me an idol, you will limit me to
one idea or interpretation, in spite of my repeatedly saying that when
the Son of Man comes he will not be here or there, but will be like
the lightning which appears in the East and West alike.[23]

When it is said, "He is risen," we may be allowed to understand
that he is not here, he cannot be located with geographical categories
or within merely historical parameters. It is as if the angel were saying that his true resurrection is his absence, his not being here or

there. He is above limited human horizons, above theological and philosophical speculations, well above any kind of worship, and yet he is present in his absence and we do not need to discover "Him" (as an object) in order for him to receive our acts, since anything we do for "the little ones" we do it unto him.[24]

But, at the same time, as the Christian Liturgy stresses at Easter, quoting from a rather free though traditional version of the Psalms of the Old Testament: "I am risen, and I am still with you."[25] Precisely because I am risen I am not here; yet precisely because I am risen, I can be with you. The presence of the living Christ is not that of an encroaching guardian or a vigilant eye, not even the ultimately alienating presence of an "Other," but the intimately liberating presence of an absence which allows us to grow, to become. The eucharistic revelation is his disappearance: only when left with the bread alone did the disciples recognize him.[26]

This Christ is certainly the living Jesus, yet this in no way prevents *him* from being present and active under as many different *whats* as there are religious traditions.

Not all problems are answered, but a breakthrough may be in sight if the contemplative joins mind and heart with the active approach.

Religious Understanding

*Loke'smin dividhā niṣṭhā purā mayā'nagha
jñāna-yogena saṁkhyānām karma-yogena yoginām.*

In this world a twofold foundation was proclaimed by me of old—
O blameless one: the discipline of wisdom for Men of reason, the discipline of action for active Men.

—BG III, 3

Ou pās o legōn moi kyrie, kyrie, eiseleusetai eis tēn basileian tōn ouranōn, all' ho poiōn to thelma toū patros mou...

Not everyone who calls me "Lord, Lord" will enter the Kingdom of Heaven, but only those who do the will of my Father...

—Matt. 7:21[27]

Necessary but Insufficient Categories. The contemplative sees, he intuits the truth, he attains a certain immediacy which makes of him a mystic; but the mystic ceases to be such the moment he speaks. Speech irradiates his experience, but also dissipates it. The Word is the Firstborn of the Father,[28] the Firstborn of the Universal Order,[29] but words are only broken fragments of that Word, and each human language is only one channel, a given system incarnating a particular cultural and religious world.

How is the contemplative to express himself if he can do so only in the language of his time and place? Each word he utters will sound to him as a lie the moment that his speech is taken literally. No living word is ever literal. On the other hand, the active method is equally as insufficient as it is necessary. Without it there would be little inter-action, but by itself it achieves understanding only at the heavy price of the surrender of one of the partners, who must submit to the rules of the encounter proposed by the other, thereby reducing its role to that of serving the interests of the other.

This latter attitude, which we describe in such a brief and crude way, is far from being unrealistic. Today many a religious dialogue is unconsciously so directed that it becomes possible only when one of the parties plays the role of servant. To ask, for instance, how Christianity can be better known in the Arabic world, and how it would learn from the Muslim experience so as to benefit from the positive riches of Muslim spirituality, would be one such example.[30]

Complementary Methods. What is needed is a twofold approach. On the one hand we need the contemplative, steeped in more than one religious world, who has achieved this wider experience not as an interesting experiment but as an excruciating yet liberating personal experience, and who at the same time has the necessary skill and intelligence to express himself in more than one theological and religious system.[31] We need the contemplative, further, to show us that, in the encounter of religions and cultures, harmony does not imply uniformity, and metaphysical oneness does not imply administrative union. Precisely because the contemplative vision discovers the oneness amidst the variegated multiformity of things and appearances, it does not tend to render them uniform. External similarity is not essential for the recognition of a deeper unity. The contemplative, to use an example from Christian ecumenism, would not push for one single administrative ecclesiastical body, but would emphasize ecclesial and sacramental unity. Here the Church is seen not so much as an *organization,* but as an *organism,* supple, open, and vital.[32]

The contemplative will also offer a salutary corrective to the haste and desire of the active approach for tangible results. Many frustrations appear because we tend both to overlook the factor of time and to overvalue it. Peace, harmony, and understanding cannot be achieved overnight. What is the result of millennia cannot be solved without reckoning with the factor of time and the proper rhythms of history. On the other hand, if the hoped-for results are delayed, the contemplative insight will prevent us from being discouraged or frustrated. It is but natural that the spiritual realization of an interior oneness is closer at hand than its external manifestations. Moreover the heart and mind of the true contemplative hold more than a private dream: it is an anticipation of a real state of affairs. The contemplative has thus a priestly-prophetic role: He mediates between issues previously irreconcilable, and anticipates a new age by realizing in his inner being what one day may also have historical repercussions. What happens in the mind and the heart of the contemplative may later irradiate on a greater scale when the time is ripe.

But there is another task to be performed. Alone, the contemplative will easily overlook or neglect other important dimensions of reality. Man also needs systems of thought, structures for action, and institutions to live in. These are the provinces of the active approach. Therefore, the contemplative and the Man of action have to be involved in a dialogical (and not merely a dialectical) dialogue, in order that the contributions of both may play their part in the growth of Man into the fullness of his own being.

What will be the criterion coordinating the active and contemplative approaches? How is mere understanding going to affect actual life; how is active interference going to modify the contemplative insight? To return to an earlier example, I may be convinced that Muslims are right to worship the form of God that they do and to believe the tenets they hold; further, I may, in a way, share in their belief from my point of view, but this may not be sufficient nor make it desirable for me to join the Muslim religion in a formal way. Acknowledging a certain transcendental unity of all creeds or the relative validity of all religions, important as this step may be, does not solve the problem of a divided humankind, for the ideological aspect of the different traditions may be at variance or even in conflict. The two methods are complementary, but the complementarity cannot be articulated in any strategic or programmatic way. Here we could apply the injunction not to be anxious about tomorrow, but have the confidence that tomorrow will look after itself.[33]

An Ongoing Process. Action and contemplation have to join hands in an act of cosmic, human and divine trust. No person, no religion, no one mode of life has the right to set the rules for this encounter. We must all recognize our insufficiency; this humble but true recognition may then put us on the right path, leading towards a new step in human growth.

Recognition of the fact that we are in an ongoing process of which we are not the masters amounts to an awareness of the radical relativity of our human situation, from which we can in no way escape. There is no such thing as an "absolute standpoint." So-called "pure objectivity" belongs to the myth of science, and has no place in the encounter of religions and cultures. Even a divine revelation is mediated by our reception of it, and the words we may use to describe it, so that we can no longer totally distinguish the "absolute" element from our understanding of it. What we can do is become more and more aware of our situation and thus of our insufficiency, maintain ourselves in an attitude of hope, a mood of expectancy. It is this attitude that makes the interreligious dialogue and the common search for truth one of the purest religious acts today. It entails not only confidence in my neighbor (impossible without love and understanding), but also faith in something which transcends us both, whatever name or no-name we may use for it.

By way of summing up this complex problematic, we return to the two mottoes of this study.

Any ultimate problem—Reality, truth, Brahman, the mystery of life, existence, human nature, God—is certainly "not understood by those who understand," for their understanding of the mystery is reduced to their capacity to understand, and is thus incomplete. Those who understand do not really completely understand; they understand only from their particular angle or from their own understanding. They understand only what they are capable of understanding, and no one Man or human group can pretend to have exhausted the understanding of truth. Brahman, or any ultimate which by this very fact would also encompass the subject, cannot be an object of anything, and thus cannot be the object of any understanding. How can you know the knower?[34] If you happened to know it, it would no longer be the knower, but the "known." You can only know along with the knower, but you cannot know it. It would be like looking for darkness with a lamp.

Moreover "it is understood by those who do not understand." And here we should take the message literally. The true, authentic nonunderstanding is the real understanding; it is the act of truly "standing under" reality and, in a way, being its foundation. The text does not say that it is understood by those who *understand that they do not understand.* Those are the intellectuals, the more or less conceited, if intelligent, people who play with the knowledge of their "ignorance." Those who are conscious of their own ignorance only play at being humble; they certainly do not understand anything. If they understand that they do not understand, they certainly understand it, i.e., their nonunderstanding. Those who really understand do not know that they do not understand, which is already a form of understanding. Real ignorance or true knowledge cannot be feigned. There is no possible pretense here. All that we are able to know is not the ultimate knowledge. Ultimate knowledge is innocent: it does not know that it does not know. It knows without knowing *it*. "Blessed are the poor in spirit" could be another way of saying this.

The second text echoes the collection of Upanishadic texts and is orchestrated by another series of sayings in the New Testament.[35] It has the same purport. The two greatest values of Man, wisdom and prudence, or intellect and acuteness, are here hopelessly shattered. There is no escape. The wisdom of the wise and the intelligence of the intellect, he, the Lord, will destroy. He will apparently make no use of any human value, nor will he build where others have built. The Kingdom is a new creation—out of nothing. It is the foolishness of the Cross, the weakness according to the world, the stupidity of Man that He will extol. Obviously, the moment we want to understand or defend those words we contradict ourselves, for if we succeed in making sense of them, we will have overcome foolishness and will have begun to manipulate the foolishness of the Cross as if it were only for others and not for us as well. If we take refuge with the scum of the world and begin, remembering the words of Paul, to feel comfortable there, then we become the worst of hypocrites, playing the publican and choosing the last places with the secret desire to be praised or to be asked to come up higher.

What does this mean? What *can* we know? It means we know that our knowledge is broken, fragmentary and distorted; we also know that the refractions of our angles may be corrected by the diffractions of our brother's or sister's and that those whom I may be inclined to consider valueless and of no interest may also contribute efficaciously to the weave of the multi-colored tunic of humankind. We know that we have no right to despise anything, or discard anyone. We have neither the right to judge others, nor to judge ourselves. We know that we must renounce the pronouncement of ultimates and final affirmations (including the ones made here), so as not to reject those who make them. What emerges here is an intuition of the *pratītyasamutpāda,* the radical relativity of all that is.[36]

I am pleading neither for an undifferentiated irenism nor for the elimination of the criteria of truth or consistency. We must stick to those latter precisely because we cannot do without them. I address myself against any kind of idolatry, to put the same idea in traditional terms. I am trying to make room for the contemplative approach, but not by saying that the contemplative has to be received with sole honors, as if he were on a higher plane than the others. I am only reflecting on those powerful words, because to put them into practice requires the supreme power of powerlessness: "Blessed are those of gentle spirit, for they shall inherit the earth."

Chapter 3

Word of Silence

Non-dualistic Polarities

Present-day ecumenism runs the risk of becoming superficial. The first commonplace, perhaps, is to assume that there is already a common place. All ways may lead to Rome, but this statement entails two conditions: that we walk on those ways, without stopping short of the end—i.e., that the ways be really ways—and that we do not jump transversally from one way to another, but follow one particular way with patience and the hope that we shall meet at least at the end of our journey if our ways do not cross earlier.

In other words, we should beware of the danger of shallowness inherent in any search for universality.

We have to recognize at the very outset that we do not (yet?) have a universal language. True ecumenism could, perhaps, be defined as a searching for one—certainly not for one tongue or idiom, but for one language as a universe of discourse.

Even today, when we are seriously concerned with spiritual life, I am too much of a Buddhist to assume that language discloses reality univocally and that we could use, if not the word, at least the reality of "God" as a common assumption and starting point. Silence is our first and perhaps our only common ground.

We could not proceed much further—at least while utilizing human language—unless we assume that language is not the whole of human reality, that reality is not exhausted in language, and that the human access to reality—and truth—is not only by means of words.

This chapter was originally published as "The Silence of the Word: Non-Dualistic Polarities," *Cross Currents* 24 (1973): 154–71, under the title "The Silence of the Word: Non-dualistic Polarities."

All the quotations in this chapter from the *śruti* (early Indian Scriptures) are from Panikkar, *The Vedic Experience: Mantramañjarî* (Berkeley: University of California Press, 1977) except text 7, on page 49, from Hume's Standard Version.

Furthermore, I would like to show that even language is precisely such because it words the silence. Silence dawns the moment we are situated at the very source of being, which is at the same time the source of the Word.

Can I, today, transcend language along with you?

Can I proceed along one concrete path—and reach that place—which is no-where and "where" we all meet?

Help me now in this venture and let us pray:

Myself listening aloud,

You listening in quietness,

All trying to hear *śruti,* Primordial Word, First-born of Silence

Word out of Silence is the overall motto of our Symposium—and rightly so, for this is understandable to everybody. Only a word coming out of silence is a real word and says something.

The Word of Silence can also be taken as the summary of my contribution—and this is appropriate, since I cannot believe that there is Silence on the one side and Word on the other.

Word of Silence does not mean Word *about* Silence (objective genitive), but the Silence that is in every Word (subjective). It does not mean the silent word, but the silence's word, the silence that is in every word, the word made of silence. By truly entering into the Word, not denying or repressing it, I may discover the source out of which the Word speaks. Then I may find that 90 percent of my words are absolutely unnecessary; I may enter into a silence that will make the few words I speak authentic, truthful. The lie, untruthfulness, is the capital sin. As the *Śatapatha Brāhmana* (II, 2, 2, 20), an Indian ritual text, says: *satyam eva upacāra,* "Worship is, above all, truthfulness." One may also say, on another level: Truth is worship. Silence is not the simple negation of words; it is not a question here of "keeping" (i.e., forcing) silence through an act of abstraction, but one of discovering Silence *in* discovering Word. Then all our words will be true words, words of worship, words of power.

Let me word that silence; the silence of the word.

We can certainly speak *about* silence as we can speak about what happened to me yesterday, or about x, or any subject matter. But the silence about which we speak is not a real silence, for silence is not an *object* (about which you can think, speak). We cannot speak about real silence, just as we cannot search for darkness with a torch in our hands. Silence cannot be spoken of without being destroyed, since it is not on the same level as speech.

We can speak *around* silence—circumscribing silence, i.e., we can speak about that which is around silence, but which silence is not. We can describe the neighbors of silence, and point out what leads to, comes from, and surrounds silence—just as we can surmise that darkness surrounds us when our flickering lamp does not illumine the entire horizon of our sight.

But we can do more: we can *speak* silence—letting silence burst into word, allowing it to explode into speech, simply and really speaking. The authentic word is not a cancer, an excretion of some concocted material on the mental level, but the expression, the revelation and intuition (*pratibhā,* as the Indian grammarians would say) of real, lived experience. Any real word is word because it comes out of silence; but it is more; it is precisely authentic word because it *is* (spoken) silence. And the Silence was made Word—and began to Speak! Creation, in the Christian context, is seen to be a splitting of the Primordial Word into thousands of different voices, melodies, cacophonies, etc. God speaks only once, but we hear it twice: the *Logos* and the world. Creation is in the Word in time. It is the business of creatures, first of all, to listen to the varied rhythms of multiplicity, and to reconstruct the Word. And the Word that emerges out of this reconstruction would be different (to speak in categorical terms) from the Word which was at the beginning. Thus, my comment to John 1:1: "And at the end, the Word shall be." And this in between, this moment of silence, is an orchestra!

The Word is the sacrifice of Silence. The self-immolation of silence brings about the word. Silence no longer exists when the word appears—but the word is there, and carries all that silence *can* express; the word *is* all that silence is—but silence is then no more; there *is* only word.

But we mortals cannot speak that Word. Who can be the Word of Silence? *Vāc,* "the Word is the Firstborn of Truth," says the Indian Revelation.[1] Through the Word everything has been produced; *vāc* was at the side of God, repeats a *Brāhmaṇa:* "And this [in the beginning,] was only the Lord of the universe. His Word was with him. This word was his second. He contemplated. He said, 'I will deliver this Word so that she will produce and bring into being all this world.' "[2]

Vāc is Brahman, echoes an *Upanishad.*[3] It is the first offspring of the absolute.[4] It is *nityā vāc,* the "eternal word," according to a famous *mantra* of the Ṛg Veda.[5] Or, in the inimitable language of the *Atharva Veda:*

That Sacred Word which was first born in the East
The Seer has revealed from the shining horizon.
He disclosed its varied aspects, high and low.
The womb of both the Existent and Nonexistent.[6]

Vāc is truly "the womb of the universe."[7] For "by that Word
of his, by that Self, he created all this [universe], whatever there
is."[8]Nobody can say that the Word is not held in the highest esteem:
"The Word is infinite, immense, beyond all this.... All the Gods, the
celestial spirits, men and animals, live in the Word. In the Word all
the worlds find their support."[9]

The sacrifice of the vedic *Prajāpati,* the total immolation of the
trinitarian Father, is the explosion of silence producing the three
worlds, uttering the Logos.[10]

In our age, still dominated by the *myth of science,* one constantly
hears the methodological advice (to students, executives, and people
who want to succeed, or have to in order to survive): "Whatever you
want to say, say it," followed by the second part of this golden rule:
"and as clearly and briefly as possible." The latter phrase betrays a
shallow, utilitarian (and, I would add, colonialistic) attitude toward
time, which is here considered as something you can manipulate,
something you can shorten and lengthen at your will. Apparently
one can "say it," and even "briefly," independently of its content.
People do not—yet—affirm that you can make a plant grow quicker
by pulling the leaves, but many assume that you can train a young
student to say in few words even things that need more words and
more time to be said. Time is considered to be a factor extrinsic to
the (temporal) thing, something you can shorten or lengthen without
changing the "thing" said. In other words, it is possible to reduce
time, just as we can simplify mathematical equations.

This presupposes that all things can be expressed clearly. Because
truth is supposed to be "clear," the human mind is also expected
to be clear, and obscurity is taken to be "black," bad, untrue. The
Cartesian dogma of "clarity and distinction" is here patent and is, I
suggest, also the Western—and even white—man's bias.

Are we so sure that we are the lords of time and the masters of
intelligibility that we should be allowed to formulate such a methodological rule? Are time and words only instruments which we can
use according to our will? We should keep in mind that most human
traditions, not excluding the *śruti* and the Bible, say that God loves
obscurity.

But I would like to linger a little more on the first part of the advice: "Say whatever you want to say." We may consider here two assumptions:

> (a) *that you can say everything that you want to say,* and
> (b) *that you can say everything, i.e., that everything can be said.*

(a) One phrase that we often and unconsciously use in a wide range of situation is, "I mean to say..." To which one could retort, "Then say it!" But the fact is that we feel it is necessary to intercalate in our discourse: "Do you know what I mean?" and "I mean to say..." because, ultimately, we cannot say what we mean and I have to know what you *mean* in spite of the fact that you have not *said* it. You only meant to say it.

There is a constitutive gap between meaning and saying. You have to jump from the meaning to the saying and I have to jump back from your saying to the meaning if the saying is really to be a saying of something—i.e., conveying something which will dawn upon me as having a meaning also for me.

A word conceals as much as it reveals. Even more, it reveals only in so far as it conceals, and it is only making you aware that it conceals something in how it reveals what it "says." In all authentic discourse there is an element of suggestion, of the unsaid, of mystery. In Sanskrit poetics this "resonance," this ineffable echo of emotion more than meaning, is called *dhvani,* and is seen as the essence of poetry and of the *kavi-pratibhā,* the "poetic genius."

You cannot say all that you mean. You can say only what you are capable of saying. You can only trans-late (in space: *trans,* and in time: *late*)[11] what you mean. You can clothe the meaning in words, but this clothing is all that you can say, for a wordless meaning cannot be said.

On the other hand, you cannot mean all that you say. You mean only a part of what you say. You mean much more and much less than what you say. And you cannot control this plus or minus by yourself. It has to be the other, the partner in dialogue, who tells you what you really have said.

The word is never a monologue; the saying is only such if it says it to someone. What you say has meaning only within a context, but you cannot control your context, much less the context of your listeners, who will inscribe the text of what you say in their context and understand you according to their own forms of apperception. What you say is not (or no longer) your private property.[12]

It is certainly not as if there were a wordless meaning that you afterwards translate. To speak is not just to translate, but to express, and the expression—the pressing it outside yourself—belongs to that which you express. There are no wordless meanings. To come to the point: Someone who keeps silent when she has many things to say is either a hypocrite or has a repressive nature on the fringe of pathology. Silence is neither a technique, nor a device, nor a matter of the will.

The word is symbol of what there is—and here we already come to our second point.

(b) *Not everything can be said:* No "thing" can be said. Only that which can be said, can be said. But this *can* does not depend upon your will. What you *want* to say is already a lie, an inauthentic word. The word you *want* to speak is not the real word. The real word is simply spoken. It speaks. And woe if you do not speak it out!

The real word neither breaks the Silence nor "trans-lates" it. The word is not an instrument or a technique. There is *no-thing* beyond or behind the word. The silence out of which the word comes and which it manifests is not another "thing," another "being," which then, because already in some way thinkable, expressible, would be in its turn the manifestation of a still more primordial being *et sic in infinitum.* The word *is* the very silence in word, made word. It is the symbol of Silence.[13] In the beginning was the Word and the Word was at the beginning—but there is no beginning when there is no word. The "Unbeginning" has no word. The word is coextensive with being: Non-being has no word, it is "unword," it does not word.

Let us pause a moment to listen to an astonishing Mayan creation hymn:

> Then he descended
> While the heavens rubbed against the earth.
> They moved among the four lights,
> Among the four layers of the stars.
> The world was not lighted;
> There was neither day nor night nor moon.
> Then they perceived that the world was being created.
> Then creation dawned upon the world.[14]

If we want to speak of Being and Non-being, then we have to realize that Being and Non-being are neither opposite nor contradictory. These two words are not reducible to the abstract formula "A and Non-A," because the *Non* of the Non-being is not the negation of being as non-A is the negation of A. If all Being is on the side of Being, even negation is on that side, so that the "negation" implied in Non-being is not a negation (which already belongs to Being).[15]

If the Word is the organ of Being and Non-being cannot be conceived as a negation of Being (which is a contradiction in terms if the negation has to be real, i.e., carrying being with it), if Non-being is an *unword,* if Being and its expression are coextensive, is there any way out of this impasse, this manifest *aporia?*

It is here that any dualistic or monistic scheme appears insufficient. In fact, there is another experience which overcomes both monism and dualism. We may call this the *trinitarian* or *advaitic* intuition. Now the real trinitarian/advaitic approach is ineffable and non-dialectical (otherwise we would have subordination of the Spirit to the Logos). We cannot understand Word and Silence through a dialectical mode of apprehension. It is only by allowing our word, our manifestation, our life, the revelation (icon) of being which we ourselves are, spirit *and* matter, to sink back into its source that the silence as source will dawn upon us.

I should immediately add that the source of being is not being, but, precisely, the *source* of being—being is already on *this side* of the curtain. Entering into silence is not an escape from the world, creating a dichotomy between the ultimate and the relative. It is to discover that the ultimate is only ultimate because I am speaking from the relative; and the relative is only relative because I discover that there is that relation which allows me to be silent from the ultimate point of view. The tension I emphasize here can neither be grasped dialectically nor is it of a dialectical nature. Rather this tension is a *dialogical* one. Perhaps a cultural digression may provide some illumination.

We are dealing with one of the basic assumptions of mankind, one of the few alternatives man has chosen, or been chosen to follow: the way of the Logos or the way of the Spirit.

There is a significant passage in the *Śatapatha Brāhmaṇa*. It describes the struggle about the primacy of *vāc* or that of *manas*. The former rests on the ultimate value of the image, the formulation, the expression, the word. The latter assumes the ultimate value of the inspiration, the experience, the thrust:

> 8. Now once there was a dispute between the Spirit and the Word. "I am excellent," said the Spirit, and the Word said, "I am excellent."
>
> 9. The Spirit said, "I am certainly better than you, because you do not utter anything that is not previously understood by me. So, as you just imitate what I am doing and simply follow me, I am certainly better than you."
>
> 10. The Word said: I am certainly better than you, because whatever you know, I make it known, I communicate it."

11. They went to Prajāpati, asking for his decision. Prajāpati
spoke in favor of the Spirit, saying [to the Word]: "The Spirit is certainly better, because you only imitate and follow what the Spirit is
doing; and he who is imitating and following what another does is
undoubtedly inferior."
12. As the Word was thus refuted, she became ashamed and mis-
carried. The Word spoke to Prajāpati: "I shall never become the
carrier of your oblation, I whom you have refuted!" Therefore, whatever in the sacrifice is performed for Prajāpati is done in a low voice,
because the Word refused to carry the oblation to Prajāpati.[16]

This text could represent the inherent polarity of the Indo-
European civilization and the emphasis put by the "West" on the
Word and by the "East" on the Spirit. For, undoubtedly, the Logos
has become *stronger* in the West and the Spirit has been considered *better* in the East—allowing for the oversimplification of such
a statement. Centuries of historical experience corroborate that the
Word without the Spirit is certainly powerful but barren, and that
the Spirit without the Word is certainly insightful but impotent. The
possibility of an authentic and balanced trinitarian approach is a
subject for another occasion.[17]

We may now offer a translation and brief commentary (concerning our subject only) rendering a basic intuition of the Indian
tradition as formulated in the *Bṛhadāraṇyaka Upanishad*.

1. In the beginning this was the Self alone, in the form of a Man.
Looking around he saw nothing whatever except himself. He said in
the beginning: "I am" and thence arose the name "I." So, even today,
when a Man is addressed, he says in the beginning, "It is I," and
then adds any other name he may have. Furthermore, since before
the world came to be he had burned up all evils; he is Man. He who
knows this also burns up whoever wants to be before him.

The text invites us to look in and out until both visions merge
into one reality encompassing subject and object, i.e., until the "i
am" coalesces with the "I AM" at the price—obviously—of burning
up the individualistic ego.

A Man: *puruṣa;* person, the primordial Man, the theandric principle, as in RV X, 90.

We have here one of the most powerful accounts of the rise of
human self-consciousness: the birth of reflection. The I is both the
aham, unique without a second, and also the I still to be liberated,
which in spite of everything has also no other name than "I." I
am: *aham asmi.* This is one of the highest revelations of reality and
should not be hypostasized upon a "He." That is to say that "I am I"

is not interchangeable with "He is I" or "I am He,"[18] the first being only a mental projection and the second sheer blasphemy.

The Sanskrit pun is untranslatable: *pūrva,* before; and *us-,* to burn, give *pur-uṣ-a,* the Man.

> 2. He was afraid; so, even today, one who is all alone is afraid. He thought to himself: "Since nothing exists except me, of what am I afraid?" Thereupon his fear vanished, for of what should he have been afraid? It is of a second that fear arises.

You are alone only when you discover that you are alone. This discovery is the beginning of finite consciousness. You discover your limits and feel alone.

But only thinking it out can help once consciousness of solitude has arisen.

Real anxiety is only fear of fear and thus dread of utter nothingness. Our own image is frightening when it reflects its hollowness.[19] A process of "conscientization" can rid us of dread, for confidence in the power of the mind tells us that, if there is nothing to frighten us, we have no reason to be fearful.

> 3. He found no joy; so, even today, one who is all alone finds no joy. He yearned for a second. He became as large as a man and a woman locked in close embrace. This self he split into two; hence arose husband and wife. Therefore, as Yājñavalkya used to observe: "Oneself is like half of a split pea." That is why this void is filled by woman. He was united with her and thence were born human beings.

Again a play with words: the Self split (*pat-*) into husband (*pati*) and wife (*patnī*). The *ardhanārīśvara* character of Man is here symbolized.[20] Man is *androgynous* as an anthropological reality. The desire for a second is only cathartic when it is a holistic movement toward integration, i.e., when it is not concupiscence but love.

Joy is here the criterion of reality as joy is the fullness of being.

> 4. She thought: "How can he unite with me, as he has brought me forth out of himself? Well, I will hide myself." She became a cow, but he became a bull and united with her. Hence cattle arose. She became a mare, he a stallion; she became a she-ass, he a male ass. He united with her and hence single-hoofed animals arose. She became a she-goat, he a he-goat; she became a sheep, he a ram. He united with her and hence goats and sheep arose. In this way he created everything that exists in pairs, down to the ants.

The theme of divine incest as the only possible way to redeem creation is here expressed by way of describing that all creatures need a second intervention, a descent of God in order to reach their destination, to continue creation (be fertile) and bring the universe to its fulfillment.[21]

5. He realized: "I indeed am this creation, for I produced all this"—for he had become the creation. And he who has this knowledge becomes [a creator] in that same creation.

To "become the creator" does not necessarily mean to be so substantially but to create along with him, i.e., to be, in the functional sense, creator, i.e., creating—because such a man really creates. No mystic would deny this experience, whatever wording one may use in order to describe it.

🍃

7. Verily, at that time the world was undifferentiated. It became differentiated just by name and form, as the saying is: "He has such a name, such a form." Even today this word is differentiated just by name and form, as the saying is: "He has such a name, such a form."
He entered in here, even to the fingernail-tips, as a razor would be hidden in a razor-case, or fire in a fire-holder. Him they see not, for (as seen) he is incomplete. When breathing, he becomes breath (*prāṇa*) by name; when speaking, voice; when seeing, the eye; when hearing, the ear; when thinking, the mind: these are merely the names of his acts. Whoever worships one or another of these—he knows not: for he is incomplete with one or another of these. One should worship with the thought that he is just one's self (*ātman*), for therein all these become one. That same thing, namely, this self, is the trace (*padanīya*) of this All, for by it one knows this All. Just as, verily, one might find by a footprint (*pada*), thus—. He finds fame and praise who knows this.

Nāma, rūpa, name and form. At variance here with the Greek *morphe,* form does not stand for the permanent "essence" but for the ephemeral shape or clothing of reality. To consider the *form* accidental or essential is, again, one of the fundamental human options.[22]
The question is here not only one of the immanence (logically as well as ontologically) and vice versa, nor can there be a part without the whole and vice versa. He who discovers this is, by this very fact, complete.

9. Thus they said: men think that by knowing Brahman they will become the All. What, then, did Brahman know by means of which it became the All?

The question is whether the epistemological order has onto-logical repercussions and again whether consciousness and self-consciousness can be identical.

> 10. In truth, in the beginning this was Brahman alone. It knew it-self only as *I am Brahman*. Hence it became the All. And as the Gods one by one awakened [to this], they too became that, and likewise the seers, and likewise men.

Real knowledge does not only mirror reality: it produces it.

We have the following equations: *idam* (this) = *aham; aham* (I) = *brahman; tat* (that) = *brahman; brahman* = (all) *sarvam*.

> 16. Now this is the Self, the world of all beings. If a man offers and sacrifices, he will attain the world of the Gods. If he recites [the Vedas], he will attain the world of the Seers. If he offers libations to the Forefathers and desires offspring, he will attain the world of the Forefathers. If he gives shelter and food to men, he will attain the human world. If he gives grass and water to animals, he will reach the animal world. If beasts and birds, [even] down to the ants, find a place in his house, he will reach their respective worlds. In the same way as a man wishes security for his own world, so all beings wish security to the one who knows thus. This is indeed known and investigated.

The whole universe is linked into a unity by the sacrament of the word and the sacrifice of action.

Known and investigated: *viditaṁ mīmāṁśitam,* i.e., known both by experience or intuition and by reflection.

The polarities we speak about are not independent positions gov-erned by the dialectical laws of thesis, antithesis and synthesis. They are not independent, nor even interdependent, but intradependent. They are not mutually exclusive so that they must be *aufgehoben,* but mutually inclusive. They need one another and they cannot be without each other. They are not parts of a whole, but rather they are the whole in a part, the whole partially (seen). Non-being, to return to our example, is not negative being; it is not a kind of mathemat-ical zero which helps in calculations with the mathematical infinite; neither is it the limit of being, as if being were limited by non-being. Non-being does not enter into a dialectical process so that one may manipulate being on the one hand and non-being on the other; Non-being is Silence, and its relationship to being (the Word) is not one of opposition but of *origination* and we do not simply go back to the origins. We take the origins with us in order to proceed ahead.

The moment we discover this we realize that this cosmic, human and divine pilgrimage is filled with origins, beginnings; we can no longer be satisfied by repeating words, or by just going back to the silence, but enter into that dance where silence and non-silence, being and non-being, form part of a whole of which we are aware *only once we have done it*—and committed the mistakes—not before.

The polarities we are speaking about have to do with the very character of reality. They need one another and *are* only in confrontation with, dialogue with, and dependence on each other. In point of fact, they are not two (anything) nor are they one. The "one and the many" is the great fallacy of our mind. It is something which the mind cannot apply to itself.

Man would not be man if there were no woman, and vice versa. God would be no God if there were no creatures, and vice versa. Goodness would not be such if evil were not its possibility, and vice versa. Freedom would be an empty concept if there were not necessity, and vice versa. Salvation would be meaningless if the opposite possibility were not a real one.

But this makes sense only if we restrain from substantivizing one of the poles or considering their relation as secondary and subsidiary to their (independent) being. An unrelated being, like an unworded word, is a sheer contradiction.

This means that only a holistic point of view will do justice to reality and that any analysis is methodologically inadequate for this kind of apprehension of reality, since the whole is more than just the sum of its parts (so that the integral of the analyzed parts would never yield the real).

Coming back to our starting point, the relationship between Silence and Word is a non-dualistic one, and neither monism nor dualism will do justice to their intra-penetration.

There is an intrinsic and constitutive polarity between Silence and Word, the one which makes possible the other. They are neither enemies nor incompatible. Of course, there are escapist silences and repressed silences, as well as empty words and nonsensical chattering; it is only such non-authentic words or silences that are at variance. Any authentic silence is pregnant with words which will be born at the right time. Any authentic word is full of silence which gives to the word its life. May our words be always words of silence and our silence always the virgin womb that does not speak, for it simply has nothing to say.

Chapter 4

The Myth of Pluralism

The Tower of Babel

To Babel, Babylon, and Santa Barbara, theandric dwellings.[1]

Introduction

I am overwhelmed, thankful, and can only say that I shall try to be up to the expectations prompted by all the fine things which have been said of me. At the same time, I must confess to a certain uneasiness. When you don't expect a reward, when you are already somewhat accustomed to working without reward—*naiṣkarmyakarma,* for those who know the *Gītā*—and a kind of reward comes...it's likely to spoil everything. You ask yourself whether you've done something wrong, because you should be transparent, like pure light, and people should not even feel the need to thank you, since it goes without saying....

Perhaps I should interrupt all this more as an *invitation,* as something which makes me *envious* of being good enough to fulfill the expectations of all that has been said these last days, and about which I still have to meditate, and to learn. Perhaps then I shall begin—as Paul Ricoeur was saying, one way to overcome one's own obituary is to show that one is still alive—begin not just by repeating things from the past, topics about which I feel somewhat safe and sure, but rather by venturing into realms where I am insecure and run the risk of capsizing. We may indeed find no solutions to some of the questions I shall raise tonight. But anything for which we have a ready solution is not a real problem. Then, we would already be

This was the major talk of the Panikkar Symposium, given as a public lecture on the campus of the University of California at Santa Barbara on the evening of February 18, 1977. It was published as "The Myth of Pluralism: The Tower of Babel—A Meditation on Non-Violence," *Cross Currents* 29 (1979): 197–230.

the masters, not pilgrims on the way, going together towards what must ever remain *terra incognita,* if it is to remain an ultimate quest. Tonight I shall speak about everything. But symbolically, and by constant innuendo, so that some of what I say tonight may come to you in dreams, tomorrow, or the day after, but not immediately. To have chosen a partial topic would not have been worthy of the occasion. But, as I say, the risk is enormous; I shall most likely be overwhelmed by the problem itself, and defeated by it—which means convinced (*convictus*). I shall try to be consistent and intelligible, but not by following any linear logic or syllogistic conclusions. I shall not speak *about* myself—which could only be a kind of inadequate autobiography—but certainly I *shall speak myself,* I shall speak *out* myself, and thus perhaps profess the sort of confession which might be expected or considered appropriate on such an occasion. I have only to add that this is not my systematic theology, which Ewert Cousins is urging me to produce. Many of you know that I have previously thought about the topics touched upon in this lecture and I have even written about them, but if you will permit me not to sub- scribe to the linearity of time, I can assure you that it is the *first* time that I am confronting them.

My presentation will have three parts. (As the *Mahābhārata* says, all perfect things are threefold.) I am going to say what I shall say (section one); I shall say it (section two); and then I shall repeat what I have said (section three).

My entire talk could be found in the words of Genesis—and this is in tribute to Fritz Buri, since when speaking with theologians present one always feels a little uncomfortable unless one takes refuge in one of the three *ratnas*—or rather, in this case, in the words of the New English Bible, which translates the passage in an admirable way. In this particular instance the chapter begins precisely as it should: "Once upon a time...," says Genesis 11 (*kaí* says the Septuagint),

> ...all the world spoke a single language and used the same words. As men journeyed in the east, they came upon a plain in the land of Shi- nar and settled there. They said to one another, "Come, let us make bricks and bake them hard"; they used bricks for stone and bitumen for mortar. "Come," they said, "let us build ourselves a city and a tower with its top in the heavens, and make a name for ourselves; or we shall be dispersed all over the earth." Then the LORD came down to see the city and tower which mortal men had built, and he said, "Here they are, one people with a single language, and now they have started to do this; henceforward nothing they have a mind to do will be beyond their reach. Come, let us go down there and confuse their

speech, so that they will not understand what they say to one another." So the LORD dispersed them from there all over the earth, and
they left off building the city. That is why it is called Babel, because
the LORD there made a babble of the language of all the world; from
that place the LORD scattered men all over the face of the earth.

"Once upon a time . . ." and time and again it is repeated, over
and over; the Babylonians, the Assyrians, the Romans, the Greeks,
the Alexanders the Great and all the rest, the Spaniards, and the
French, and the British, and the Americans, and the Technocrats of
Modern Times, they all thought themselves to be alone bearers of
a flag with absolute standards.[2] They journeyed towards the East,
they journeyed towards the West to find new techniques, new ways
to make stronger bricks, or better mortar, or more useful tools or
powerful weapons, or whatever. It was perhaps the spear, it was the
discovery of iron, it was—big jump—the atomic bomb. And then
they said: "Let us spend some time together and build a big tower,
one single city, one single civilization, one single construct . . . and
worship one single God, because now we have got the better bricks,
with which we can make something really durable, and go up to
heaven and this time really build the classless society, the true justice on earth, on single culture of whatever sort, the paradise of
Democracy, the Proletariat mastering its own destiny," and so forth
and so on. Once upon a time . . . it was Mankind's dream (a dream
which seems somehow built into the heart of Man)[3] to build one
single tower, one big ladder to heaven, one great construct. And
the Lord—who seems here to be perhaps envious, or wants to keep
his prerogatives, or is playing a nasty game—the Lord appears not
to favor such human enterprises and, once upon a time, time and
again, Nebuchadnezzar falls, the *augustus imperator* dies, the colos-
sal empires collapse, the great hordes fade away. . . . And yet we go on
dreaming the same dream of a big city enclosing everything. Perhaps,
after all, the Lord God knew better: that the nature of Man is not
gregarious, collective, but each human being is a king, a microcosm
and the cosmos is a pluriverse and not a universe. God, as the symbol
for the infinite, seems to be in his proper role when he is destroying
all human endeavors towards comfortable finitudes.

In any case, after sixty centuries of human memory in the historical realm, is there no way for us to awaken to the futility of this
dream? What would happen if we simply gave up wanting to build
this tremendous unitarian tower? What if instead we were to remain
in our small beautiful huts and houses and homes and domes and
start building roads of communication (instead of just transporta-

tion), which could in time be converted into ways of communion between and among the different tribes, life-styles, religions, philosophies, colors, races, and all the rest? And even if we cannot quite give up the dream of a unitarian Mankind—this dream in the monolithic system of the tower of Babel which has become our recurring nightmare—could it not be met by just building roads of communication rather than some gigantic new empire, ways of communion instead of coercion, paths which might lead us to overstep our provincialisms without tossing us all into a single sack, into a single cult, into the monotony of a single culture?

This, in sum, is what I want to say.

The Problem of Pluralism

I am not referring exclusively to so-called "political pluralism," in great evidence during the first half of this century, nor to the ideal of a "pluralistic society" as in contemporary sociological discussion. I am not going to discuss "ontological pluralism," as the phrase has it, either. My problem is related to all these concerns and its treatment would like to offer a critical support to sociology and ontology; but it attempts to touch upon a more radical issue lying at the very basis of the use of this word "pluralism" as a living symbol whose purview includes both the nature of Man and that of the World.

Irreducibility of the Praxis to Theoria

We are here facing one of those existential problems which both arises out of a challenge from the *praxis* and only in the *praxis* finds its "theoretical" solution. The present-day problem of pluralism stems from a genuine experience of disorientation and chaos, and not from any merely theoretical problematic. There is nothing very peculiar in this, since most real problems come from having to face situations which set the mind tottering. The peculiarity in such types of existential problem comes from their touching an ultimate, something irreducible in principle, and thus inviting a return to the *praxis*. No purely theoretical solution can ever be adequate to the problem of pluralism; and this almost by definition. A problem which has a theoretical answer is not a pluralistic problem. We should therefore not expect a theoretical solution merely because we are now in an academic setting. We should avoid the superiority complex and dominion of the intellectual as much as that of the Man of action. *Theoria* and *praxis* are as mutually subservient as they are consistent.

I call this an *ontonomic* relation. However this may be, the solution belongs as well to the *praxis* (although we can, of course, also reflect on the solution and its meaning). If this is the case, the relation between theory and practice is not a dialectical relation, which would only put the burden on the *logos* and thus amount to another ideology: "We know better and now we come with our own solution; all the previous towers were wrong, but we are now going to tell you the secret for building the real, the everlasting, tower. 'We,' the Marxists, the Civilized, the Technocrats, the Artists, the Scientists, the Rationalists, the Christians..." No!

As I am still preparing the ground, let me point out that there has been a shift of meaning in the word "pluralism." If we consult any dictionary, we are taught that it is either a sociological concept or a philosophical notion. In the first case we are told that pluralism deals with political theories of how to structure the interrelation between human societies, especially the state, and the other human groupings. In the second case we find that pluralism is distinguished from monism and dualism, and that pluralism can be atomic, absolute, substantial, etc., depending upon whether you refer to Bertrand Russell and his logical atomism, or to William James, or to Gilbert Ryle, or whomever. In short, pluralism has classically been considered a metaphysical concept which raises certain questions about reality—in the abstract, so to speak. Today the meaning of the word is shifting from a sociological and metaphysical to an existential locus, which helps us to discover its roots. Pluralism is today a human existential problem which raises acute questions about how we are going to live our lives in the midst of so many options. Pluralism is no longer just the old schoolbook question about the One and the Many; it has become a concrete day-to-day dilemma occasioned by the encounter of mutually incompatible worldviews and philosophies. Today we face pluralism as the very practical question of planetary human coexistence.

Now, of course, the great temptation is and has always been to create a super-system: "Here I am, the tolerant one, who has made a place for everybody and for all the different systems. Obviously you will have to stay in the place I have allotted you, I—the great *jīvanmukta* of the Vedāntic persuasion—I know that I am above all the differences, and I have a place for Muslims, for Christians, for Jews, for everyone... provided, of course, that they behave, and sit at the places I have assigned them, they will feel happy and contented because I—the enlightened Man of Science and Reason—I have an overarching, superior vision which allows me to be totally tolerant and to keep all the other people in the world content in their little places. I, the Philosopher, the Christian, the King..." Enough. This is certainly not an attitude of pluralism. Needless to say that those are caricatures. A genuine *jīvanmukta* like Śrī Ramakrishna was saying the opposite.

The question of pluralism is also not the quandary presented by a *plurality* of irreducible entities. To be tolerant of a plurality of religions or world markets or schools of art as long as we can go along with our own idiosyncrasies, doing business as usual, being only respectful of the otherwise noninterfering whims of the others, has little to do with religious, economic or artistic pluralism. The plurality of absolutely sovereign nations which promise not to meddle in their neighbors' affairs, because they implicitly recognize that there are at the most international, but not supranational, problems like human rights, universal social issues or planetary concerns, has again little to do with pluralism. Pluralism begins when the *praxis* compels us to take a stance in the effective presence of the other, when the *praxis* makes it impossible to avoid mutual interference, and the conflict cannot be solved by the victory of one part or party. Pluralism emerges when the conflict looms unavoidable.

The problem of pluralism arises only when we feel—we suffer— the incompatibility of differing worldviews and are at the same time forced by the *praxis* of our factual coexistence to seek survival. The problem becomes acute today because contemporary *praxis* throws us into the arms of one another; we can no longer live cut off from one another in geographical boxes, closeted in neat little compartments and departments, segregated into economical capsules, cultural areas, racial ghettoes, and so forth. Perhaps the greatest, albeit indirect, achievement of technology is to have brought people and peoples together. Today isolation is no longer possible, and the problem of pluralism has become the first order of business. Neither Chinese walls, oceans, secret police nor armies can protect us against mass-media and atomic bombs.

Importance of the Problem

The problem of pluralism is in a certain sense the problem of *the other.* How can we tolerate, or even understand, the other when this is in no way—rationally, reasonably or intelligibly—feasible? The world is perhaps no longer in the arms of Greek *moira,* or the Indian *karma,* or in the hands of the Abrahamic *providence.* The world nowadays appears to be in *our* hands, and it seems to be in rather worse shape than in those days when we could at least curse the fates, charge destiny, or dispute like Job with his God as to whether or not he had acted justly. We no longer have anyone to blame for our woes but ourselves. What in Man has become more unfathomable and distant to human beings than any traditional Deity? *How can we deal with incompatible systems?* How can we deal with the ultimate problems of Man? How can we deal in justice with the problem of the other? It is worth noting that practically every so-called civilization has reached its ascendancy at the expense of some "marginal" people ... the aboriginal, the goyim, the kaffir, the infidel, the pagan, the poor, the illiterate, the savage, the black, the third world ... in a word: the barbarian.

And here I cannot but feel the tremendous power of the words. You know, at least, all of you who live in Santa Barbara, what the name *barbara* means. The name *barbara* is a Sanskrit word, from an Indo-European root, and from there it went to the *barbaros* of the Greeks, and then the Latins, and then the Barbarians. Ibn Khaldun refers to Qays b. Ṣayfī, a legendary king of South Arabia and contemporary of Moses, who gave the Berbers that name after hearing their "barbarah" jargon. *Barbara* is an onomatopoeic name; it means a kind of ... *ba, ba;* it means stammering ... because you are a foreigner, a non-Aryan, a *niger,* have curly hair (which is the secondary meaning of the word), and speak in a way which I cannot understand. Thus you may perhaps feel that I speak with an accent, without realizing that you also speak with another accent. And here we have Santa Barbara: *the canonization of the barbarian.* The bare fact that you today, here, are accepting my barbarous speech may perhaps help us to understand this symbol. Let this then be the *kairological* moment when we begin to discover that the barbarian has not only to be tolerated, but also blessed, canonized, sanctified. Perhaps now we begin to discover that the problem of the barbarians can no longer be solved at their expense, or provisionally solved, in the expectation that "one day they will become *cives romani,* civilized; one day they, too, will become Christians, one day we will make of them 'developed countries,' one day the slaves will be freed and be allowed all the gadgets of freedom and democracy, one day all the wetbacks and coolies will come and live with us in this great tower of Babel we are meanwhile forcing them to build for us.... "

And the barbarian? What has he to say about all this? There is even a Babylonian word *barbaru* meaning also foreigner, stranger. *Santa Barbara* ... has a great symbolism. And that the barbarian can come to us in this place and time with the claim of canonizing the *barbaros:* I find it not without a very deep meaning. And let me sur-reptitiously intercalate that this I assume to be a central question for Religious Studies in a time of pluralism.

The problem of the other *qua* other: How can we pretend to deal with the ultimate problems of Man if we insist on reducing the human being to only the American, or to only the Russian, or to the Christian, or to the black, or the male, or the exclusively het-erosexual, or the healthy and "normal," or the so-called civilized? Obviously we cannot. What I shall say is that the true foundation of a pluralistic society is not pragmatism, is not common sense, is not tolerance, is not just the lesser evil, but rather that pluralism is rooted in the deepest nature of things.

An important objection should be met here. In saying that the jus-tification for pluralism is not on the level of pragmatism—out of sheer necessity to put up with the other—but is grounded in the nature of Man and Reality, am I not securing a theoretical basis for pluralism and thus contradicting my initial statement that the pluralistic problem set by *praxis* cannot be solved by any *theory?*

Two observations may dispel this objection. The first is to recall that I began telling the *Myth of Pluralism* not by dispelling the myth, but by clarifying that pluralism is indeed a myth in the most rig-orous sense: an ever-elusive horizon in which we situate things in order to be conscious of them without ever converting the horizon into an object. The myth is irreducible to the logos—despite their common origin—and thus not reducible to theory either. The second observation will simply remind us that nowhere is it said that the nature of Man and Reality are totally transparent to theory or, in other words, that Man is synonymous with anthropology or Reality with philosophy—even as objects of consciousness. Affirming, then, that the nature of Man and of Reality is pluralistic, I am contending that no anthropology (or anthropologies), no philosophy (or philoso-phies), has ever exhausted—not even theoretically—Man and Reality. Neither can theory offer the last justification for the praxis (on what is theory itself based?), nor can praxis offer the ultimate foundation for theory (on what is praxis itself justified?).

Let me be clear about this, betraying one of my most cherished metaphysical insights: The ultimate metaphysical assumption of the greatest part of Western civilization, since the Presocratics, is the con-viction of the intimate correspondence between thinking and being. They may be ultimately the same or different, but they "theoret-ically" match each other. And my contention is that this genial intuition is not humanly universal and thus not universalizable if we want to encompass the whole range of the human experience—or of the human fact. The Buddhist world, for instance, does not make such an assumption.

Genesis of the Problem

As an interlude, permit me to present a few remarks under this heading.

1. *Pluralism is meaningless (Uniformity).* Except at the exceptional, and generally mythical, beginnings, the community (family, tribe, nation, group, church...) precedes the individual. The individual enters or is born into a society he has not shaped. Here rites of initiation (name-giving, circumcision, baptism, contract, vows...) have their place. Before this everything is indiscriminately undifferentiated: "all young men are uncles"; "all Chinese look alike." There is an *undifferentiated consciousness:* all the others are thrown into a single sack, all the others are "third world." (What indeed do the people of the so-called third world have in common, except a certain type of GNP?) The other *qua* other does not exist; and if he exists at all, he is "non-persona," unreckoned with, ignored. We live in an undifferentiated world, however big or small this world may be. The tribe is the world.

2. *Pluralism amounts to plurality (Difference).* At a certain moment, the individual begins to notice that his group is not the only such group existing in the world (there are other families, tribes, nations, churches, religions). He becomes conscious of *multiplicity.* This could be called the *de facto* recognition of *plurality.* It is the reign of Quantity. The many peoples set up Babel. In *plurality,* the question of the compatibility or incompatibility of *multiplicity* does not arise. It is a fact. It does not create unbearable frictions because the boundaries are clearly drawn and zealously guarded. One nation is just another nation, one group simply another group, one individual merely another individual, and the like. Multiplicity is taken for granted, and there is no question about unity. (Bertrand Russell, defending the "absolute pluralism" he at first called "logical atomism," could serve as an example here.)

3. *Pluralism means pluriformity (Variety).* At another moment the individual becomes aware that he has a particular vision of his own group. He realizes that his interpretation, although obviously the best for him, is not the only possible one. Other people in the same group hold different opinions, and these notions crystallize in different forms (political parties, religious persuasions, various sectors,

roles and functions) within the one given community. Man becomes aware of *variety*. This could be called the awareness of *pluriformity*. Again, the reign of Quality; the different peoples with different skills begin to construct Babel. In *pluriformity*, the question of the compatibility or incompatibility of *variety* does not arise because the unity of the group is already an accepted fact. There is the nation, and within it political parties and a variety of agencies. There is the church, and within it a variety of works, activities, and callings. Unity is taken for granted, and variety is not seen as a challenge to it. Here we all live within a single myth. But this can become the erroneous assumption of philosophies and worldviews when they try to be universal, extrapolating from any one such unified horizon. (Post-medieval Christianity could be a typical example, or Process Theology: they want to be universal from a perspective which is seen as universal only from within the system.)

4. *Pluralism connotes unattainable harmony (Diversity)*. There is another moment in the evolution of individuals and societies when Man becomes conscious of *diversities* which, if pushed to the limit, would break the unity. Man becomes aware of *both* the need for diversity and the need for unity. But harmony between the two needs has suddenly become problematic; they seem to be incompatible. "Deutschland über alles" and the United States as "the greatest nation in the world" ultimately cannot coexist. Christianity as the "absolute religion" and Hinduism as the "everlasting dharma" are incompatible. A philosophy based on the real difference between essence and existence, as the very foundation for human freedom and for distinction between creator and creature, cannot be reconciled with a Scotistic position; a Thomist can neither agree with a Scotist nor really understand how the latter can avoid pantheism and call himself a Christian—and, obviously, vice versa. Or again, St. Paul did not think it was possible for married people to be so undivided as to be fully consecrated to God. In other words, as long as Germany and the United States are independent nations, Christianity and Hinduism unrelated religions, Thomism and Scotism autonomous philosophies, as long as worldly matters are kept apart from those of God, there is no problem. The problem appears when interaction becomes inevitable and we discover we have only one word for both Germany and the United States, only one truth for Hinduism and Christianity, only one church for Thomism and Scotism, only one perfection for married and celibate alike. The builders of Babel cannot each construct a tower for himself. They not only have to communicate about the means (tools), but share the goals (the one Tower). Isolation is

no longer possible and unity is not convincing since it destroys one of the parties.

At this moment, the alternatives seem to be either despair with all that it entails or hope with all that it demands. This second half of our century can be called both the age of despair and the age of hope. Time is running short: either it will have to begin all over again (liturgy and death) or it will blow up (eschatology and revolution). *"Los extremos se tocan."*

Approaches to Pluralism

At this point I shall have to try to say just what pluralism is. I would approach the formulation by means of three different avenues: the *philosophical,* the *phenomenological,* and the *anthropological.*

The Philosophical Approach

From a philosophical viewpoint, the conflict between the One and the Many, which has occupied Man at least since Plato in the West and the Upanishads in the East, is perhaps the central question of the human mind. Here, instead of a whole course in philosophy, I shall confine myself to presenting, as it were, an exhibit in art, focusing on metahistorical sketches, which will attempt to indicate some ways Man has dealt with the problems of *ultimate human diversities.* The problem of the *hén kaì pollá, ekam evādvitīyam,* or, as we may put in here, (a) monism, (b) dualism, (c) non-dualism, could be formulated as follows: (a) one *or* many, and the one at the end succeeds; (b) one *and* many, and the many wins; and (c) neither one nor two, and the tensile polarity is maintained. Because of brevity, some caricatures are inevitable, but you will understand, I am sure, with *esprit de finesse.* This tripartite division is cross-cultural and must be understood against the background of our problematic on pluralism. We say neither that the West is dualist nor the East non-dualist or monistic, nor that these three concepts are not richer in meaning than the description we give of them.

(a) *Monism.* Reality is one, being is univocal, plurality is secondary, provisional or even apparent. But this plurality appears and therefore needs to be interpreted. The first way is governed by the law of the jungle: what academia might call the law of history, science the law of nature, and philosophy the law of power. The monism here may be latent, or implicit; it need not show its true colors immediately. The stronger in claws, intelligence, or weapons shall win—unless, of course, the equilibrium is maintained by an equal proliferation of prey and predator. This is the so-called law of nature. The secret of culture is to *postpone* the confrontation long enough for it to be "solved" eventually by the victory of the most powerful. We have to tolerate the other until we can conquer, convert, convince, or indoctrinate him as the weaker party. Patience, also called prudence and tolerance, are the key words here, along with strategy, apostolate, conversion, victory and the like. One Empire, one God, one Civilization, one Party, one Church, one Technology, etc. are so many general expressions of this first attitude. *Monism* is its final expression. Monotheism, as distinct from theism, could be another key word. Colonialism and imperialism would be the polemical descriptions. And eschatology may be the most refined way of taming the conflict by postponing the solution until the end. With a linear conception of time, this is perfect for the stronger; he can wait in the hope of final victory. For the weaker party, all is lost if time is linear. If time is circular, each moment is independent of its final outcome and one does not need to assume that the real beauty of a symphony lies only in its finale. No wonder that monistic exploitation has found it easier to dominate peoples indifferent to the oneway flow of history. Theological eschatology puts in a vertical transcendence what historical eschatology puts in a horizontal future.

In a monistic worldview, there is no legitimate place for pluralism. It is at most *tolerated*—with kindness and patience (or sometimes without them)—to avoid a greater evil. Plurality is always provisional.

I am not saying that monism offers a bad solution. Well understood, it may well be that it maintains the polarity of helping us to strive for an ultimate unity and to put up with pluralities for the time being, during the itinerant condition of Man and being. Man has then a goal, and at the same time an awareness of his fallen or provisory condition, so that patience becomes the central virtue—by which we possess our lives, to quote the Gospel.

(b) *Dualism.* The second way to deal with the problem of ultimate diversities is the genuine dialectical method. Here, in a sense, pluralism is *tamed.* The tension between the One and the Many is solved by the so-called rules of the mind seeking a balance, and eventually a synthesis, between the *sic et non.* The differing opinions, worldviews, and attitudes are permitted a "free" dialectical interaction; Man allows this free interplay of the various factors in full confidence that the conflict will be channeled and eventually resolved. Coexistence is the ground rule which enables the dialectical exchange to take place on all levels. Theoretically any opinion could be represented, provided it is willing to descend into the dialectical arena and struggle there on its own behalf. If it is defeated, it will lose the right to exist. Democracy and freedom are key words here; numbers (votes, points, dollars...) are considered decisive, the result of a dialectical process by which these very numbers are gained. It is not quite so simple as "one man, one vote," because the more responsibilities, the more votes you win and the cleverer you are, the more money you earn, so that power and influence are "justly" distributed according to talents. Liberalism, free enterprise, interplay, propaganda, and so forth are other expressions of the same attitude. *Dualism* is its final expression. But true dualism implies that both parties accept the dialectical game. It works only so long as the one and the many are more or less equally powerful (dualism works when you have Tory and Labour, the United States and the Union of Soviet Socialist Republics), but why should the white South Africans accept a Round Table Conference or the U.S. government allow the Symbionese Liberation Army to exist if they are convinced that the aim of the other is to destroy the opponent totally? Monism is lurking here. We allow coexistence as long as the other does not question our existence. Some compromise in good faith because they would not wipe you out if they could (the democratic opposition, for instance, belongs to the system). Others compromise in bad faith because they realize that they cannot eliminate you. What then is to be done—"écraser l'infâme"? (Invade South Africa or the Soviet Union? Or should they attack first, knowing their adversary's intentions?)

Again I am not saying that dualism is a bad or wrong option. Perhaps in some instances it is the only "realistic" one. Perhaps the factual human situation does not allow for any other form of survival; perhaps it trusts the spontaneous intuition of Man, the divine animal, endowed certainly with what the Greeks called *zoé* (spiritual, infinite life), but also with what they called *bíos* (animal, finite, or, we may even say, "vital" life). In any case, the problem of pluralism is not solved by accusing others as the villains and presenting ourselves as the heroes.

(c) *Nondualism.* There is still a third way, of which our epoch is becoming increasingly aware, although it has existed along with the others since the very beginning. The first way tries to solve ultimate conflict by promoting the triumph of the strongest party, although the words it uses are not only power, but also truth, God, law and order, etc. and, indeed, it succeeds in curbing the disruptive forces of a given *status quo*. The second way tries to solve the incompatibility by a provisional and dynamic balance between the different positions, and it certainly works as long as we believe in the same myth. The third way is sensitive to both the right of power and the wisdom of tension, but attempts a radically different approach from a monolithic solution in favor of the most powerful and a dualistic solution which is bound either to stiffen into an unstable and explosive balance or fall into a compromise in which the minority is given only a consolation prize. *Nondualism* would be its expression. Here pluralism appears as an awareness leading to a *positive* acceptance of *diversity*—an acceptance which neither forces the different attitudes into an artificial unity, nor alienates them by reductionistic manipulations. Here power does not have the last word, nor is majority rule the decisive factor.

As we saw, the problem of pluralism arises when we cannot dismiss the other from a unity which somehow encompasses both of us even though we are unable to agree with (or often even understand) the other party. We can neither dispense with nor break unity—it is above us. We cannot leave the country or the language or the planet, for instance—nor approve of or understand diversity—again obliged by a power superior to our will. "We" cannot condone torture or capitalism or dictatorship. As the poet once said speaking of love: *nec tecum nec sine te,* neither with you nor without you can I live.

Seen from another angle, the problem of pluralism arises when we face an insoluble conflict of ultimate values: on the one hand we cannot renounce the claims of our personal *conscience,* and on the other we cannot renounce the claim of our personal *consciousness.* For Abraham the problem of sacrificing his own son was not a pluralistic problem because God was the absolute master of both his conscience and consciousness. Here there is no ultimate conflict. For Arjuna in the *Bhagavad Gītā,* however, the problem was one of pluralism. Arjuna was torn between his conscience, which told him to follow the sacred duty of his caste, and his consciousness, which told him that waging war would not solve anything. The problem of pluralism is the problem of the limit case, the ultimate instance: God or Man, Conscience or Consciousness, Family or Country, Church or World, Fidelity to myself or Loyalty to my society. The problem arises when I feel that I have inalienable rights whose preservation has become an ultimate duty for me. Pluralism arises in the area of that which is non-negotiable for us. All the rest is a matter of acceptance, or compromise, or prudence, or "savoir faire"; but pluralism itself is non-manipulable. Pluralism begins its course in the world when Man, having lost his innocence, tries desperately to gain a new innocence. If philosophy and religion ignore this problem, we can well understand why they have little credibility when they try to give us a compass for orientation in our world. Authentic human life is facing death constantly: "to be or not to be," as young Naciketas exclaims in the *Kathopanishad*.

I should end the short description of this third attitude repeating what was emphasized in the other two cases, namely, that this fundamental option may be both a valid one, allowing us to overcome tensions without destruction of positive values, and a stifling attitude enervating us in the face of conflictive situations.

I should include a sort of footnote to the overcondensed philosophical treatment of the three attitudes: Man has often tried to resolve the dilemma by introducing a moral factor and absolutizing goodness when he could not succeed with truth. "The other is bad because he wants to kill me." "We are convinced that the Turks are a danger for Christendom, and so we organize a crusade; we are convinced that the Asian communists are a danger for the free world, and so we wage a war." Or we exploit the earth because we want more paper or oil, and so on. As long as we are on the top, "we"—Christians, whites, males, Hindu in India, Muslims in Pakistan, Westerners, rich people, the Educated, the Technocrats, the Trade-Unionists, the humans (against the earth)—as long as "we" are on top, we find ways of soothing, of making things palatable, of arranging things so that the other is somewhat happy in his subordinate position. But when the other begins to kick back, we are obliged to come to terms...and then what happens? Only a truce, until we have better weapons? Or?

The Phenomenological Approach

The problem of pluralism reaches the critical phase when we simply do not know what we have to say or to do. Let me proceed a little further by attempting what will amount to a simplified phenomenology. A phenomenological approach might say that pluralism appears as a problem when every other means for dealing with diversity fails. I have chosen three sorts of failure, which I shall present to you in short order. I am not defending a pessimistic vision of human nature as if there were a Platonic paradigm of what Man is supposed to be; but I am not indulging in an optimistic evaluation either, as if we should only look toward a rosy future, afraid to look into the errors of the past. A realistic attitude should not be discouraged by the failures of the past but cannot ignore them either.

Any writer is already a privileged being, any listener and reader of a reflection on the human condition already stands out from the average of his fellow humans. The underdogs don't give lectures, nor listen to them, nor have they much time for reflection. Even when they are not directly persecuted and tortured or starving, they live under the ever-present danger of losing a precarious balance whose absence might leave them at the mercy of human insensitivity. When we say Man, do we forget the slaves, for generations without number, the untouchables, who have no place in their own country, those exploited by foreign and domestic lords, the serfs, the armies of soldiers, workers in the service of causes they don't even understand, the multitudes of displaced, deprived, and hungry specimens of our human race? Who can be spokesman for them if they cannot even begin to articulate what they want or need? The subdued majority has not even a voice and, if we were to give them one in order to let them speak in our terms, we would easily convince them that they are pitiable, ignorant, and degraded fellows who deserve their lot. No wonder that their leaders are not prophets (who speak) or priests (who perform) but heroes who kill, retaliate, howl and destroy. But there are outstanding exceptions, Dr. Ambedkar for the untouchables, Martin Luther King, Jr., for the blacks, and others less well known. It is against this background that we should reflect on the meaning of pluralism. All the rest is "edifying" literature.

(a) The Historico-Political Failure. A pluralistic problem arises when the question cannot be solved by democratic means because we cannot abide by the rule of the majority in regard to those values most vital to us. It would amount to suicide, and even suicide may not be an option. You vote only on means, never on ultimate ends. Can you tolerate the intolerant? But if you don't, then you become as intolerant as he. Is balance of power the only solution?

No need for us to linger over the political failure of all civilizations. History shouldn't be, but in fact is, a collection of successive and often simultaneous wars which each time seem more or less justified to the parties concerned while even the victors often wonder *a posteriori* if the prize was worthwhile or even if the victory was really such. The law of the jungle and dialectics, monism and dualism, cannot boast of a great record. Shouldn't we be concerned at this turning point of humanity? The question of pluralism may be like looking for a white lotus in a dirty pond or a lily emerging from a dung-heap. But out of the ruins of both victor and vanquished pluralism may thrust itself up like a flower—alas, even more fragile than the lotus and the lily.

Millennia of repression, dominion, and power-policy (and not only political)—all those systems based on either monistic or dualistic bases—have only triggered more injustice, exploitation, and hunger. On a world scale the system has not worked. It might have worked for you and me but the Ukrainian, the Jew, the Quechua, the Black, the Chinese, to name just a few, have not been included. And in fact the positive changes—and there are many—came thanks to Socrates, Buddha, Jesus, Gandhi...and not Alexander, Akbar, Napoleon, Churchill (not to name villains).

The problem of keeping peace is not a new problem. The syndrome of being menaced and in danger of being attacked and annihilated is almost a constant factor in the history of peoples. Violence meets violence and arms are opposed with arms. "Defense" is justified by fear of a possible "offense." What the Russians are today for the "first world," what the Vietnamese for the Cambodians, or the Chinese for the Vietnamese, the Americans for the Russians, etc., the Moors, Saracens, and Turks were—for almost three centuries—for the West. Europe since the twelfth century lived in perpetual fear of Islam. So did part of the Indian subcontinent. We know about the Maratha king, Shivajī, a national hero, who fought against the Muslims and vanquished them. For Europe the response was the Crusades. But after the first experiences, Crusades were no longer possible. To the pathetic calls of some popes and princes, most of the nobility and the people did not respond. In 1453 Constantinople falls. Europe lives in paroxysm. A respite is given when in 1492 Grenada is conquered by Fernando el Católico. But there is no Council, no major political event without the reminder of the imminent danger to "Christendom." It is not until 1571 that Juan de Austria wins the victory of Lepanto, which became a universal feast for the entire Church, understandably enough. But the danger is not even conjured away after Lepanto.

Yet—and this is my point—a handful of people take another turn. Ramón Llull, Nicholas of Cusa, Pico della Mirandola, Erasmus, Luis Vives, and many others, in the East and in the West, do not believe in violence and war and propose a true ecumenism: dialogue, persuasion, understanding. They are not popular, they are considered idealists and often have to suffer, but they offer an alternative. Perhaps we should begin to realize that it is less risky to venture a peaceful attitude than to trust in a deterrent and menacing counter-power.

(b) The Philosophico-Dialectical Failure. A pluralistic problem arises when the issue cannot be dealt with dialectically because it calls into question the very foundation of dialectics. In fact, Man is so made that in many fields of human existence, even if dialectically "cornered"—convicted of contradiction, lack of intellectual proof, or logical impasse—he will not cease believing, hoping, or loving that which he holds to be the case. Many people do not stop believing or disbelieving in God or in the reality of the World even if the issue is proven or disproven by accepted dialectical means and every possible intellectual reasoning. To say that astrology is irrational, for instance, leaves astrology unconcerned and astrology lovers happy. There are, in other words, sources of human convictions, beliefs, hopes, and loves which defy the power of reason and are apparently stronger than and superior to it. And this is a fact: I may be convinced, and yet that conviction may not carry strength or force.

The instances of European thought from Descartes onwards or of buddhistic philosophy after Nāgārjuna exemplify this failure. The rationale behind these efforts is clear: "Given the scandal produced by the divergent opinions of the best people regarding the most important questions of life and death, let us establish an infallible system based on reason alone or on the dialectical effort to transcend dialectics." And after centuries of philosophizing, what we have is a new proliferation of mutually exclusive systems of thought, whatever names they apply to themselves and qualifications they seem to make. The Tower of Babel has not yet been constructed and no *philosophia perennis* has reached the second floor. Neither reason nor even a "broadminded" philosophy has succeeded in constructing a worldview, a Tower of Babel, where people might live, at least theoretically, in justice and peace.

(c) The Religio-Cultural Failure. A pluralistic problem arises when the conflict cannot be resolved by violence or power because we cannot bring ourselves to yield to pressure, even if threatened unto death. The Roman Empire had to yield to Christians, the Soviet Union has had to recognize the presence of dissidents, and the histories of the Kurds, Armenians, Jainas and so many others offer equally valid examples. There is something in Man which neither power, nor violence, nor domination can succeed in controlling or reducing to unity. The history of any religion is more the adventure of its heresies than the evolution of its orthodoxy.

We must not drown ourselves in euphemisms: the ancient empires wanted to conquer the whole world; Christianity and Islam—to cite two striking but hardly exclusive examples—aspired to become not only the number one religion, but ideally the one religion; scientific civilization and humanistic culture have similar claims today. What we so clearly discern as utopian if not ridiculous in the *urbi et orbe* of the Roman Romans and the Catholic Romans we seem not to detect in our own dreams of universality. Although many agree that man cannot build Babel, they go on believing that they at least have the plans. "If everyone were a good Christian! If everyone practiced Transcendental Meditation every day! If everyone followed the dictates of Science!... If everyone thought and behaved like me!"

And this is why, after at least sixty centuries of human civilization, we still have to ask ourselves this fundamental question: What is there in Man which makes him irreducible to unity and yet unable to renounce the quest for it? (If this isn't a religious question, I don't know what Religious Studies means.) After the fiasco of the Tower of Babel, can we not foresee some possibility for the world other than of a paneconomic system and a single technological megamachine? "*Tu quoqué?*"

The Anthropological Approach

(a) Three Anthropological Chapters. In facing such concrete and existential problems modern Man is again asking the question about himself which perhaps begins to close the wider circle opened by the first Western Man, Augustine (an African): *Quaestio mihi factus sum,* "I have made a question of myself." The dative has slowly become an ablative. "What *am* I for myself?" has become "What *is* Man for me?"—i.e., as known by me that I might know him better, and eventually have *it* in my hand? I am suggesting that we may be taking a third step in Man's self-reflection upon himself in the overall context of the world civilizations.

(i) What is Man? This is the Western way of formulating the anthropological question. Man is an object of research—even of introspection—and the science of Man would be an integration of all the results of the specific disciplines dealing with one or another aspect of the human being. We call it integral anthropology and today even theologians pay tribute to it when they speak of "theological anthropology." What is that being which we call Man that can think, speak, build...?

(ii) Who am I? would be the typical Indian way of formulating the same question, as Śrī Ramanamaharshi, the contemporary sage

of Arunāchala, in South India, reminded us. Man is here the scrutinizing subject trying to eat the cake even if he cannot have it. Man tries to assist at the very origins of his *I-consciousness* and pushes it deeper and deeper until the I has been peeled off from every layer of contingency. We call it wisdom, and its aim is to reconstruct the entire body of knowledge from that supracosmic intuition.

I would not wish to oversimplify these two extraordinary and fecund approaches which still remain the two basic pillars for human self-understanding. But in our time of encounter and the mutual fecundation of cultures, a third equally fundamental way remains to be explored with the same thoroughness as the other two.

(iii) Who are you? is the third question. I shall try to explain what this means because (since the Indo-European languages have lost the dual) the sentence is ambiguous. Not "What is Man?" (objectification, even if we call it a subject); not "What am I?" (subjectification, even if we find it in the *ātman*); but "What are *you?*" And this is a radically different question for it not only cannot be answered without *you,* but it requires you as a fellow-questioner (*Mitfragenden*)—and the "you" is the Pygmy, and the Muslim, and the woman, and the Communist, and the Christian, and the Democrat, and the wife, and the worker, and the poor . . . if I want to know what Man is in a more comprehensive way than a reified "is," I must listen to myself and I must also ask *you.* The question "What am I?," the question "What is it (he or she)?," is simply not enough. I have to ask "What are you?," look you in the eye, and formulate it better: "*Who* are you?" Who can say what Man *is* if none of us has access to the total range of human experience? The question about Man belongs to Man and not exclusively to me, even if I make an effort to speak on behalf of a large human group. Either we take pluralism seriously, or it becomes just another label for our philosophical imperialism. And if we take it seriously, we cannot bypass the you of *any* human being.

What I am getting at here is simple and straightforward: Man is not an object of research . . . alone or mainly; he himself is a searching subject. But this searching subject is not only my ego, it is also you. In more simplified terms: Man's self-understanding belongs to Man's being. Even more plainly: self-understanding is part of any understanding. But the *self* is not my ego alone or "we" alone. No encounter of cultures or religions can really take place without a new anthropology, a cross-cultural religious anthropology, if you will, such as some of us here in Santa Barbara are presently pursuing.

We now come to a sort of anti-climax, for obviously I cannot in this context describe the whole process of becoming aware of the I, the thou, the he/she/it, the we, the you and the they—which would be the proper way to lay the groundwork for an anthropology capable of at least discerning the problem. With the Hellenic categories, on the one hand, which have shaped most of the objective anthropological vision, and with the Upanishadic ones, which have been at the basis of most of the subjective experience of Man, we should now forge a third type of basic symbol for the integration of the three perspectives under which Man sees himself: as an I, a thou, and an it. Instead I shall simply sketch some insights which might serve as stepping stones toward the cross-cultural religious anthropology, using the common Western categories as starting points without further elaboration.

(b) Overcoming a Threefold Reductionism. In order to make my point, I shall speak of a threefold reductionism which seems to plague the modern conception of the human being.

(i) Reason is not the whole of Logos. Here I refer to the famous *animal rationale,* which is a rather constricted translation of Aristotle's definition of Man as *zōon lógon échon,* i.e., as a living being—or an animal—through which or through whom the logos *transits:* "Among the animals Man is the only one endowed with logos." Reasoning reason is only one aspect, almost a technique, of the logos. The logos is a certain intelligibility (the *lógos* is the *enérgeia* of the *noũs,* following Plato's definition), but it is not primarily reason. Rather is it word, *verbum,* verb; but *verbum entis* much more than just *verbum mentis:* it is the revelation, the very symbol of Being—the *lógos* is, along with the *épos,* the *mythós* and the *aínos,* one of the four ingredients of consciousness. I repeat: Reason belongs to logos, but it is not identical with it. Logos is also sound, it is content and intent, it is spiritual and material. And saying this I am in fellowship with Israel's *dābār,* India's *vāc,* and the Christian *lógos,* but here I am only sketching the problematic, and limit myself to affirming that reason does not exhaust the logos and thus the terms *irrational* and *arational* are not synonymous with *illogical* and *alogical.*

We could put this in a more existential way, using another perspective, and simply say that *the individual is not the whole of Man.* On this I do not want to elaborate now.

(ii) Logos is not the whole of Man. This is the second reductionism. There is also myth, there is body, there are feelings, there is world . . . but here I should prevent a possible misunderstanding: the

moment I say that the logos is not the whole Man, I am saying it *with the logos;* it is the logos which allows me to say this. What this means is that *all the efforts to transcend the logos have the logos as a fellow-traveler.* What does this tell us? It tells us that just as reason permeates the whole of the logos without being the whole of it, so the logos permeates the whole of Man without being the whole of him. It tells us that the constituent elements of the human reality are not like parts of a macrophysical body (*Körper* not *Leib*). The relation is not a spatial one—as if here we have one little thing and there another thing, and so we are made of all these things stuck together—but there *is* a mutual interaction and interpenetration so that there is nothing which I can separate from the logos, and yet the logos itself can make me aware that not everything is logos. We cannot recover the innocence we had to lose to become who we are, but we may perhaps acquire—or conquer or perhaps simply accept or receive—a new innocence. And precisely here cross-cultural studies are indispensable; they show us other forms of intelligibility, other perspectives of understanding, other forms of awareness . . . forms which cannot be reduced to one common denominator.

Let me give an example here, daring to contradict the great utterance of Husserl which seems to maintain that consciousness has always to be *consciousness of.* And this indeed appears to be the way in which Western intelligibility has customarily functioned. But there is also, as many Eastern traditions would affirm, a *pure consciousness,* a consciousness which is not a consciousness *of.* Of course, the way to attain this pure consciousness is not by looking for an object, not even by looking for consciousness, but rather by becoming *self-transparent* as subject. Here you cannot become a sage unless you become a saint. The quest for pure consciousness is not the quest for knowledge; it is of another type altogether. It could perhaps be called mystical awareness, but here I can only point out stepping stones toward a new anthropology. The necessary ambiguity of the word "pure" applied to consciousness has often led to the belief that "pure consciousness" is a consciousness so pure that only a few shamans, mystics, and ecstatics can reach it, forgetting that pure, i.e., unmixed and mere consciousness, is the very basis for having "consciousness of" something. And undoubtedly "pure consciousness" is not "consciousness *of* pure consciousness," as the *Tao-te-Ching,* the *Kenopanishad,* the *Gītā* and the Gospels again and again repeat to us.

Another way to say this would be to affirm that *Man is not the whole of Humanity.* Once again, I shall refrain from elaborating.

(iii) Man is not the whole of Being. It should be clear, of course, that nothing is unrelated to Man, that all that there is, is there with Man... neither the Divine, nor the Material is separable from Man. As Thomas Berry has reminded us, quoting from the Confucian *Chung Yung,* Man is the heart—heart and mind—of the entire reality, the third between Heaven and Earth.

Consciousness may be all-pervading, and there is surely no way for us to deny that consciousness and being are coextensive. There is nothing beyond consciousness because the beyond already belongs to consciousness. And to interpret this statement as saying that *there is* Nothingness beyond consciousness is a plain contradiction. And yet consciousness itself witnesses to Man that he is not alone in the universe, nor even the center of it but just one pole.

The other way to put this would be to say that *Humanity is not the whole of Reality.*

All this has not been a digression but an overcondensed presentation of the foundations of pluralism. Short of these and similar considerations, pluralism would be reduced to one, *our* more comprehensive and tolerant vision of the world. Many uses of the word imply a sort of "pluralistic society" in which you are allowed to appear odd in the eyes of the other because nobody cares, nobody interferes, and we are all happy in our little boxes. This may be many things but not pluralism. The problem of pluralism is neither just a practical problem (a kind of stopgap because we do not know how to behave with the other and thus have to tolerate his foolishness), nor merely or simply a human problem (because we are limited beings and thus have to put up with imperfection). The problem of pluralism arises, I would contend, because the very nature of reality is pluralistic. The underlying myths for the doctrines of the Trinity and nondualism and many other myths, might stand for this insight. Or, to go back to our original Jewish parable at Babel, the Lord confused Man's dream of a monolithic and totalitarian vision of reality.

(c) Pluralistic Man. I am saying that Man himself is a pluralistic being, that he is not reducible to an unqualified unity, nor can anything human be said to have a oneness we can grasp. To say human nature is one, or to say Truth is one, or even to say God is one, is philosophically ambiguous. Either the statement refers to a non-numerical transcendental one, and then we have simply the principle

of identity, or it is a categorical, and hence purely formal statement—
or, if filled with my particular contents, it is wrong outright; it is
either a tautology or an empty statement with no proper contents. If
we fill it with any meaning, we will have to ask: One what? To say
there is no other Man, or no other Truth, or no other God, staying
with our threefold example: What do we mean by it? If other Man,
other Truth, other God, means that there is no other Man than Man
and so on, then we have the necessary tautology of the principle of
identity: Man is Man, Truth Truth, God God. But if we mean by this
that there is no *other* Man, Truth, or God than what we take Man,
Truth, or God to be—i.e., other than what tallies with our conception
of it, then those entities are made dependant on our concepts: "There
is no other Man, Truth, or God than what we consider Man, Truth,
and God, to be!" We establish a closed system and ask the others to
become members of our club if they want discussion with us! Here
I subscribe to the principles Benjamin Nelson enumerated this after-
noon. We may bring the symphony of the different civilizations of
humankind into a tube of harmony not by lopping off all the differences and imposing some *a priori* schema of intelligibility, perfect as
this may be, but rather by allowing all of these different civilizations
to say their word, or dance their dance, or sing their song, and by
striving to understand what all of them are trying to say. This is not
just the lesser evil, or a concession to the limitations of our being.
Pluralism is an exigency rooted in the pluralistic nature of reality.
Pluralistic Man renders false all the absolutisms, fanaticisms, and re-
ductionisms to artificial unities. Only the one is nondualistic. There
is no second Man, Truth or God; but we do not exhaust what Man
is, or Truth, or God. There is no second Man, God, or Truth, but
Man is not monistic, nor God monotheistic, nor Truth monolithic.
A reasoning reason which closes or locks our awareness or compre-
hension into *one* intelligibility is a plain fallacy. There is a kind of
perichoresis, a "dwelling within one another," of these three dimensions of Reality: the Divine, the Human and the Cosmic—the *I,* the
you, and the *it.*

The Pluralistic Myth

It is time to recapitulate. I have said that pluralism is a myth and have
tried to describe the garniture of it. We may now go back and ask this
myth what it tells us theoretically, what it does for us practically, and
how it looks as a myth for our times.

The Awareness of Otherness and of the Other: *aliud et alius*

That the problem of pluralism is the question of the other needs some further elaboration. First of all, it is the question of an awareness of otherness (*aliud*). This is more than just an awareness of differences, necessary for the recognition of any plurality. It is an awareness that there are or there may be other entities besides those which we take into account, the awareness that logos is other than mere reason, Man other than logos, and Being other than Man; it ultimately implies an awareness that I (my reason, my consciousness, my being) do not exhaust the real nor am its center—but only one of its poles, if anything at all. There is another: *aliud,* otherness. And this not only besides the *my* and the *me,* but also against them and even beyond them. Solipsism is asphyxia. Or, using an Upanishadic metaphor, the windows of the senses, including the spiritual senses, not only allow us to peep into the outer world but allow the world to penetrate into us as well. I am not alone. Solitude, which allows me to be myself, is not to be confounded with isolation, which would suffocate my own being. Pluralism begins with the recognition of otherness, which already implies my sameness. I am in relation.

But this is not all. The *aliud* is not the *alius;* otherness is not *the* other. The other, the other subject of love and knowledge, the other person, is not pure otherness. Even more, the other does not see himself as other, but as *ego,* as I myself see myself. To have treated the other as otherness instead of an *alius,* to have reified the other and not to have allowed him a place in my-self, is one of the greatest confusions the human being can fall into. It is true that Western and Eastern traditions ask me to love my fellow being as *myself,* but we fix walls of separation and at best allow him to be an-other with the same rights as *my*self—without, however, sharing in the Self.

I have already made a passing reference to the impoverishment of Modern languages, amounting to a human catastrophe of cosmic proportions, in their loss of the dual and treating of the *you* as an *it* (in spite of calling it he or she). The reason for the dual is not concern for two as a number as many grammars still blindly repeat. Why not, then, also a case for three and four and so on? One may infer, therefore, that grammarians welcome the simplification of language; the *Encyclopedia Britannica,* for instance, includes no entry on the dual, apparently considering it unworthy of attention. The reason for the dual is to allow expression of the I-Thou: the you is not an it. The dual: I speak, you speak, they speak, but we-two speak; and even when they-two speak, the connotation is different from the speaking of they–the many. The moment that the other becomes the you, all changes. The awareness of the other as other (*alius*) and not just as otherness makes of him a fellow, a companion, a subject (and not an object), a source of knowledge, a principle of initiative as I myself am. This alone allows me to listen to the other, to be known by him and not just to know him. There can be no true pluralism until the other is discovered. I mean the other (*alius*) as source of (self) understanding and not only as term (*aliud*) of intelligibility.

This other does not always need to be a good fellow, a person with good intentions, or with the same feelings I have and the same opinions I hold. The other can be my enemy—although always with a human face, a Thou and not an it, an anonymous entity beneath the clouds or inside the house or shelter that I bomb from miles above....

Does pluralism allow us to deal with conflictual situations? This is something I have already indicated and may now elaborate a little more.

Dialogical Tension instead of Dialectical Conflict

This contrast between the dialectical and the dialogical modes of dwelling in our pluralistic reality may be the great difficulty and yet it is the proof of all that I have tried to say. Not accepting the dialectical conflict and transforming it into a *dialogical tension*—is this not what the Christian and Jain martyrs, for instance, did, and what contemporary resisters and dissidents are still doing? The risk is real. What is a tiny little group or an individual before the Kremlin, the Pentagon, a powerful Corporation, an all-powerful bureaucratic machinery? The prophetic role of Man here comes to the fore, and you cannot be a prophet of mere reasonableness, or of statistical probabilities, or of economic calculations, however learned you may be. To accept the dialectical strategy, important as it is in its own realm, only produces a regress to never-ending pendular reactions when extended into the total human situation. Let me submit a few considerations on this dialogical way of dealing with conflicting positions:

1. A pluralistic society can subsist only if it recognizes a center which transcends the understanding of it by any particular member or even by the totality of the members at any given moment. If king, party, or people is the absolute sovereign, there may be tolerance but not pluralism. Only an open society can be pluralistic, but this needs a transcendent force to prevent it from closing on its own self-interpretation. If we do not accept an un-understandable tran-

scending point, then obviously, if I am right, you are wrong and we cannot accept any higher qualifying understanding of our respective positions.

Example: a society arrogating to itself the right to mete out capital punishment, be it Church, State or Nation, cannot be called in our day a pluralistic society.

2. The recognition of this center is a given fact, a gift (theologically speaking). It implies a certain degree of awareness, which differs according to time, place, and the individuals concerned, that is never covered by the object of awareness; in other words, pluralism assumes that there is always a remnant of (pure) consciousness that is not consciousness of.

Example: if the welfare of the Basque people cannot be separated from the independence of the Basque nation, and this is seen as an absolute and non-debatable value, any conflict with it will have to yield uncompromisingly to the supreme value, and conflict with Spain will be inevitable. If the United States of America is an absolute sovereign nation, it will not tolerate any conflict of interest which puts in jeopardy the welfare of that nation. If you feel threatened to death and your life is for you an absolute value, you will have to yield to such a threat.

3. The way to handle a pluralistic conflict is not through each side trying to convince the other, nor by the dialectical procedure alone, but through a *dialogical dialogue* which leads to a mutual opening up to the concern of the other, to a sharing in a common charisma, difficulty, suspicion, guidance, inspiration, light, ideal, or whatever higher value both parties acknowledge and neither party controls. The dialogical dialogue is art as much as it is knowledge, involves *technē* and *práxis* as much as *gnōsis* and *theoría* and the difficulty is to re-enact it, even when one of the partners refuses to enter into such a relation.

Example: if the Pope's infallibility is essential to Christianity according to Roman Catholics and is only a historical accident according to Protestants, no way out of the impasse will be found through argument alone; also required will be a common search in loyalty to a common spirit superior to both parties.

4. Not only discussion but also prayer, not mere words but perhaps silence, not decisions but rather allowing situations to take care of themselves, not authority but a mutual and higher obedience, not knowing solutions but mutual searching, not mere exegesis of rules or constitutions, but freedom of initiative even at the risk of rupture, etc., are the proper attitudes in dealing with truly pluralistic problems

(not to be confused with problems of pluriformity). The pluralistic attitude does not assume *a priori* non-negotiable issues. It is in each case a new creation.

Example: if the corpuscular physical theory of matter and energy seems incompatible with the wave theory, it is fitting to hold in abeyance any ultimate explanation and wait until some further input may solve the problem or shift the question.

5. There is a continuum between pluriformity and pluralism, and the dividing line is a function of time, place, culture, society and the spiritual resistance and flexibility of the particular group, tribe, province or individuals involved. What for some is merely an issue of pluriformity is for others a problem of pluralism. Whoever sees a particular issue as one of pluriformity should not forget that for the other party the issue may appear to be of an altogether different nature, and thus needs to be dealt with in a different way.

Example: for one party marriage is a permanent sacrament, and a transient contract is—and was—no marriage; for the other party permanent and transitory marriages may simply be different types of marriage. A pluralistic problem arises when we do not agree regarding the very essence of what we are discussing—marriage, democracy, justice, Christianity, goodness....

6. The problem of pluralism need not always be solved by maintaining unity. Each human group has its own proper coefficient of coherence, uniformity, and harmony. What may not break up the unity of a culture or religion may very well disrupt a nation or a church. The strength of this coefficient is again a given—a gift—and yet one may reinforce it. The spiritual attitude of the members of a society positively influences the strength of this coefficient. As a general rule, each society should strive to be as pluralistic as it can allow itself to be. But each society has its own limits.

Example: a modern group within a traditionally celibate religious congregation may wish to have married people as full-fledged members of the same institution. Some congregations may be so structured existentially as to allow it, whereas others may have to start a new foundation altogether.

The occasion is too tempting not to bring in another instructive example: as anybody in India knows, and the last chapters of the second book of the *Rāmāyaṇa* so forcefully reiterate, the husband is the highest deity (*param daivataṁ patiḥ*) for the wife and should be loved whether he is bad tempered or poor, or even licentious and disloyal. We should say the same of the husband regarding the wife, but this is not my point. My point is that equilibrium is easy to maintain within equity and when equality is present: I am loyal to you because you also keep your fidelity. The problem arises when you are no longer that trustworthy person. We may divorce, part, break the unity (of family, country, church, group, or association), but we cannot keep unity if one of the parties has not decided to stay through "thick and thin." Should we—or anyone else—disarm even if the adversary goes on accumulating weapons?

7. The passage, the *pascha* from plurality to pluriformity and thence to pluralism, belongs to the growing pains of creation, to the very dynamism of the universe.

Example: the monolithic character of the Catholic Church some decades ago and its plurifaceted aspect today, the totalitarian nation-state of some centuries ago and its evolution into liberal democracy, offer instances of this "transit."

The Exigencies of Pluralism

Since I began with the Bible, permit me to conclude by citing one of the most daring sentences of Jesus' kerygma, which comes at a certain moment in the Sermon on the Mount: "Do not resist evil!" If we take these words to mean what they say, either the foolishness, or the optimism, or the innocence behind them is unfathomable... or else the whole thing is nonsensical. I suggest a neither/nor answer to this dilemma, and consider these words an adequate motto for our meditation on pluralism.

"Do not resist, do not oppose, evil." We may translate the Revised Version, "Resist not him that is evil" or with the New English Bible, "Do not set yourself against the man who wrongs you," as the word can mean evil, the devil, or a wicked man: however, the third reading is to be preferred, as text and context show. We may oppose evil, we have to resist the devil as James says, but we should not withstand the Man who does evil; instead we should turn the left cheek and, offering him our coat as well, go along the extra mile. Why? Because otherwise you will be drawn into the dialectical game; you will have to build another power to oppose the first one, and so forth and so on. Thus from reaction to counter-reaction, from swing to counter-swing, we have the all-too-familiar pendular movement of the world. "God" was with the right, now "God" is with the left; at first the males dominated, now some females want to do the bossing; the colonial powers have exploited other peoples, now the other peoples are going to kick back with whatever arms they have at their disposal... and we go on and on and on. "Now it is our turn to build the Tower of Babel up to paradise! We, the Proletariat, the Chinese, the Liberals, Scientists. . . . " Yet we read: Do not stand against an evil action because evil can only be resisted by evil and two evils do not make a good; because evil is not an absolute, and, exasperating the evil Man by resisting him, you only increase evil—by opposing it, you are contaminated by it. If somebody hits you, there is no end to the retaliation until you have piled up bigger bombs which will destroy us all. If you do not stop this flow of bad *karma* by ceasing to assimilate and embrace it, the end will be the destruction of the world. Christians speak of the Lamb that has taken upon himself the sin of the cosmos; Buddhists set universal *karuṇā* or compassion as the only way to enlightenment, to mention just two universalistic religions. Or as the *Rāmāyaṇa* says, mercy to all beings is the highest virtue (*bhūta-dayā-param*).

"Do not resist the evil Man." Once you declare war on evil, you become not only immersed in but also dependent on it. You are no longer free to live on your terms. You are caught in the net of the evil itself, and it is irrelevant whether you win or are defeated. The poison is already in you. Evil can be fought and even negated only on its own plane. You can no longer overcome it. The "strategy" should be a more subtle one. "Do not resist the evil Man" because evil is not an absolute. Overcome it but do not be tainted by it, do not fall into the temptation to fight back, to hit as you are beaten, to enter the only place that evil allows you to move: its own arena. This is not minimizing the power of evil. You have to be very firmly grounded not to yield to the allurement of evil. Is it not true that when we decide to fight evil, we "think" we are going to be the winners and defeat evil? A defeated evil permeates the entire body of the victor, as any historian knows. We are difficult to convince only when we are intoxicated by the thought of the possible victory: we are really not so pure and uncontaminated. Or, in philosophical terms, often misinterpreted: evil is not a separate and positive entity but only a privation. And you do not directly fight an absence. Otherwise, how could the author of the words just quoted have said in the most decisive moment of his life: "Father, forgive them, for they do not know what they are doing"? Only forgiveness cancels evil.

I am not saying we should be indifferent to evil or abolish all value judgments. I am not defending sheer passivity in front of, say, Nazism (it is always more comfortable to speak of things past—should I have said, instead, Communism? capitalism? military regimes?). I am saying that the way to struggle with what everyone considers the forces of evil is not by dialectically opposing to evil what we believe to be non-evil, but by transforming, converting, convincing, evolving, contesting—and all this mainly from within, as leaven, as witness, as martyr.

It is not the place here to enter into some exegesis. We know well that the *antistenai* of Matthew's Gospel has no Hebrew equivalent. The so-called "non-resistance" to evil or to the devil could be interpreted as not to hasten to react, not to compete with the same means or on the same level, or not to care entering into competition. And this amounts to breaking the circle which consists in defeating evil by evil. The text of Jesus does not encourage passivity or fatalism but it is an invitation not to play the same game with the devil. One could here add other references to Jesus' teaching. "Blessed are those who are persecuted for righteousness' sake" certainly implies that they have fought against the evil of injustice. And his own attitude was not less forthright.

Pluralism, therefore, does not mean that we recognize many ways (plurality) but that we detect many forms which we cannot recognize as ways leading to the goal. Pluralism does not mean just tolerance of the many ways. It is rather that human attitude which faces intolerance without being broken.

After our accumulated experience of the fiasco of other aggressive means which were supposed to be more effective and immediate, we may be readier today to handle human conflicts by increasing our own energy and capacity for endurance so as to be able to carry the burden without being crushed by it, to assume and assimilate evil rather than add our own energies as so much fuel for its fires. Here again, drinking poison and not being harmed by it has always been one of the signs of those who believe. Taking into oneself the poison, like Shiva, assimilating the evil, this kind of tolerance obviously demands a deeper insight into the nature of Man and Reality and a stronger hold on the source of inner power. Here, maybe, one begins to glimpse the proportions of a radical *metanoia*—a mutation not of Man alone, or of the World alone, or of God alone, but of all three dimensions of the Real—in concert and cooperation. The Lamb that takes away the sin of the world, the scapegoat that is sacrificed on neutral ground, the holocaust that is performed for the healing of the people—in one word, the ritual aspect of Man's life that, despite exaggerated superstitions and undeniable aberrations, forms part of Man's nature—are all nonviolent or less violent attempts at dealing with conflicts in a way other than annihilating the opponent. They are non-dialectical ways of handling a conflict; they act not through opposition but by assimilation, not through countermeasures but by redemption or taking upon one's self the common burden, not through defeat of the adversary but by (mutual) conversion to a higher value.

The "realist" will immediately remind me that we are not God and that with such pacifistic attitudes we blur any distinction between good and evil; we might split India into a dozen states, undermine the United States' role as guardian of Democracy, ruin Catholicism, destroy society, allow the "criminals" (always the others) to overrun "us," pervert human institutions and let chaos dominate the world.

True to my proposed method, I will not plainly oppose my thesis to the foregoing affirmations, but first reexamine my position and see whether we would not agree perhaps that the line has to be drawn somewhere (in the sense that pluralism has definite limits for each situation). Secondly, I should invite the others to see whether the current method of meeting violence with violence has yielded better results so that the "chaos" of which they warn us may not be better than the present apparent peace by institutionalized violence—in a time when in absolute numbers never have more human beings been in chains, suffering, and distress. Third, it would be a contradiction *in adjecto* to impose nonviolent methods.

To the first point it may be said that only an infinite being, surely, can encompass good and evil—that each human being and each human society has its own coefficient of magnanimity: only Shiva can drink the entire poison of the world or a divine redeemer be charged with the fullness of its sin. We inevitably suffer from our incapacity to assimilate a larger proportion of evil into our human metabolism. As to the second point, we should not pretend to purity but explore forms of human life other than those dominated by single immutable principles. The third point should caution us that institutionalized nonviolence could become as deleterious as other tougher forms of compulsion. Any erecting of absolutes leads to the disappearance of pluralism.

Let me offer an example: I am personally convinced that today slavery as a social institution is an evil. Yet I am also convinced that at a certain time in history, the majority of people (at least among the non-slaves) found a justification for it. I am not committing the methodological error that I have called the catachronic: judging with meters of the present furlongs of the past. My point here is that slavery at that time was not such an intolerable evil precisely because most of the people found it justifiably tolerable. Something similar occurs with Communism, Nazism, Capitalism, Colonialism, Apartheid, the armaments race, etc. Some people find these examples as inhuman and cruel as slavery. Others may not be of the same opinion. We may fight back and engage in battle, build another tower, or we may begin to speak another language, and simply refuse to pay taxes or go into the military or collaborate with the regime and the like. I am convinced that the first method only perpetuates evil. Once upon a time, we learn in the *Rāmāyaṇa,* a pious ascetic was living his saintly life in the forest. The mischievous temptor, divine Indra, came to his hermitage in the form of a soldier. He left a magnificent sword in deposit with the sage. In order to keep it with the required care the hermit would constantly carry the weapon with him. Slowly the sage became negligent of his duties, turned to cruelty, and was led astray by *adharma,* ending in hell. He who has ears, let him hear. Or, with the very words of the selfsame Princess Jānakī: "With great subtlety a noble soul is led to adharma." In other words, a pluralistic society is a flexible reality that depends on the spiritual health or power of its members.

But it is time to conclude.

I have said that there is an urgent need for a new fantasy, a new vision, a mystical experience touching the very core of the Real *kat' exochen*—and not only of the individual human being, or only of the human race. We have witnessed what amounts to probably forty centuries of specialization, of breaking down the different pieces and, following in the footsteps of Descartes, becoming more and more knowledgeable about less and less (a process we should *not* sneer at, because without it we would not even have survived). But now, perhaps, the moment has come to gather all these broken pieces into a new whole which neither ignores nor despises diversity and which therefore cannot be reduced to any bland or monolithic uniformity.

The human predicament today should by rights cure us of all the messianisms and unrealistic dreams of new world empires, even if heralded by great bombastic trumpetings of Freedom, God, and Truth—which are indeed positive symbols; but we have neither all of them, nor a monopoly on them.

I have said that we were dealing with a myth, and a myth is something on which we cannot put our finger without dispelling it. It is something we cannot manipulate. We are not pluralistic by integrating everything in one "pluralistic" worldview. We are pluralistic by believing that none of us possesses the philosophers' stone, the key to the secret of the world, access to the center of the universe if such there is; by having the restraint not to think through everything lest we destroy the "thought" (*das Gedachte,* not *der Gedanke*) and the thinker. This is not irrationalism. It is intellectual humility or common sense.

Let me say it again in strict philosophical parlance. If we think out (*ausdenken*) the Eucharist, we destroy it; if God, he vanishes; if an atom, it disappears; if a person, we miss him; if a tree, we do not understand it. In other words, thinking has a corrosive power; it destroys what it really thinks through. When it touches the surface of a thing, it is all right—the thing still has a depth untouched by thinking. The price of understanding is that we transform, assimilate, and thus change, absorb, and ultimately destroy the thing understood, making of it an object, a concept, a conception conceived by our thinking. As long as we do not think a thing exhaustively, that thing still stands outside our thinking—i.e., exists (*ek-sists*, sticks its neck out). But by this very fact, we gain a decisive insight regarding the nature of reality. It is this: the criterion of reality is precisely to be "thought-proof"—viz., resistant to thinking. When something does not obey our thinking, when it offers resistance, it shows its reality by this very fact. Indeed we cannot "think through" (in the sense of think exhaustively) the Eucharist or God or an atom, a person or a tree. They offer resistance of another type from that of, say, a triangle or a logical syllogism. These latter are unfathomable, they yield more and more and we do not discover their limits; there may always be more properties to a triangle and more refinements to a logical argument. They offer the resistance of the Siberian forest: there is nobody there and you do not know what is beyond and if it will ever end. The former offer the resistance of the Chinese Wall. You know that all the glory of the empire is behind it and that you cannot break the wall. But you also know that if you succeed you will have destroyed the Kingdom of the Rising Sun (with apologies to historians for my turning historical facts into philosophical metaphors!). A tree, for instance, simply stops our thinking at a certain point. It possesses an enclosure forbidden to or rather impenetrable to our thinking. If we could think it through, we would destroy the tree (and some of you may recall the power of *tapas* and concentration); the tree would become totally an object of our mind. This is the fundamental difference between an idea of God, which has infinite possibilities, and a real God who stops and silences our thinking.

This limit is something which nothing can impose on us except the resistance of the thing itself. And paradoxically (as I have already suggested), we are then convinced that the thing is true and exists; we are convicts, defeated, overpowered by the thing, and our accusations—i.e., our categories with which we tried to understand the thing—return to us as if rebounding from the power of the thing themselves. Jacob fought with God in the form of an angel and experienced his reality the next day when he felt that he had been hurt. Human reflection, when it is not a solipsistic spinning on our own constructs, always brings back the scar of the thing it has touched, the thing it has tried to "flect," to bend so that it might give us its secret. Reflection hurts more than a laser beam.

If this is the case, the foundation of pluralism implies the recognition of a weakness, not in our mind—so that if we were more intelligent we could come to a single theoretical truth on which all we humans would agree—but in the nature of reality, i.e., both in our thinking power and in the things themselves. It is more than an example of perspectivism because in this case we could always argue that, despite the fact that there is another perspective that sees things differently, or own perspective is the proper one for that particular purpose—which is the "real" purpose. To acknowledge different perspectives upon a question only shifts the problem because we then have to begin all over again to discuss what the right perspective is for that particular case, and so forth and so on. Pluralism is not the mere justification for a plurality of opinions, but the realization that the real is more than the sum of all possible opinions. The "intelligence" of Laplace cannot exist: it would destroy everything, and beside it would not know itself. There is no "intelligence" as Laplace imagined. Pluralism affirms that Parmenides was wrong, if you will, but that we are equally wrong if we want Heraclitus to contradict him and be right. Reality is not dialectical; although dialectics, of course, has a place in reality.

We may feel disoriented in the face of so many "orients," so many compasses, medicines, and prophets. Yet we should not be resigned and try to withdraw into selfish individualisms, but instead recognize that Man himself and Reality are pluralistic (neither monistic nor dualistic), and thus that the immense variety of what appear to be conflicts (when viewed dialectically) can be transformed (I would even say converted, but this is not an automatic process) into *dialogical tensions* and *creative polarities*. All that is needed is for us to experience, to touch, to reach that very core of reality which makes us so differently unique that we are each incomparable, and so uniquely unique that all our differences appear as so many colorful beams of an unfathomable light.

In simpler words, I have said that no group, no truth, no society, ideology or religion can have a total claim on Man, because Man is ever elusive, not finished, not finite, infinite—still in the making, on the way, itinerant—as is the entire reality in which Man is an *active* participant. It is this free and active participation, and yet only participation, that makes our lives really worth living. And it is this that I wanted to share with you.

Epilogue

Once upon a time all the world was one planet and became a single gigantic city, the *megalē polis,* Babylon. The children of Man had found Science and Technology, believed in Reason and Civilization, and had already succeeded in using (one cannot say speaking) one single basic—scientific and rational—Esperanto. As Men journeyed so easily to the East and the West, they came upon the realization that they were living on the plains of a land they called Earth and decided to remain there where their ancestors had already settled. They said to one another:

"Come, let us make United Nations and create United States, Common Markets, and Internationals of all types; come, let us limit our armaments to no more than the capacity to destroy the planets a thousand times; let us make machines that will work for us and have perhaps, if need be, some "fourth-" or "fifth-world" people to work for the machines; let's use Duralumin and Gold and Plutonium and enriched Uranium. Come, they said, let us make one World, one civilization, really one Planet for the first time, and not be like our naive and foolish ancestors who believed that the Roman Empire was the entire world, Christianity the religion of humankind, the Chinese Wall the enclosure of all culture, and similar utopian dreams. With our supersonic conveyances and transplanetarian flights, we have broken the sound barrier and even that of space; we shall soon break the barrier of time also. Let us build a perfect (who can cheat with a perfect computer data-bank?) welfare-classless-socio-capitalist-paneconomic society, combining the best of our efforts, and build a human tower with its top on the moon for the time being, so as not to incite jealousies and not to imitate our credulous ancestors who still believed in heaven. Let us make a name for ourselves, sending messages to outer space to let the universe know how brave we are, united and happy. Otherwise we shall be scattered all over the inhospitable places and lose our identity. Our evolutionary dogmas tell us that we have come a long way from nebulous nebula via apes and primates and that we are travelling to an omega point via the galaxy alpha."

Then the Lord came down to rejoice at the marvels of enlightened

Humanism and Scientific civilization and to see the Tower that Men had built. He had heard some other different but also human voices that feared all was not so shiny, and suspected that all was cloaked in propaganda-politics, statistical studies, and great conferences. They were crying out that the world was living on the credit of time and space, postponing real living and real issues as if time and space were infinite.

"Space [these zealots were crying in the wildernesses] has begun to show its limits, the oceans are full of pollution and the Earth is empty of its energy. Even the future has been showing signs of not being unlimited, not only in personal lives (death) but also on a cosmic scale: we will run out of time. The monetary credit of a single nation, to give a more concrete example, will require a minimum of four years' exclusive work of all its citizens for it to be redeemed—and new markets will soon not be available.... "

At the time of the evening breeze the Lord went for a walk to see for himself. People did not know for certain in which suburb of the megalopolis the Tower had to have its Capitol and He sensed they might come to a confrontation, but they were too absorbed in their competitions to want to disrupt the balance of power which had already brought the Tower to such an advanced state of construction. They had almost finished it, so much so that they had reduced the "curse" of the old Babel, which left the world with over four thousand languages, to (for all serious—i.e., practical—purposes) a mere half dozen tongues. To be sure, their present languages were very peculiar. Blasphemies, oaths and swearing had practically disappeared from the face of the earth, and thus fidelity to the given word as well. Apparently a tremendous inflation of words had obliged Men to use paper-words instead. They had papers on the one hand and signs on the other, so civilized had the race literate Men become; they were Men of letters, not of words. Of course, human "signaletics" were well organized by delicate computers and could make flights come on time, parcels arrive punctually, and the working hours, especially, run to the minute—and the "needs" of customers well known to commercial agencies. The race of Men had become old or perhaps intelligent with a different form of wisdom than the traditional one. In order to escape the confusion of the first Babel the new civilization was converting words, which once were living symbols and thus polysemic, into terms, which were mere signs, and thus univocal. Univocity was the ideal and suspected unscientific metaphors were on the wane—at least for all "important" matters. The ideal was to reduce everything to quantitative formulae. Only then would ill-fated discussions be eradicated. The "now," for instance, had been reduced to 20, 57 hours of the month two of 1977, and if somebody contested such a "fact," he would be simply sent to a psychiatric ward. Justice, to give another specimen, was also on its way to find quantitative parameters. It was being reduced to 2,000 calories for each stomach, some amount of money for each pocket, and to three or ten or more months' or years' jail for each breaking of the rules. Idle talk without elucidating anything, about the nature of beauty or love or dharma or karma and the like was becoming obsolete. People would no longer need their own fallible opinions. The majority would decide. Research was possible, but not dialogue. To be sure, there were still some who wanted again fire from heaven, but heaven was no longer the dwelling-place of the Lord.

And the Lord God did not listen to the prayers of the "believers" to summon his angels to build another tower so that from the stronger angelic fortress his hosts could easily smash down Babel. The Lord still remembered his ironic policy at Paradise, inciting Man to eat from the Tree of Knowledge of good and evil by forbidding him to do so. This time the Lord did not forbid the sons of Woman to build the Tower of their dreams. And Babylon was built and the ziggurats are still there, although empty and in ruins. Babel was dispersed but not so Babylon (Athens, Rome, and all its successors) which resisted Oholibah (Jerusalem and its successors) when dialectically attacked. Only a former Manichean could write of "Two Cities" and trigger the dialectics of Western Christianity. This was long ago. The fact is that the Lord did not resist Men's evil purposes; he simply allowed selfish individualism to penetrate their heads and impregnate their tongues so that there was no longer a common language. His past irony, which at that time he took for "esprit de finesse," that cross-cultural pun that he had allowed himself to make did not satisfy him any longer. He wanted to convert every Man into a poet; that is why he gave everyone a language. Instead Babel as Babylon, "the Gate of God," became Babel as *bālal,* "to confuse." He would not dare say now that Art (*techne*) and Word (*logos*) had become "technology." Instead, the Lord said:

"Here they are, they believe that they are one because all those who can afford it use the same vitamins, gadgets, and plastic materials; even the literate use (let's not say speak) one of the major languages for which there is simultaneous translation. And now that they are nearing the end of construction, they will not waste their precious time, like Penelope, undoing in the night the work of the day, because there are no suitors left: they will start fighting each other for the highest jobs, for they understand one another too well, know the whole game, and have theoretically abolished privileges; they have excelled in watching each other. Yet they are somewhat innocent for they do not know—otherwise they would commit collective suicide—how lonely they are, how much they work under compulsion. If they would stop working—how seriously they have taken what we told them long ago in paradise!—they would devour themselves and each other. They do not recognize how addicted they have become, like ants, to the building of the Tower and the City. What will they do if they succeed in finishing it? Learned as they are, they have not read the signs of the times and have not understood the meaning of world wars, famines, crises and revolutions, so busy are they deciphering their mutually encoded signals. All seem to be ecstatically absorbed in acquiring or conserving power. Come, let us go down there," the Lord said, "and confuse their meanings so that when they say 'democracy' some may mean people's dictatorship, some licentious individualism, some a bowing to the majority, and others the manipulating of public opinion; when they say 'justice' some may mean maintenance of the status quo at any cost, some state ownership, some upheaval, some violence, and some nonviolence; when they say 'love' some may mean rape, others flirtation, and still others conquest, pleasure, and even pain, self-abnegation, or self-gratification. Apparently they have not yet realized that language is the concrete personal symbol and that a *lingua universalis* would not be language. Come, let us see if, like our own Trinitarian Mystery which is neither a numerical one nor a quantitative three, or like our Non-Dualistic Nature which is neither one nor many but a pluralistic symbol in which they also share—let us see if perhaps they will come to their senses so that it dawns upon them that each one of these children of Man is unique and in a way the entire reality, reflecting it like a mirror the better and purer he or she is. Come, let us go down, but now there is no point sending an avatār, or a prophet, or a sage, or even my son. They are too advanced for believing in such innocent theophanies; they would not even care to stone or ban or crucify them. They would simply tolerate and ignore them, they would allow them freedom of speech to render them innocuous and even, perhaps, with enough guarantees, allow them to found a small new sect for a select and enlightened elite. In olden times we sent them mediators, but they took them for intermediaries; some ruins of our interventions still preserve the *pontifical* name, but they are also busy building some special domes of the tower and have forgotten how to make *bridges* among themselves, roads of communication between people. They have forgotten that each one has his own center, and it is the symphony of these centers that makes the music of the spheres about which they have dreamed ever since the sons of God saw that the daughters of Men were beautiful, precisely because each single human language is as unique and beautiful as any child of God."

And the Lord hesitated to call another assembly of the Gods. It was very present in his mind that in one of those assemblies they decided to put the Cherubim at the Gate in order to prevent Man looking back with nostalgia and to encourage him to continue on his pilgrimage. And still Mankind wants always to go back to Paradise and has not understood that the essence of Eden is its existence as Lost Paradise. Only a lost paradise is real. That is why it can not be searched for by looking back, but forward. The sons of Man have taken the Falling too seriously without integrating it in an equally original and regenerating Raising at the same time. They have taken Babel as a curse instead of as our concern for pluralisms and abhorrence of finite monolithic systems; they have overlooked that immediately after Babel we proceeded to the calling of Abram. And the Lord pondered anew that in another of such assemblies when they decided that the Spirit should descend again, she (the spirit) did not reduce all the languages of Babel to one single idiom as if the full truth were with one single language; her purpose was not to create a great single Dome to shelter the whole of humankind as if creation were bad and needed an extra protection; she simply let people understand each other and yet speak different tongues, not one tongue; she let them have different religions and not one single system of beliefs, love each other and not love the same things. Babel has occurred and remains ambivalent, like all living and real things, because the Kingdom is neither a private property within, nor a public affair outside, but *between* everything that there is. And the Lord went up again, wondering whether the Tower would be finished or whether people would learn that the fullness of life is neither isolation in individualistic monads nor agglomeration in collectivistic units but communion in interdependent wholes. He wanted to leave a message of hope or at least a single word of love but did not dare...after all, his counsellors had told the Lord that now Man is of age and does not so easily accept advice from alien sources. The Lord kept silent: *upararâma*.

Chapter 5

The Pluralism of Truth

Our Human Situation

The Geographic Panorama

Let me reflect on the geographic upsetting of the modern world. Over a century ago 80 percent of people did not move more than fifty miles from their birthplaces. Now in North America, every family changes dwelling places every four and one-half years. The Atlantic is crossed by the millions. In eight hours you can be in Kathmandu, and here today there is an audience of an immense variety of races, languages, and religions. The geographic upsetting escalates in intermingling of people and cultures, but also in tensions and strife. Now we mingle, we are ready to tolerate the other, we are no longer scandalized by anything, we imitate, we reject, we are upset, but, after all, we have to go along with that and put up with as much as we can. We try to find our way within this jungle of varieties of all kinds of opinions and behaviors. We are forced to deal with each other, and, thus, in spite of our respective masks (for self-defense) we are almost obliged to try to understand each other.

The Question of Understanding

In olden times people understood that they didn't understand one another. People understood that they did not understand those exotic fellows, those strange costumes, and those foreign religions, but since they did not meet them every day, it was not a great challenge. The foreigners lived in beautiful countries, primitive jungles, or neglected ghettos, but always far away, geographically or spiritually. Now and then some anthropologists would tell us stories, which we

This essay was published as "The Pluralism of Truth," *World Faiths Insight* 26 (1990): 7–16.

found more or less interesting, funny, or irritating. The skirmishes were only among neighboring religions, often tinged with economic and political problems, or among some intellectuals worried with the negative results of religious divergences.

Now the problems are before our own eyes and we need to understand them. Please bear with me the only English philosophical pun that I allow myself: To understand is to stand-under the spell of the thing which we under-stand, it is to be got by the spell of the thing, and stand under it in admiration, or perhaps skepticism. It is an existential attitude, we stand really under the power of the risky act of knowing (*inter-legere*). To know, as the Upanishads and Thomas Aquinas (following Aristotle) explicitly said, meant to identify ourselves with the thing known. Now, due to the shift of meaning of the notion of knowledge, introduced and popularized by the modern so-called natural sciences, to understand has been reduced to being able to foresee, calculate, and dominate. In a word, we claim to understand by "overstanding." If we "overstand," we simply apply our own categories or superstructures. We superimpose them in order to recognize the object, and no longer to understand the thing. Should I interject here a footnote on the Kantian categories and Shankara's critique *ante litteram* with his notion of *adhyâsa* (super imposition)?

I am only preparing the ground to indicate that there is an unavoidably epistemological problem undergirding our question.

If we "overstand," like a pretended universal scientific "knowledge," we approach reality from a standpoint superior to that of the things themselves. We are not listening to the things, obeying them; we are integrating objects into our mental scheme. We "overstand" from a higher platform: Reason, Science, Revelation, or whatever, to which, of course, "we" have a privileged access. Intelligibility comes then from a single superior principle. On the other hand, if we truly understand we shall humbly recognize that, while we have access to a source of intelligibility, other people may tap on other sources as well, or on other streams of the same source. Human history has shown us that Man has many different self-understandings. Can we by-pass the different human self-understandings by our exclusive interpretation? We may recognize objects, but here we have to deal not with an object, but with Man, whose very nature is to be endowed with self-understanding, so that to know Man includes to know Man's self-understandings—and not just to know our own interpretations of an object called *anthrôpos*. *This is the problem.*

Something happened to a Sicilian at the beginning of the century. He was caught, taken to court, manacled. It seems that he was innocent, but he didn't utter a word when the judge was asking him to defend himself. When the advocate later asked him why he didn't speak, he said, "How could I speak if I had my hands tied?" For him the word was still something more than meaning; it was gesture. How could he speak without using the hands at the same time as the tongue?

A Universal Understanding?

We have suffered and still suffer so much of fanaticisms, political, religious, and cultural, that we are legitimately thirsty for a universal understanding. A typical example of this mentality is the global village syndrome. Noble as the intention is, to me it appears as just another worthy successor to the colonialist mentality. Colonialism believes in the monophormism of culture: that there is ultimately only one civilization: "And now comes the unification of the world into a global village. Now we can have a universal theology which will make a comfortable little hole for the Muslim, another for the unbeliever, and everybody will be happy because we now are tolerant, we don't enforce anything, we accept everything, and everybody has a place. Everyone can welcome a universal theology which is based on openness, tolerance, and self-criticism." So far so good, but is it so easy to be really open to the fanatic, tolerant with the intolerant, and to accept the criticism of those who do not agree with our universal theology?

Yet there is a thirst for real understanding. We cannot live compartmentalized. The other becomes a problem precisely because it encroaches upon my life and is irreducible to my views. If one extreme is that we are right and the others wrong, the other extreme is that we all can fit into a kind of global village. I submit that it is not given to any of us to encompass the universal range of the human experience. In a village everyone knows everybody and the different dialectics are understood. Do we still dream that a universal television will bring real "communication" to 5.2 billion people? There is an *inertia of the mind* very visible in most of the modern efforts to deal with this problem. I have the hunch that we have to face a radically new vision of reality.

This is the challenge.

Pluralism

In between these two extremes, the word "pluralism" has emerged more and more as representing a third attitude; and this is the second point of my presentation.

Accepted Pluralisms

There are a number of pluralisms which are accepted today. A philosopher can be a good philosopher, and does not need to be a follower of Kant or whomever. One philosopher may disagree with another and yet both may be accepted as good philosophers. The pluralism of philosophy is accepted. Theological pluralism is also practically recognized. Cultural pluralism is also something which we boast of, although I don't think we have achieved it. What we have is a certain type of cultural tolerance which allows Greeks, Pakistanis and Gypsies to have their own folklores—but they all have to pay the taxes...and accept *our* Laws and Constitutions. At any rate we are theoretically ready to accept cultural pluralism. Religious pluralism, which cannot be severed from cultural pluralism, is probably the last and most difficult notion to accept. It touches our personal identity.

Preliminaries to Pluralism

We have become aware of *plurality*. This is a fact. But plurality is not yet pluralism. Plurality is the recognition of *different* ways, moods, colors. It is a quantitative notion.

A second step is *pluriformity*. There are not only differences, there is also *variety*. This is a qualitative notion. We become sensitive to varieties about which we cannot pass a quantitative measurement. Blue is not green and in no way can I say that green is nicer than blue. We cannot measure what is better, what is nicer, and it depends on the context. But this is not yet pluralism.

Pluralism goes a step further than the recognition of differences (plurality) and varieties (pluriformity). Pluralism has to do with radical *diversity*. This further step has had two forerunners.

The first step is *perspectivism*. Those conversant with the Indic fable of the elephant in a dark place remember how the one said that it was something like a bare bone, others said it was like a heavy pillar, a thick container, a rough skin and the like. This would be an example of perspectivism. Perspectivism is common sense. People see from different perspectives, and we have to respect them. The difficulty is, as in our example, that somebody has to know that it is an elephant. When I know the elephant I can say you are simply describing the tusk, you the foot, and you another member, but if no one knows the elephant, how are we going to defend perspectivism? Who knows the elephant? Obviously "we," the Vedântins, the Christians, the scientists, ... "we" know the elephant!

The second step is *relativity*, which should not be confused with relativism. Relativism defeats its purpose. Relativism is self-defeating agnosticism. You can not even know that you don't know. If there are no criteria for discernment, relativism is also not a criterion. Relativity, on the other hand, is a much more serious thing. Relativity tells us that everything depends on a set of collations in which that particular case, statement, fact, or situation can be expressed, and also falsified, verified or whatever. It abolishes any kind of absolutistic claim. But I dare say that pluralism in its deepest sense goes still a step further and this is what I would like still to describe in brief sketches.

Description of Pluralism

In six points, I try to sum up what I mean.

1. Pluralism does not mean plurality or a reduction of plurality to unity. It is a fact that there is a plurality of religions. It is also a fact that these religions cannot be reduced to any sort of unity. Pluralism means something more than sheer acknowledgment of plurality and the mere wishful thinking of unity.

2. Pluralism does not consider unity an indispensable ideal, even if allowance is made for variations within that unity. Pluralism accepts the irreconcilable aspects of religions without being blind to the common aspects. Pluralism is not the eschatological expectation that at the end all shall be one.

3. Pluralism does not allow for a universal system. A pluralistic system would be a contradiction in terms. The incommensurability of ultimate systems is unbridgeable. This incommensurability does not need to be a lesser evil, but it could be a revelation itself of the nature of reality. Nothing can encompass reality.

4. Pluralism makes us aware of our contingency and the nontransparency of reality. It is incompatible with the monotheistic assumption of a totally intelligible Being, that is, with an omniscient consciousness identified with Being. Yet pluralism does not shun intelligibility. The pluralist attitude tries to reach intelligibility as much

as possible, but it does not need the ideal of a total comprehensibility of the real.

5. Pluralism is a symbol which expresses an attitude of cosmic confidence which allows for a polar and tensile coexistence between ultimate human attitudes, cosmologies, and religions. It neither eliminates nor absolutizes evil or error.

6. Pluralism does not deny the function of the *logos* and its inalienable rights. The principle of non-contradiction, for instance, cannot be eliminated. But pluralism belongs also to the order of *mythos*. It incorporates *mythos*, not, of course, as an object of thinking but as a horizon that makes thinking possible. Brevity compels me not to develop these points as I have done elsewhere.

The Pluralism of Truth

Truth Is beyond Unity and Plurality

Pluralism affirms neither that truth is one, nor that it is many. If truth were one, we could not accept the positive tolerance of a pluralistic attitude and would have to consider pluralism a connivance with error. We could, at best, refrain from any judgement regarding disputable or irrelevant matters. But how can we abstain from condemning what we judge evil or error? How can we postpone practical decisions, all the more when mere postponement is already an uncritical decision?

But truth is not manifold either. If truth were many, we would fall into plain contradiction. We said already that pluralism does not stand for plurality, the plurality of truth in this case. Pluralism adopts a non-dualistic or advaitic attitude that defends the pluralism of truth because reality itself is pluralistic; that is, incommensurable with either unity or plurality. Being as such, even if encompassed by, or coexistent with the *logos* or a supreme intelligence does not need to be reduced to consciousness. In fact, the perfect self-mirroring of Being is truth, but even if the perfect image of Being is identical to Being, Being does not need to be exhausted in its image—unless we previously assume that Being is (only) Consciousness.

Truth Has No Center

In theological circles these are today interesting discussions regarding whether christocentrism or theocentrism or any other center should be the point of reference for Christian theology. In sociological and anthropological circles, questions of ethnocentrism, Eurocentric attitudes, and technocentrism are debated. All those discussions implicitly recognize that it has to be a center if we have to reach intelligibility. The center, if at all, is mobile. I say to "christocentrists" and "theocentrists" alike, "You are right!" But I emphasize the *you*, the context within which the particular theologian thinks. What is not necessarily true is that truth needs always the same center.

Let me cite the story of a wise rabbi who was heading a congregation long ago. Jews were quarrelling with one another, and one party went to expose its grievances to the rabbi, who would say, "You are right! You are right!" The other party of the congregation having learned that, went also to the rabbi and explained their plight. The rabbi listens attentively and says, "You are right!" You are right!" Obviously the quarrel began all over again. So the intellectuals and scribes of the congregation, who knew better, formed a small commission and went to the rabbi stating with due respect: "Master, you have said today this was right, and yesterday that the other party was right. Obviously both cannot be right." The rabbi said, "You are right! You are right!" Who is right? Or only the rabbi is wrong?

The relation between the three statements is of course dialectical. But the relation between the two discussing groups of living people is not dialectical. The rabbi saw the relative completeness of each position, although it entailed the mutual contradiction of the intellectual statements, as the third existentially uninvolved party saw.

What I am trying to say is that pluralism enters when we discover the mutual incommensurability of human attitudes. It is the recognition of incompatibility of ultimate beliefs. We should take seriously the human experiences and struggles of the last 8,000 years of historical memory, each party thinking to do the right thing, and the other one believing that this is not so. We should hear once again Solomon's wisdom. Our many solutions want to cut the child in two when we cannot keep it for ourselves. Truth, like the child, is ours. But to keep the child alive, to keep humanity alive, to keep the polarity of the human realities alive, to keep the good faith of the people alive, to keep alive freedom as the highest dignity, we cannot judge by Reason *alone*. Solomon has shown us that his final judgement was the correct one, because when love intervenes, when the child is yours, you prefer to lose, you prefer even to be trodden down, but the child should live. I guess that our present situation demands of all of us to be able to say, "I don't understand you too well, even I think you are wrong, but the fact that you are wrong does not tell me much about my being right, or my being perhaps also wrong."

We need this intercourse with one another. The "interfaith" meeting is not just a dialectical affair. It requires also love, dialogue, and human touch. We belong together, even if our notions and codes are incompatible. The radius and the circumference belong together even if they are mutually incommensurable. Pluralism belongs to the human condition.

Truth Is Polar

The insight that truth itself is pluralistic may be described by saying that the very nature of truth is polar. Truth qua truth is itself a polarity. Whatever philosophical theory of truth we may espouse (correspondence, coherence, pragmatic, and the like), one thing remains common to all. Truth is always a relation, be it subject/object, or subject/predicate, or knower/known, or user/used, etc. There is still more. One of the terms of the relation, explicitly or implicitly, is us. Men. Even if we speak of the metaphysical truth of Being or theological truth of the Godhead itself, we humans cannot be totally bracketed out. And this is all the more the case when dealing with religious truth. We are coinvolved in the enterprise. In other words, truth has always an element of subjectivity in the sense that we, Men, are somewhat sharing in that statement, entity, process, or state of affairs which we call truth. Truth is always a relation which makes reference to us Men, for which the truth is truth (and not only objectively true).

Now, if this referee is only me, or only us, in a particular spatio-temporal culture, this I or this we cannot exhaust the total relation. This for two reasons: First this I or we is limited and can never know that it has totally known the other side in question. Secondly, the subject (I, we) is in itself unobjectifiable and this with no guaranty it could not change. We are one of the poles of the relationship, and we cannot be "sure" we cannot change. We cannot have control over ourselves except from the objective pole, which at its turn is related to the subjective one. A clear example is the so-called evolution of dogma. If the subjects change their perceptions and presuppositions, the "objective truths" of the dogma need to change accordingly, precisely to keep constant the relationship.

If this referee is not "we" but an infinite intellect, besides the fact that we can have only a limited human interpretation of this absolute intelligence, there is also no necessity whatsoever that this infinite intellect knows all Being. There is nothing hidden to an infinite intelligence; it is omniscient, and, as such, what it knows is the

Truth. One could even grant that it is the very source of truth, so that truth is precisely what the divine intellect knows. Truth would then be originally on the part of the Subject, not being conditioned by any object. This would be all the more in favor of a pluralism of truth, for Truth would utterly depend on Divine Pleasure and there would be no objective foundation whatsoever for a persistence of the "same" truth, or rather, the sameness would be derobed of any point of reference to affirm itself as such. We could not say whether truth is one or many.

The traditional position will defend that truth is one because this infinite intellect cannot change. This line of argument already implies the identification of Being with Consciousness. But this is a gratuitous assumption not warranted by the acceptance of an infinite Consciousness. The divine Consciousness, in fact, should know All, i.e., all that is knowable, but not all that is not all (of) Being, unless we identify previously Being with Consciousness. An infinite intelligence has no limits in its proper field: nothing is unintelligible to it, but this field does not need to be totally identical with reality. In short, it might well be that Reality has an opaque face impervious to Intelligibility. In Christian parlance the Divinity cannot be reduced to an infinite Logos. There "is" also an apophatic Source. There is also the Spirit, neither inferior to nor different from the Logos, but not reducible to it either. The Truth of God, the *logos,* to put it paradoxically, is not the Whole of God, because God being Truth, Logos, and infinite Truth, God "is" only this. It "is" Trinity.

We could formulate the pluralism of truth in a more yogic and Buddhist manner. We would comment then on the *citta-vrttinirodha,* or cessation of all mental activity, as in the beginning of the *Yogasûtra,* or on *ākimcanya âyatana,* or the abode of non-existence, as in primitive Buddhism. In both cases the mental is overcome and the ultimate insight is beyond the tetralemmic dialectic (of A, non-A, A and non-A, neither A nor non-A). Truth is not abolished, but its dwelling place (*âyatana*) is no longer the mansion of language. Are you so stupid as really believing that your opinion is the correct one and all the others are in error, hints discreetly the *Suttanipâta.*

These latter considerations are only ways of speaking within particular schools. And yet almost all theologies, as Ibn 'Arabî so pointedly stressed with his theory of *jam' al-diddayn (coincidentia oppositorum),* are forced to use antinomic language and paradoxes when referring to the Divine: the truth of one statement has to be contradicted by another affirmation which is equally true. Truth cannot have a unique and univocal expression, stressed *al-chaykh al-*

akbar (the greatest master), as tradition called him. This would be an example of our point which is directly concerned with the problem of religious truth in the very encounter of religions. Let me spell some of the corollaries without now elaborating on the intrinsic polarity of truth and the fact that we are, at least, partially involved in one of the poles.

By Way of Conclusion

The pluralism of truth entails among other corollaries:

1. The religious truth of a particular tradition can be properly understood only within the very tradition which has elaborated it. Each tradition has its language.

2. From one religious intellectual system one can legitimately criticize another system, provided one arrives at a certain common area where the dialogue and the critique is meaningful to both parties. We have to speak, at least partially, a common language.

3. At any given moment in human history there are prevalent *mythoi* which allow cross-cultural and transreligious criticism of held opinions. Human sacrifice and slavery can be fairly said to have elicited today a universal consensus which justifies calling them wrong straightaway. But there are today burning issues which no merely intellectual approach should minimize. Unless we quibble about words, is violence to be avoided at all costs? Is God a necessary hypothesis for a just world? Is present-day capitalism a dehumanizing force? We may have our own strong opinions on these questions, but should not present them as non-negotiable "truths."

The pluralism of truth is an eye-opener, first of all, for contingency; I don't have a 360-degree vision; nobody has. Second, and here is the most daring notion, truth is pluralistic because reality itself is pluralistic, not being an objectifiable entity. We subjects are also part of it. We are not only spectators of the Real, we are also co-actors and even co-authors of it. *This is precisely our human dignity.*

I do feel that this brief sketch, imperfect as it is, touches an essential question of the very nature of Reality, and touching the nature of Reality rebounds, as it were, into the nature of all our enterprises. This third millennium of the Western world, pointing towards a mutation in our situation, requires from us a notion of what it means to be *human,* of what it means to be *divine,* of what is the *world* in which we live and for which we share the responsibility.

Chapter 6

Philosophy and Revolution

The Text, the Context, and the Texture

The Text

Revolution

The dictionary meaning of "revolution" is a very broad one: from its mathematical, astronomical, and physical use to a merely metaphorical and spiritual sense. All have in common an underlying spatial metaphor: a revolving, a certain putting upside down of a set of given entities. We detect, then, from the very beginning a certain prominence given to the experience of *space.*

We shall restrict ourselves, however, to the more common use of the word today in the sociological field.[1] Here, significantly enough, the accent lies on the *temporal factor.*

The various written and oral "texts" about revolution, specially the modern ones, situate the issue under the heading of liberation[2]— a highly religious and theological word.[3] The aim of revolution is the liberation of Man. The two words, however, are not synonymous. Two important restrictions have to be noted: (a) the *contents* and (b) the *form* of the revolutionary liberation are specific and peculiar.

Whereas religions have to do with the liberation of Man—and one could even define religion as a way to liberation or of salvation—revolutions aim at a particular type of liberation only. We may understand liberation or salvation as referring to the fullness or end of Man in whatever sense it may be interpreted. This is the reason why revolution and religion are so closely related: be it to coalesce or to clash with one another, both deal with the same central human

This essay was originally published in *Philosophy East and West* 23 (July 1973): 315–22, under this title.

problem: the liberation of Man. Revolution, then, is a theological problem.[4]

(a) Revolutionary movements understand the *contents* of liberation in a more specific or restricted way than most traditional religions. Revolutions want to liberate Man from oppressive temporal or historical structures, from economic and social injustice, and further, this neither by denying nor transcending them (like spiritualistic movements), nor by reforming them (like rebellion of all sorts), but by radically changing or overthrowing them.[5] It would be a *metábasis eis állo génos,* an unwarranted extrapolation, to include under the word revolution, spiritual paths claiming to liberate Man by denying the reality of the historical structures or by escaping into an ahistorical realm or mode of existence. They may eventually be the answer to the revolutionary challenge, but they are not revolutions in the proper sense of the word.[6]

(b) The specific revolutionary *form* is also peculiar: it is that form of bringing about the desired radical change by speeding up time, by modifying the "natural" rhythms, by doing a kind of temporal violence to the temporal development of things, by carrying out the revolution by means of a man-made or artificial span of time. Revolution is more than evolution.

These considerations lead us to understand revolution as a process tending to liberate Man from historical structures felt oppressive, by overthrowing those very structures in a man-guided span of time.[7]

We may detect immediately a common assumption basic to all revolutions: the centrality of time and history and their real grip on the human being. Without this assumption, talk about revolution is idle.[8]

Philosophy

We can discover four different *kairological* moments in the self-understanding of the philosophical enterprise.[9] I call them kairological moments because they are somehow temporal without being merely chronological.

(1) The most ancient conception of the supreme wisdom, which only later began to call itself "sophia" or more discretely "philosophy," was nothing but the intellectual aspect of religion, the reflective awareness on the nature of religion, the conscious effort at understanding the truth (orthodoxy) of the existential religious path (orthopraxis). What people do when handling their human situation, that is what philosophy reflects upon. Philosophy is here the intellectual aspect of religion. No wonder that philosophy and religion were

bound together either in collaboration (apologetics, handmaiden of theology, etc.), or in fight (substituting religion, enlightenment, human adulthood, etc.). During this first period, philosophy was inextricably tied to the whole religious pilgrimage of Man.[10] It was more than symbiosis; it was a single life.

(2) Reason, being the main instrument of philosophy, soon fought for its independence from religion. Its main strength was its claim to be free from human credulity and superstition, and thus, to be the "science" of truth. Philosophy had to pay a heavy price for its independence. It had to renounce the temporal realm of fleeting events, it had to abandon what Aristotle would call the singular, Thomas Aquinas, the mere accidental contingencies, and Leibniz, the *vérités de fait* and to concentrate on the nontemporal realm of unchanging, general, and necessary ideas. Philosophy bought its independence from religion by abandoning the temporal world. Scholasticisms of all types furnish adequate examples. History as the realm of contingency and individual action was outside the scope of philosophy.

(3) Philosophy recovered its lost link with temporality in two stages. The first one was the critical revolution of which Kant could be considered the exponent: philosophy became aware of its own assumptions and discovered that before being able to say anything about the world, the "thing in itself," reality and the like, it had to examine its own laws, structure, and assumptions. The alleged intemporality of the ideas was thus tempered by the discovered temporal structure of the thinking mind. This incursion of temporality into the human mind became more apparent and pressing in the second stage of this same period, after the collapse of the Hegelian system. It took the form of philosophical historicisms and Marxist and post-Marxist philosophies: not only time and thinking but also time and being were considered indissolubly connected: the temporal factor ceased to be seen as being accidental to human thinking or even to reality itself. We come thus to a fourth period: a secular one.

(4) Once the historical dimension is regained for philosophy, this latter either becomes a religion in itself or it reconciles itself with traditional religions. We have then either the ideologies performing the role of ancient religions, or an encounter and embrace of traditional religion with philosophy.

We may now formulate our hypothesis regarding the topic of philosophy and revolution from the perspective of comparative philosophy.

The Context

Philosophy of Revolution

So long as philosophy was considered to be outside the temporal flux and dealing mainly with eternal and everlasting or at least necessary truths, philosophy had little to do with revolution. It could deal only with moral issues, for example, whether or not it is ethically correct to kill the tyrant, to use violence, to utilize certain means for some kind of ends, etc. The context of philosophy was the intemporal realm, and revolution was considered to lie outside the competence of philosophical speculation.

Philosophy, thus, could be considered by the revolutionary movements only as a reactionary and counterrevolutionary force, for such an intemporal philosophy could be only in favor of the status quo. It could, at best, try to understand change, once this had already occurred and been successful, but never bring it forth.[11]

Only when philosophy became more and more entangled in the temporal process itself could it contribute to effecting or countereffecting revolutions.

The Revolution of Philosophy

Only in the first, the second half of the third, and the fourth period of the philosophical evolution can philosophy be said to bear an intrinsic link with revolution. In the first period philosophy reflects the same changes of the complex religious setup of which it forms a part—with the subsequent danger of transgressing its limits and becoming an instrument in the hands of all sorts of totalitarianisms.

In the fourth period, bringing the third to completion, the relation between philosophy and revolution begins to dawn as an *ontonomic* or constitutive relation.[12] Philosophy is here no longer outside the human struggle, looking down upon the temporal events of man's life on earth, it is no longer only passing moral judgments as to how things ought to develop, but is involved in the same temporal melting pot of human consciousness and historical development. One could speak of an internal revolution in the philosophical field itself, of which not even linguistic analysis could be an exception, for languages themselves are intrinsically connected with time and history.

This brings us to the point of formulating a kind of law regarding the revolutionary stage of mankind from the perspective of comparative philosophy, which is here submitted as a working hypothesis.

The Texture

Revolution as a Philosophical Theory

We could formulate this law in the following terms: not only every revolution has its philosophy but no revolution is possible without an undergirding philosophy, so that if this latter is lacking, no revolution can take place. A revolution is doomed to fail if the cadres and under-cadres of men and women on the different levels of society are not taken account of, but a revolution cannot even take place if the intellectual structures and substructures cannot be articulated in the underlying philosophy of the peoples concerned.[13] In other words, the philosophical undergirding of the aims and means of a revolution belongs to the revolution itself. Revolution is, in itself, a philosophical problem; it is, first of all, a philosophical endeavor and not only a fact or the concept of a fact that can be, later on, philosophically evaluated.[14] Revolution takes place first in the mind—but not in every mind.[15] It is not a bare fact—even if bare facts were possible—but a cosmo-anthropological complex, meaningful, and thus real, within a particular context.

We are living today in a special texture which renders the contexts of the different philosophical texts somewhat obsolete. On the one hand, philosophies and ideologies have subjects and citizens according to geographical and historical provinces, that is, there are different philosophical texts only valid over against the background of their respective contexts. On the other hand, there is a wind of universality, which has not yet found an accepted formulation but which is blowing in mythical and still timid forms. There is a subtle texture which begins to encompass the different contexts of the several worldviews. It is this texture which offers the only possible background for comparative philosophy. Philosophies are not simply different readings or different texts about the mystery of reality (just to use this expression), but different contexts, which can only be understood over against the background of a common texture which challenges any verbalization. Now, revolution does not belong to the universal texture but only to the context of very few philosophies, and it is part and parcel of one philosophical text, which now strives to become more universal. What once was done under the name of

God, or Church, or Civilization now would like to be effected under the flag of Revolution (technical or social).

We may try to clarify this complex situation by adducing an example.

The inadequacy felt today by certain groups in India between their understanding of social justice and the historical situation they see, leads them to the conviction that a revolution like those of the West or of China is just and needed. They have arrived at this conviction because, having been exposed to a way of thinking alien to the traditional Indian one—for which even the word "revolution" has to be almost artificially constructed—they have arrived at what is for them an unbearable social situation.[16]

The difficulty they are facing lies in the fact that there are no philosophical tools in the traditional thought of India to handle such a revolution and that most of the population of India nurtured in the ancient culture would not even understand what it all is about.[17]

Any "intemporal" philosophy, any monistic and pantheistic worldview, any ahistorical culture, will not be able to understand and try to carry out the necessary philosophical and psychological preparation for the "needed" revolution. To superimpose an alien trend of thought will only add confusion and will not directly lead to a revolution.[18] It may, rather, lead to a mere reactionary resistance or sheer rebellion. Revolution is neither a universal value nor a universal human fact. It is at home in a particular philosophy and tends to become a myth outside its proper context. This leads us to our final point.

The Idiosyncrasy of Revolution

The morphological character of any colonial or neocolonial attitude is the ideal of cultural monophormism, be this in the form of one religion, one church, one king or kingdom, one technological age or one world-culture, or even one revolution. And yet this does not justify the opposite extreme of a disconnected plurality: pluralism does not mean chaotic confusion.

If a true "revolution" has to take place in India, to continue with our example, there has to be an undergirding philosophy which gives due importance to space and time and to the historical dimension of Man and which allows the paradigm idea to have an influence on the external fact.[19] Now, it is the task of philosophy and the incumbency of comparative philosophy to bring forth an understanding of time and history congenial and homogeneous with the tradition of the peoples in question.[20] A superimposition of ready-made conceptions of time and history as foreign bodies into an alien culture will not succeed in creating the necessary understanding or the tools needed for a constructive revolution. To put something upside down, you must first have a certain spatial orientation of the transformation you are to bring about. The Indian revolution has to be endogenous, like the conception of time, space, and history necessary to articulate and carry out such a revolution has to correspond to the experience of the temporal reality of the peoples of India. It will be the task of philosophy to develop such a conception. The very concept and also the techniques of revolution will change accordingly.[21] The Indian revolution cannot originate, like most of the modern revolutions of the West, out of impatience for the *parousia*. It has to strike another root.[22] By the same token such an enterprise would demythologize time and history and get rid of its monopoly by the modern Western world. Such a task is still to be done.[23] Here philosophy regains its existential, practical, and even political character, its risk and also its beauty and life. It may well be the task of comparative philosophy to contribute, to discover, to weave, to create, or however we would like to articulate it, the common human texture, which will neither eliminate the variegated texts of human reason nor destroy the various contexts of human experience, but present to the world at large the polychromic harmony of the human texture.

Chapter 7

Is the Notion of Human Rights a Western Concept?

The Mythical Horizon of Every Human Right: A Tale for Our Time

I am a self-supporting villager with a small farm of my own and have three children. I do not see why I have to pay some strange taxes to maintain, they say, an army and a social infrastructure which make possible my security. Our family has lived for generations without such qualms. My son has also refused to go to what they call the military "service."

And now I hear grand talk about Human Rights. I am not undermining the power of the State, I am not intending to establish a *new* style of life. My son is not challenging any of the "sacred" principles of democracy. We are not isolated individuals either. We have lively relations with a vast number of people and have an enriching net of exchanges in all senses of the word. We had our own well and animals. Now they have put strange pipelines in and ask us to contribute to the "service" they do to us—which we have neither asked for nor do we see it bringing real advantages. It makes us more dependent on who opens or closes the faucet (which word, incidentally, I am told, comes from "falsifying"). I am ready, just to make a compromise, to pay some compensation for the alleged "service." But not for the militarization and industrialization of the country, which they say extends far beyond the limits of the real history of the people who speak our own language, which they call a dialect.

This essay is an expanded and revised version of the presentation at the "Entretien de Dakar," Senegal, to the annual session of the "Institut International de Philosophie" on *Philosophical Foundations of Human Rights*. It appeared previously as "Is the Notion of Human Rights a Western Concept?" *Diogenes* 120 (Winter 1982): 75–102. It is introduced by a section originally published separately as "The Mythical Horizon of Every Human Right," *Jeevadhara* 21 (1991): 48–52.

Now, I am fined, punished, and so is my son. Do we not have the *right to be ourselves?* Do we not have the right to decide about our lives, provided we do not harm others? Have we *rights* only if we join the train of modernity which has to move on prefabricated tracks?

They speak about the voice of the voiceless, but it is always their voices—and their languages. They say that feudalism is over, but I fail to see the difference. The only difference is that it is now practically impossible to escape their computerized controls. Before, it was all done as a matter of fact and fate. Now, the attempt they make at justifying it and the entire talk about Human Rights, backfires, for we have lost our innocence and are not convinced by their arguments. I wonder if we have really "progressed."

I am not speaking about "revolutionary" people as those who want, for instance, a separate country or region, or who upset the status quo. What right has a State to declare its proper limits sacred and untouchable when people within those limits seem to question both the sacredness and the inviolability? My case is milder. It is the query of the Human Right to a dissent which does not upset anything—except, perhaps, they say, that this will set a precedent and trigger a "domino effect." If they preach democracy I do not understand their fear of people's opinions. I am merely asking whether I have the Right of not playing the game, of abstaining. We are not subversive. We are peace-loving people. And my simple question is about the meaning of Human Rights, of individual human rights—since I hear that the Human Rights are precisely there to protect the right of individuals against coercions from higher powers.

So far the query. Let us listen now to the sociologist, the psychologist, and the philosopher.

The *sociologist* will argue like this:

You do not realize that you are not alone, that you are forming part of a great nation which needs your collaboration precisely to make possible what you are dreaming of. You are living under a democratic constitution which states that we, the sovereign people, have given us that charter in order to live in peace. So you should bow to the will of the majority who through their representatives have decided that the common good demands from you these services.

No need to say that our Man will not be convinced. He has not framed the Constitution nor was he asked anything of what the sociologist is talking about. He even has different ideals. And our Man is sufficiently self-taught so as not to abide by the argument that his abstentionism produces a great evil. He is not tempted to organize a political party in order to fight for his rights. He has neither the means nor the liking, nor the faith that such is the way. He is precisely contesting the very rules of the game of the so-called democratic set-up. They say one Man, one vote. His experience tells him: one rupee, one vote. His only reaction will be one of resignation, apathy, loss of enthusiasm, and will simply yield to the pressures, and eventually compensate the injustice he feels victim of by going "the way of friends," which is what others call corruption.

The *psychologist* may take a different route. He will say something like this: Your reactions are diachronical. You live in another time, you have not yet evolved and fail to realize that the world today lives on another wavelength—and you have got to play the game. You have the right to dissent only within the limits set up by the Constitution, but meanwhile you have to abide by the rules of society. You have now plenty of rights which you did not have before, let alone that of voicing your discontent. But you should not contest the very democratic foundations of our rights.

To which our Man may answer, taking the hint from the psychological jargon, that perhaps his position is not diachronical, out of time, but diatopical, out of place. Has he to accept psychological homogenization in the same way that they impose agricultural homogene programs and monocultures of all types? Has one not the right to live in a different time and also on a different space? Are Human Rights only for modern democrats?

The *philosopher* will ponder within and will feel incapable of talking to the peasant. The problem is not of the *logos*—and thus no rational word will do—but of the *mythos*. That petty landowner lives another world and not just another vision of the (same) world. This is what I call the *Conflict of Kosmologies*.

Human Rights have been presented as universal rights, but they are such only within a very particular mythical world. It is, to be sure, the predominant mythical world of the "developed" nations and the "elites" profiteering from the "developing" countries. The "Human Rights" come from the mythos of that predominant culture which sees as mythical the world of the "undeveloped" peoples, but is unable to discover its own myth.

The alternative is not "Human Rights" or nothing, anarchy, the exploitation of the poor and no bridle to the abuses of power. "Human Rights" try precisely to counteract. The alternative is to find the *homeomorphic equivalents* in each culture so that human dignity and the sacredness of reality may be safeguarded—as I have tried to explicate above.

Our philosopher may still ponder how easily under the cloak of "Human Rights" a particular "civilization" may penetrate into others and disrupt the fabric of different cultures. Our philosopher may have sympathy with our peasant, but remain speechless in front of him and his son. The philosophical talk about myth and logos, about cosmology and kosmology, individual and person requires not only theoretical knowledge. Of this the Man of our example is fully capable. The responsible philosophical approach is not a lifeless abstraction in the realm of ideas. A meaningful philosophical reaction to his questions requires *praxis*. It has to take into account the *Sitz im Leben* of the discussion. Philosophy cannot abstract from power and politics. And present-day philosophy has been often devitalized because made to function in an ideal world. Philosophy has severed its links with science, on the one hand, and theology on the other. The three now suffer from the split.

Within the concrete context of present-day India our philosopher may still think in serene but melancholic mood: We are in a situation which has yet hardly reflected on the meeting of cultures and encounter of religions in "post-independent" India. We hurried, for political and historical reasons, to imitate the model of Western civilization. It is undoubtedly one of the greatest civilizations of the planet, but certainly neither the only one, nor perhaps the most congenial to the Indian subcontinent. We acted as if our traditional cultures were either dead or inferior, and superimposed a political pattern borrowed from the Anglo-Saxon world. Perhaps there was no other viable alternative. Now the West is having second thoughts, but we are already thrown into the technocratic complex. If we retrieve traditional culture, we may perish. If we do not, we will certainly do so.

The philosopher feels paralyzed to speak. To incite rebellion courts total fiasco. The allure to obey undermines the nerve of sane people. Our philosopher is thankful for the questions of the peasant but is now going to meet the intellectuals and urge them not to be satisfied with some amendments here and there. These are urgently necessary. But a thorough transformation is essentially required. If the four millennia of the culture of the Indian subcontinent mean anything, it is taking into account that political and human problems have to be tackled. We can strive for success in international markets, but no people can truly live from a borrowed myth.

BT 83.85 K63

BR 127 .C558

BR 127 .K56   BR 85 .P25

BT 202 .M44   BL 87 .R26

Edelson, Stephen.

    What you doctor may not tell you about autoimmune disorders : the revolutionary drug-free treatments for thyroid disease, lupus, MS, IBD, chronic fatigue, rheumatoid arthritis, and other diseases / Stephen B. Edelson and Deborah Mitchell.   New York : Warner Books, c2003.

    xx, 348 p. ; 21 cm.

    "A Lynn Sonberg book."
    Includes bibliographical references (p. 337-338) and index.
    ISBN 0-446-67924-0 (pbk.)

    1. Autoimmune diseases—Alternative treatment. 2. Autoimmune diseases—Popular works. I. Mitchell, Deborah R. II. Title.

RC600.E344   2003   616.97'806—dc21

                                     2002068972

Library of Congress   r0303;   COMARC

The Notion of Human Rights

We should approach the topic of Human Rights with great fear and respect. It is not a merely "academic" issue. Human rights are trampled upon in the East as in the West, in the North as in the South of our planet. Granting the part of human greed and sheer evil in this universal transgression, could it not also be that Human Rights are not observed because in their present form they do not represent a universal symbol powerful enough to elicit understanding and agreement?

No culture, tradition, ideology, or religion can today speak for the whole of humankind, let alone solve its problems. Dialogue and intercourse leading to a mutual fecundation are necessary. But sometimes the very conditions for dialogue are not given, because there are unspoken conditions which most partners cannot meet. It is a fact that the present-day formulation of Human Rights is the fruit of a very partial dialogue among the cultures of the world. It is only recently that this question has been acutely felt.[1] I shall not enter into the details of the history of Human Rights, nor into an analysis of their nature. I shall confine myself to the interrogation implied in the title: Are Human Rights a universal invariant?

The Method of Inquiry

Diatopical Hermeneutics

It is claimed that Human Rights are universal. This alone entails a major philosophical query. Does it make sense to ask about conditions of universality when the very question about conditions of universality is far from universal? Philosophy can no longer ignore this intercultural problematic. Can we extrapolate the concept of Human Rights from the context of the culture and history in which it was conceived into a globally valid notion? Could it at least *become* a universal symbol? Or is it only one particular way of expressing—and saving—the *humanum?*

Although the question posed in the title is a legitimate one, there is something disturbing in this formulation as it was given to me. At least at first glance, it would seem to offer only one alternative: either the notion of Universal Human Rights is a Western notion, or it is not. If it is, besides being a tacit indictment against those who do not possess such a valuable concept, its introduction into other cultures, even if necessary, would appear as a plain imposition from outside. It would appear, once again, as a continuation of the colonial syndrome, namely the belief that the constructs of one particular culture (God, Church, Empire, Western civilization, Science, Modern Technology, etc.) have, if not the monopoly, at least the privilege of possessing a universal value which entitles them to be spread over all the Earth. If not, that is, if the concept of Universal Human Rights is not exclusively a Western concept, it would be difficult to deny that many a culture has let it slumber, thus again giving rise to an impression of the indisputable superiority of Western culture. There is nothing wrong in admitting a hierarchy of cultures, but this hierarchical order cannot be assumed as the starting point, nor can one side alone lay down the criteria necessary for establishing such a hierarchy. There is then a prior question implied by asking whether the notion of Human Rights is a Western concept. It is the question regarding the very nature of Human Rights, and it directly submits this notion to cross-cultural scrutiny.

Our question is a case in point of *diatopical hermeneutics*: the problem is how, from the *topos* of one culture, to understand the constructs of another.[2] It is wrong-headed methodology to begin by asking: Does another culture also have the notion of Human Rights?—assuming that such a notion is absolutely indispensable to guarantee human dignity. No question is neutral, for every question conditions its possible answers.

The Homeomorphic Equivalent

I was once asked to give the Sanskrit equivalents of the twenty-five key Latin words supposed to be emblematic of Western culture. I declined, on the grounds that that which is the foundation of one culture need not be the foundation for another. Meanings are not transferable here. Translations are more delicate than heart transplants. So what must we do? We must dig down to where a homogeneous soil or a similar problematic appears: we must search out the *homeomorphic equivalent*—to the concept of Human Rights in this case. "Homeomorphism is not the same as analogy; it represents a peculiar functional equivalence discovered through a topological transformation." It is "a kind of existential functional analogy."[3]

Thus we are not seeking merely to transliterate Human Rights into other cultural languages, nor should we be looking for mere analogies; we try instead to find the homeomorphic equivalent. If, for instance, Human Rights are considered to be the basis for the exercise of and respect for human dignity, we should investigate how another culture satisfies the equivalent need—and this can be done only once a common ground (a mutually understandable language) has been worked out between the two cultures. Or perhaps we should ask how the idea of a just social and political order could be formulated within a certain culture, and investigate whether the concept of Human Rights is a particularly appropriate way of expressing this order. A traditional Confucian might see this problem of order and rights as a question of "good manners" or in terms of his profoundly ceremonial or ritual conception of human intercourse, in terms of *Li*. A Hindu might see it another way, and so on.

In order to clarify the question on our title, I shall indicate some of the assumptions on which the notion of Human Rights is based and immediately insert some cross-cultural reflections which shall lead us to the *locus*—the context—of the question and the justification for my answer, which I would like to anticipate by means of a simile: Human Rights are one window through which one particular culture envisages a just human order for its individuals. But those who live in that culture do not see the window. For this they need the help of another culture which sees through another window. Now I assume that the human landscape as seen through the one window is both similar to and different from the vision of the other. If this is the case, should we smash the windows and make of the many portals a single gaping aperture, with the consequent danger of structural collapse, or should we enlarge the viewpoints as much as possible and, most of all, make people aware that there are—and have to be—a plurality of windows? This latter option would be the one in favor of a healthy pluralism. This is much more than a merely academic question. There can be no serious talk about cultural pluralism without a genuine socio-economic-political pluralism. This is, for example, what has led intellectual groups in India to ask whether "civil rights" are not incompatible with "economic rights." At any rate, to speak of cultural pluralism within what could be called a paneconomic ideology makes little sense and amounts to treating the other cultures of the world as mere folklore. The example of the notion of Dharma from the Indian tradition will offer us a point of reference from which to formulate our conclusion.

Assumptions and Implications of the Western Concept

I take the expression "Human Rights" in the sense of the Universal Declaration of Human Rights adopted by the General Assembly of the United Nations in 1948.[4] The Western, mainly liberal Protestant roots of the Human Rights Declaration are well-known.[5] The Western world has known of the struggle for citizens' rights since the Middle Ages.[6] This struggle for concrete rights, rooted in the practices and value system of a particular nation or country, is felt with greater urgency after the French Revolution.[7] Western Man passes from a corporate belonging in a community of blood, work, and historical destiny, based on practically accepted custom and theoretically acknowledged authority, to a society based on impersonal law and ideally free contract, to the modern State, for which explicitly rational norms and duties are required. The problem becomes increasingly acute with the growth of individualism.

This essay assumes knowledge of the history of Human Rights, as well as of the fact that this transition from one form of collective life to another more modern form is said today to have acquired a worldwide character. We would like to concentrate on the more strictly philosophical *assumptions* which seem to be at the basis of Declaration.

1. At the basis of the discourse on Human Rights there is the assumption of a *universal human nature* common to all peoples. Otherwise, a Universal Declaration could not logically have been proclaimed. This idea in its turn is connected with the old notion of a Natural Law.

But the contemporary Declaration of Human Rights further *implies:*

(a) that this human nature must be *knowable*. For it is one thing to accept human nature uncritically or mythically, and another to know it. Otherwise, the Declaration could not speak and legislate about Rights that are universal.

(b) that this human nature is known by means of an equally universal organ of knowledge, generally called *reason*. Otherwise, if its knowledge should depend on a special intuition, revelation, faith, decree of a prophet or the like, Human Rights could not be taken as *natural* rights—inherent in Man. This must be commonly-held knowledge. Otherwise, Human Rights could not be declared universal by an Assembly which does not claim to have a privileged epistemological status. This is made plain by the use of the word "declaration," which stresses the fact that it is not an imposition from above but a public explicitation, a making clear of what is inherent in the very nature of Man.[8]

(c) that this human nature is essentially *different* from the rest of reality. Other living beings inferior to Man obviously have no Human

Rights, and creatures superior to Man are likely not to exist. Man is the master of himself and the universe. He is the supreme legislator on Earth—the question of whether a Supreme Being exists or not remains open, but ineffective.[9]

2. The second assumption is that of the *dignity of the individual.* Each individual is, in a certain sense, absolute, irreducible to another. This is probably the major thrust of the Modern question of Human Rights. Human Rights defend the dignity of the individual vis-à-vis Society at large, and the State in particular.

But this in turn implies:

(a) not only the distinction but also the *separation* between individual and society. In this view the human being is fundamentally the individual. Society is a kind of superstructure, which can easily become a menace and also an alienating factor for the individual. Human Rights are there primarily to protect the individual.

(b) the *autonomy* of humankind vis-à-vis and often versus the Cosmos. This is clearly shown in the ironic ambivalence of the English expression, which means at the same time "Menschenrechte," "droits de l'Homme," and also "Menschliche Rechte," "droits humains" (human rights). The Cosmos is a kind of understructure. The individual stands in between Society and World. Human Rights defend the autonomy of the human individual.

(c) resonances of the idea of Man as *microcosmos* and reverberations of the conviction that Man is *imago dei,* and at the same time the relative independence of this conviction from ontological and theological formulations. The individual has an inalienable dignity because he is an end in himself and a kind of absolute. You can cut off a finger for the sake of the entire body, but can you kill one person to save another?[10]

3. The third assumption is that of a *democratic social order.* Society is assumed to be not a hierarchical order founded on a divine will or law or mythical origin, but a sum of "free" individuals organized to achieve otherwise unreachable goals. Human Rights, once again, serve mainly to protect the individual. Society here is not seen as a family or a protection, but as something unavoidable which can easily abuse the power conferred on it (precisely by the assent of the sum of its individuals). This Society crystallizes in the State, which theoretically expresses the will of the people, or at least of the majority. The idea of an Empire, or a People or a Nation with a transcendent destiny—whose duty it is to carry through the entrusted mission independent of the will of the members of that society—still exists today in some theocratic states, but even

most of these try to palliate their messianic vocation by democratic endorsements.

This implies:

(a) that each individual is seen as equally important and thus equally responsible for the welfare of society. Hence the individual has the right to stand by his or her convictions and propagate them or to resist impositions against his or her inherent freedom.

(b) that Society is nothing but the sum total of the individuals whose wills are sovereign and ultimately decisive.[11] There is no instance superior to Society. Even if there were to exist a God or a superhuman Reality, this too would be filtered through human consciousness and human institutions.

(c) that the rights and freedoms of the individual can be limited only when they impinge upon the rights and freedoms of other individuals, and in this way majority rule is rationally justified.[12] And when the rights of an individual are curtailed by "reasons of State," this is allegedly justified by the fact that the State is supposed to embody the will and the interests of the majority. It is interesting to note that the "Universal Declaration" speaks of "freedoms" in the plural and, even more intriguing, of "fundamental freedoms." The individualization does not stop at the individual, but divides this segregated entity even further into separated freedoms.

In enumerating these Assumptions and Implications I do not mean to say that they were actually in the minds of the framers of the Declaration. In fact, there is evidence to suggest that no unanimity could be found regarding the basis of the rights that were being declared. But the Declaration clearly was articulated along the lines of the historical trends of the Western world during the last three centuries, and in tune with a certain philosophical anthropology or individualistic humanism which helped justify them.

Cross-cultural Reflection

Is the Concept of Human Rights a Universal Concept?

The answer is plain *no*. Three reasons vouch for it.

(a) No concept as such is universal. Each concept is valid primarily where it was conceived. If we want to extend its validity beyond its own context we shall have to justify the extrapolation. Even mathematical concepts imply the previous acknowledgment of a limited field defined by the axioms we postulate. Furthermore, every concept tends to be univocal. To accept the possibility of universal concepts would imply a strictly rationalistic conception of reality. But even if this were the theoretical truth it would not be the actual case, because *de facto* humankind presents a plurality of universes of discourse. To accept the fact that the concept of Human Rights *is* not universal does not yet mean that it *should* not *become* so. Now in order for a concept to become universally valid it should fulfill at least two conditions. It should, on the one hand, eliminate all the other contradictory concepts. This may seem improbable, but there is a logical necessity here and, theoretically, it would all be for the best. On the other hand, it should be the universal point of reference for any problematic regarding human dignity. In other words, it should displace all other homeomorphic equivalents and be the pivotal center of a just social order. To put it another way, the culture which has given birth to the concept of Human Rights should also be called upon to become a universal culture. This may well be one of the causes of a certain uneasiness one senses in non-Western thinkers who study the question of Human Rights. They fear for the identity of their own cultures.

(b) Within the vast field of Western culture itself, the very assumptions which serve to situate our problematic are not universally recognized. The particular origin of the formulation of Human Rights is sufficiently well-known. Probably the most important sources of dissent are three.[13]

Theology. Human Rights need to be grounded, says the theological view, in a superior, transcendent and therefore unmanipulable value, whose traditional symbol is God as origin and guarantor of both human rights and duties. Otherwise, they are only a political device in the hands of the powerful. According to this view, the Declaration suffers from a naive optimism regarding the goodness and autonomy of human nature. Moreover, it implies a deficient anthropology, inasmuch as it seems to view the human person as merely a bundle of needs, material and psychological, of which it then proceeds to make an inventory.[14] And finally, in case of doubt or conflict, who is going to decide? Majority rule is only a euphemism for the law of the jungle: the power of the strongest.

Marxism. For Marxists, so-called Human Rights are merely *Klassenrechte*, class rights.[15] "There are no rights without duties and no duties without rights."[16] They reflect the interests of a certain class and in many cases only its aspirations. There is no mention of the economic conditions for the effective realization of what are said to be universal human claims. Furthermore, there is something abstract and too general about most of these rights; they are not sufficiently grounded in the material and cultural reality of particular groups. Finally, their individualism is evident. The individual is conceived as being in confrontation with (rather than included in) society, although the latter is said to be the result of freely contracting individuals. Society is not merely the sum total of individuals and it has rights which the individual may not violate. History has transcendent power.

History. "Human Rights" appear to some students of recent history as another example of the more or less conscious domination exerted by the powerful nations to maintain their privileges and defend the *status quo*. Human rights continue to be a political weapon. Human rights were known long ago but only for the noblemen, or the free citizen, or for whites or Christians or males, etc., and when they were hastily applied to "human beings" it was often defined just which groups belonging to the race could properly be styled "human." If not all humans had human rights, the claim of human rights on behalf of animals, plants and things would seem and still does seem bizarre, not to say ridiculous, in spite of occasional remonstrances delivered by Societies for the Protection of Animals. Animals and such may very well have rights, but not human ones. And, as we have seen, this particular notion of the "human" has not always been very humane. And who is to speak for the whole? History discloses that only the victors declare and promulgate "rights," which are simply what the powerful consider right at any given time.

(c) From a cross-cultural stance the problem appears exclusively Western, i.e., the question itself is at stake. Most of the assumptions and implications enumerated earlier are simply not given in other cultures. Furthermore, for a non-Western point of view the problem itself is not seen as such, so that it is not merely a question of agreeing or disagreeing with the answer. If anything, the problem is that the issue is experienced in a radically different way. A *diatopical* hermeneutic does not deal with just another point of view on the *same* problem. At issue here is not simply the answer, but the problem itself.

Now is it possible to have access to other *topoi* so that we may be able to understand other cultures from within, i.e., as they understand themselves? We may not be able to jump over our own categories of understanding, but it may not be impossible to have one foot in one culture and another in a second. Generally, we have only one culture as we have only one mother-tongue—but we may also have a father-tongue. We cannot a priori deny this possibility. I recall that, in certain parts of the East, to be illiterate means to know only a single language. It is in dialogue with others that we can encompass our common ground. We may not integrate more than one culture in ourselves but we may open the possibility of a wider and deeper integration by opening ourselves, in dialogue, to others.

The following parallelism may be instructive. To assume that without the explicit recognition of Human Rights life would be chaotic and have no meaning belongs to the same order of ideas as to think that without the belief in one God as understood in the Abrahamic tradition human life would dissolve itself in total anarchy. This line of thinking leads to the belief that Atheists, Buddhists and Animists, for instance, should be considered as human aberrations. In the same vein: either Human Rights, or chaos. This attitude does not belong exclusively to Western culture. To call the stranger a barbarian is all too common an attitude among the peoples of the world. And, as we shall mention later, there is a legitimate and inbuilt claim to universality in any affirmation of truth. The problem is that we tend to identify the limits of our own vision with the human horizon.

Cross-Cultural Critique

There *are* no trans-cultural values, for the simple reason that a value exists as such only in a given cultural context.[17] But there *may be* cross-cultural values, and a cross-cultural critique is indeed possible. The latter does not consist in evaluating one cultural construct with the categories of another, but in trying to understand and criticize one particular human problem with the tools of understanding of the different cultures concerned, at the same time taking thematically into consideration that the very awareness and, much more, the formulation of the problem is already culturally bound. Our question is then to examine the possible cross-cultural value of the issue of Human Rights, an effort which begins by delimiting the cultural boundaries of the concept. The dangers of cultural westocentrism are only too patent today.

(a) We have already mentioned the particular historical origins of the Declaration of Human Rights. To claim universal validity for Human Rights in the formulated sense implies the belief that most of the peoples of the world today are engaged in much the same way as the Western nations in a process of transition from more or less mythical *Gemeinschaften* (feudal principalities, self-governing cities, guilds, local communities, tribal institutions...) to a "rationally" and "contractually" organized "modernity" as known to the Western industrialized world. This is a questionable assumption. No one can predict the evolution (or eventual disintegration) of those traditional societies which have started from different material and cultural bases and whose reaction to modern Western civilization may therefore follow hitherto unknown lines.

Further, the very powerful Declaration of Human Rights also shows its weakness from another point of view. Something has been lost when it has to be explicitly declared. As the Chinese say: it is when *yi* (justice) declines that *li* (ritual) arises.[18] Or as the British and Spaniards repeat: There are things which you take for granted and about which you do not speak. And in some traditional societies, you cannot boast of being noble or a friend of the royal family because the very moment you do so, you lose your nobility and your friendship with the reigning house.[19] When Human Rights are declared this is a sign that the very foundation on which they rest has already been weakened. The Declaration only postpones the collapse. In traditional words, when the tabu of the sacred disappears sacredness fades away. If you have to teach a mother to love her child, something is amiss with motherhood. Or, as some theoreticians of Human Rights have also recognized, the legislation of Human Rights is introduced in order to find a justification for contravening somebody else's freedom. Putting it positively, you need some justification to encroach on somebody's field of activity.

I am not saying this in order to revert to utopian dreams of an earthly paradise, but just to sound another voice. You may promulgate laws, but you do not declare what is the case—unless it has ceased to be evident; you do not proclaim an "ought" if there are no transgressions at all.

We may now briefly reconsider the three Assumptions mentioned above. They may pass muster, insofar as they express an authentically valid human issue from one particular context. But the very context may be susceptible to a legitimate critique from the perspective of other cultures. To do this systematically would require that we choose one culture after another and examine the Assumptions of the Declaration in the light of each culture chosen. We shall limit ourselves here to token reflections under the very broad umbrella of a pre-Modern, non-Western state of mind.

(i) There is certainly a *universal human nature* but, first of all, this nature does not need to be segregated and fundamentally distinct from the nature of all living beings and/or the entire reality. Thus exclusively *Human* Rights would be seen as a violation of "Cosmic Rights" and an example of self-defeating anthropocentrism, a novel kind of apartheid. To retort that "Cosmic Rights" is a meaningless expression would only betray the underlying cosmology of the objection, for which the phrase makes no sense. But the existence of a different cosmology is precisely what is at stake here. We speak of the laws of nature; why not also of her rights?

Secondly, the interpretation of this "universal human nature," i.e., Man's self-understanding, belongs equally to this human nature. Thus to single out one particular interpretation of it may be valid, but it is not universal and may not apply to the entirety of human nature.

Thirdly, to proclaim the undoubtedly positive concept of Human Rights may turn out to be a Trojan horse, surreptitiously introduced into other civilizations which will then all but be obliged to accept those ways of living, thinking and feeling for which Human Rights is the proper solution in cases of conflict. It is a little like the way technology is often introduced in many parts of the world: it is imported to solve the problems that it has itself created. We have already made reference to this when criticizing the universalization of the concept of Human Rights.

(ii) Nothing could be more important than to underscore and defend the *dignity of the human person*. But the person should be distinguished from the individual. The individual is just an abstraction, i.e., a selection of a few aspects of the person for practical purposes. My person, on the other hand, is also in "my" parents, children, friends, foes, ancestors and successors. "My" person is also in "my" ideas and feelings and in "my" belongings. If you hurt "me," you are equally damaging my whole clan, and possibly yourself as well. Rights cannot be individualized in this way. Is it the right of the mother, or the child?—in the case of abortion. Or perhaps of the father and relatives as well? Rights cannot be abstracted from duties; the two are correlated. The dignity of the human person may equally be violated by your language, or by your desecrating a place I consider holy, even though it does not "belong" to me in the sense of individualized private property. You may have "bought" it for a sum of money, while it belongs to me by virtue of another order altogether. An individual is an isolated knot; a person is the entire fabric around that knot, woven from the total fabric of the real. The limits to a person are not fixed, they depend utterly on his or her personality. Certainly without the knots the net would collapse; but without the net, the knots would not even exist.

To aggressively defend my individual rights, for instance, may have negative, i.e., unjust, repercussions on others and perhaps even on myself. The need for consensus in many traditions—instead of majority opinion—is based precisely on the corporate nature of human rights.

A paragraph on language is required here. Each language has its own genius and its own particular way to see the world and even to be it and in it. But from a cross-cultural perspective, each language has to show the flexibility necessary to incorporate other human experiences. I know that in current English "individual" is synonymous with "person," but this should not prevent me from using these two words in the sense I have suggested, and from recognizing a particular human trend which tends to identify the human being with the most salient features of a gross "individualized" body or at least to inscribe it within that framework. In drawing the distinction between individual and person I would put much more content in it than a French moral philosophy would do nowadays, for instance. I would like to adduce this case as a particular instance of two radically different anthropologies.

(iii) *Democracy* is also a great value and infinitely better than any dictatorship. But it amounts to tyranny to put the peoples of the world under the alternative of choosing either democracy or dictatorship. Human Rights are tied to democracy. Individuals need to be protected when the structure which is above them (Society, the State of the Dictator—by whatever name) is not qualitatively superior to them, i.e., when it does not belong to a higher order. Human rights is a legal device for the protection of smaller numbers of people (the minority or the individual) faced with the power of greater numbers. This implies a quantitative reductionism; the person is reduced to the individual and the individual to the basis of society. I may put it more positively by saying that it is the way by which the individual as cornerstone of society is protected, and his or her dignity recognized. In a hierarchical conception of reality, the particular human being cannot defend his or her rights by demanding or exacting them independently of the whole. The wounded order has to be set straight again, or it has to change altogether. Other traditional societies have different means to more or less successfully restore the order. The rāja may fail in his duty to protect the people, but will a Declaration of Human Rights be a corrective unless it also has the power to constrain the rāja? Can a democracy be imposed and remain democratic?[20]

The policy of non-alignment subscribed to by many countries of

Africa and Asia here strikes a much deeper chord than possible political opportunism, or just another way of being relevant in the contemporary political scene. It represents precisely this refusal to admit the vision of the world as a function of the just mentioned set of dilemmas represented by the so-called superpowers.

In short, the cross-cultural critique does not invalidate the Declaration of Human Rights, but offers new perspectives for an internal criticism and sets the limits of validity of Human Rights, offering at the same time both possibilities for enlarging its realm, if the context changes, and of a mutual fecundation with other conceptions of Man and Reality.

Should the Symbol of Human Rights Be a Universal Symbol?

It should be noted that I speak here of Human Rights as a symbol which, unlike a concept, is by its nature polyvalent and polysemic.

The answer is yes, and no.

(a) *Yes.* When a culture as a whole discovers certain values as ultimate, these values must have a certain universal meaning. Only collective and culturally expressed universal values may be said to be human values. A mere private value cannot be called a *human* value. It is a humane value, but not necessarily a value for every human—as *Human* Rights claim to be. As a matter of fact, Human Rights come as a corrective to the former exclusive rights of the Whites, the Believers, the Rich, the Brahmans and others—without meaning to touch legitimate privileges in the traditional sense of the word. The Declaration of Human Rights must needs be considered, at least in its intention, as a declaration with universal validity. To say that Human Rights are not universal would amount to saying that they are not human; they would cease to be *Human* Rights. The whole novelty of the Declaration lies precisely here, in the assertion that every human being, by the mere fact of being human, is endowed with inalienable rights that everybody should respect.

In that sense we may have here something rather unique and revolutionary in the Declaration of Human Rights. Here indeed we have the positive side of the individual vis-à-vis the person. Every single human being in its individuality, by the very fact of being born, has a dignity and rights equal to any other. It is not one's place in society, or degree of civilization, or intellectual, moral or religious endowments that count. Certainly, limits will immediately appear: you may be subnormal or abnormal, and not only physically, but also morally—or, others would also add, intellectually or religiously. But the naked fact of being born is the universal symbol on which Human Rights is based. From this point of view, the claim to universality of Human Rights has found a solid basis.

Paradoxically enough, the Christian origin of this belief had been the cause of some of its degradation, i.e., when it became an ideology, a doctrine to serve the interests of one particular group. Everybody is born free and equal; all human beings are equal in the sight of God; every human person has the same rights as any other. Nonetheless, in order to justify the fact that the unbaptized, or the negro or slave or female or whoever did not have the same rights, one was compelled to claim that they were not fully human beings, as history cruelly witnesses.

(b) *No.* Because each culture expresses its experience of reality and of the *humanum* in concepts and symbols which are proper to that tradition and are as such not universal, and most likely not universalizable. This relationship between truth and the expression of truth in concepts and symbols is one of the most central philosophical problems. Truth has the inbuilt claim to be universally valid, here and there, yesterday and tomorrow, for you and for me. Yet my grasping and formulating it cannot sustain that same claim without charging all the others who do not agree with me with stupidity or wickedness. Hence the necessary *via media* between agnostic relativism and dogmatic absolutism. This is what can be called *relativity.*

Our particular case is a typical example of the *pars pro toto:* from the optic of the inside it looks like the whole; from the outside it looks like a part, a fragment. Similarly, Human Rights are universal from the vantage point of modern Western culture, and not universal from the outside looking in. Now, if we take from the inside the *pars pro toto,* are we able to take from the outside to *totum in parte?* Can another culture see in the Human Rights issue a universal language? Or should we say that it is only one way of looking at things, one way of speaking?

The answer which claims to discover the *totum in parte* is appealing, but not convincing. This is the temptation of the intellectual, who senses that any affirmation has the inbuilt tendency to be universally valid—or of the politician who, having neither the time nor the inclination to engage in such reflections, would like to see the *totum* in the *parte* of his party. But then we tend to become the self-appointed judges of all humankind. Now philosophy, being a situated reflection, makes us aware that nobody has direct access to the universal range of human experience. We can only indirectly and through a limited perspective come to know the totality. Even were we to know all the existing human opinions, ours would amount to just another opinion. One cannot view the *totum* except in and through one's own window. This is the case not only because the whole is more than the sum of its parts, but also because that *totum* does not exist independently from the *parte* through which it is seen. It is only seen in and through the respective *parte* and there is no stance from which one could proceed to the integration of all the parts. Co-existence is only possible on a common ground, a *co-esse* recognized by the different parties

Here lies the crux. We cannot but aim at the *totum,* and yet we often forget that all we see is the *pars,* which we then take *pro toto.* If a Christian, to put another example, were to say that Christ is not the universal savior, according to accepted custom he or she would cease to be a Christian. But a non-Christian cannot, and should not, agree with this. It is only in mutual dialogue that their respective views will change or evolve. Christ will be for the Christian the symbol of the totality; for the non-Christian, only the symbol of the Christians. Myriad examples from the past, especially regarding the West, are all too striking for one not to be wary of the danger of repeating what was done in the name of the one God, the one Empire, the one Religion, and what is nowadays being done under the aegis of the one Science and the one Technology.

In brief, we need a new hermeneutic: the diatopical hermeneutic that can only be developed in a dialogical dialogue. This would show us that we must take neither the *pars pro toto,* nor believe that we see the *totum in parte.* We must accept what our partner tells us: simply that we take the *totum pro parte,* when we are aware of the *pars pro toto;* which is obviously what we will retort right back to him. This is the human condition and I would not consider it to be an imperfection. This, again, is the topic of pluralism.

Let us consider now an example of a different perspective without attempting to present any homeomorphic equivalent.

An Indian Reflection

The word "Indian" here has no political connotations. It does not refer to the "nation" with the third largest Islamic population in the world, but to the traditional Hindu, Jain, and Buddhist conceptions of reality.

Dharma (dhamma) is perhaps the most fundamental word in the Indian tradition which could lead us to the discovery of a possible homeomorphic symbol corresponding to the Western notion of "Human Rights." I am not advancing the idea that Dharma is the homeomorphic equivalent of Human Rights. I am only indicating that a reflection at the level of Dharma may help us find our footing on a common ground, so that we may know what we are looking for when we set out on our search for "Human Rights" in the classical Indian context.

As is well-known, the meaning of the word Dharma is multivocal: besides element, data, quality and origination, it means law, norm of conduct, character of things, right, truth, ritual, morality, justice, righteousness, religion, destiny, and many other things. It would not lead us anywhere to try to find an English common denominator for all these names, but perhaps etymology can show us the root metaphor underlying the many meanings of the word.[21] Dharma is that which maintains, gives cohesion and thus strength to any given thing, to reality, and ultimately to the three words (*triloka*). Justice keeps human relations together; morality keeps oneself in harmony; law is the binding principle for human relations; religion is what maintains the universe in existence; destiny is that which links us with our future; truth is the internal cohesion of a thing; a quality is what pervades a thing with an homogenous character; an element is the minimum consistent particle, spiritual or material; and the like.

Now a world in which the notion of Dharma is central and nearly all-pervasive is not concerned with finding the "right" of one individual against another or of the individual vis-à-vis society, but rather with assaying the *dharmic (right, true,* consistent...) or *adharmic* character of a thing or an action within the entire theanthropocosmic complex of reality.

Dharma is primordial. We cannot hope to understand it if we approach it with moral categories (cf. the case of the Gītā) or even epistemological ones. It embraces both the conflict and the resolution; both the ought and the ought not. There is no universal dharma above and independent of the *svadharma,* the dharma which is inherent in every being. And this *svadharma* is at the same time a result of and a reaction to the dharma of everyone else.

The starting point here is not the individual, but the whole complex concatenation of the Real. In order to protect the world, for the sake of the protection of this universe, says Manu, He Svayambhū, the Self-existent, arranged the castes and their duties.[22] Dharma is the order of the entire reality, that which keeps the world together.[23] The individual's duty is to maintain his "rights"; it is to find one's place in relation to Society, to the Cosmos, and to the transcendent world.

It is obvious from these brief paragraphs that here is the discourse on "Human Rights" would take on an altogether different character. It would distract us from the purpose of this article to look now for the homeomorphic equivalent of Human Rights in a culture pervaded with the conception of Dharma. We adduce this Indian example only to be able to elaborate in a fuller way the question of our title.

Only one submission and one observation may be allowed here so as not to leave this thought incomplete. I submit that the homeomorphic equivalent is *svadharma,* and I make the observation that the homeomorphic equivalent does not mean the corresponding counterpart, as if all that is conveyed by Human Rights is also borne by *svadharma* or vice versa. Cultures are wholes, and do not fit into one-to-one correspondences. In order to have a just society, the modern West stresses the notion of Human Rights. In order to have a dharmic order, classical India stresses the notion of *svadharma.*

We shall now attempt to formulate without further development some reactions to the Western discourse on Human rights from this Indian perspective. We should add immediately that this Indian critique does not imply that the Indian model is better, or that Indian culture has been faithful to its fundamental intuition—as the existence of the outcastes and the degeneration of the caste system sufficiently prove.

In confrontation and dialogue with the Western model, the Indian critique would stress fundamentally that Human Rights should not be absolutized. It would contest that one can speak of Human Rights as "objective" entities standing on their own in isolation from the rest of the Real. This is what seems to be implied in the very first article of the Declaration: "All human beings are born free and equal in dignity and rights. They are endowed with reason and conscience and should act towards one another in a spirit of brotherhood." Particular rights, privileges due to a special position in society, i.e., a relativization of rights does not seem to be compatible with this article.

Developing this point, the Indian vision would insist on the following points among others:

1. Human Rights are not individual Human Rights only. The *humanum* is not incarnated in the individual *only.* The individual as such is an abstraction, and an abstraction as such cannot be an ultimate subject of rights. As we have already indicated, the individual is only the knot in and of the net of relationships which form the fabric of the Real. The knots may individually be all the same (either *jīva,*

ātman or *anātman*), but it is mainly their position in the net which determines the set of "right" an individual may have. Individuality is not a substantial category, but a functional one. The structure of the universe is hierarchical, but this does not imply that the higher echelons have the right to trample upon the rights of the lower ones—in spite of the dangers of this happening the moment the harmony of the whole is disturbed.

I am not entering into the merits or demerits of this worldview. We should however bear in mind that this conception is intimately linked with the conception of karma, and thus should not be evaluated outside its proper context.

2. Human Rights are not Human only. They concern equally the entire cosmic display of the universe, from which even the Gods are not absent. The animals, all the sentient beings and the supposedly inanimate creatures, are also involved in the interaction concerning "human" rights. Man is a peculiar being, to be sure, but neither alone nor so essentially distinct. One could even ask whether there are specific human rights, or if this specificity is again only an abstraction for pragmatic reasons which defeats it own purpose the moment we forget its merely practical character.

Here again, another cosmology and another theology provide the justification for this conception. Whether modern India, accepting and adopting modern Science as it is, will be able to maintain this conception for very long is another matter altogether. But we know also about the persistence of mythical patterns.

3. Human Rights are not Rights only. They are also duties and both are interdependent. Humankind has the "right" to survive only insofar as it performs the duty of maintaining the world (*lokasamgraha*). We have the "right" to eat only inasmuch as we fulfill the duty of allowing ourselves to be eaten by a hierarchically higher agency. Our right is only a participation in the entire metabolic function of the universe.

We should have, if anything, a Declaration of Universal Rights and Duties in which the whole of Reality would be encompassed. Obviously, this demands not only a different anthropology but also a different cosmology and an altogether different theology—beginning with its name. That only human beings and not animals could make this Declaration would invalidate it only to the same extent that the Declaration of Human Rights could be contested because the Nagas and the Masai did not take part in the discussion and framing of the Declaration.

4. Human Rights are not mutually isolatable. They are related not

only to the whole cosmos and all their corresponding duties; they form, among themselves as well, a harmonious whole. It is for this reason that a material list of definitive Human Rights is not theoretically feasible. It is the universal harmony that ultimately counts. This is not invalidated by the fact that India, as so many other countries, knows the codification of laws. India suffers, perhaps more than most countries, from legalistic *minutiae*, precisely because no juridical legislation will ever suffice.[24]

5. Human Rights are not absolute. They are intrinsically relative, they are relationships among entities. Moreover, these entities are determined by the relationships themselves. To say that my human value depends on my position in the universe would be a caricature of what has been said if we start by thinking of an individual in itself, whose dignity is then made to depend on whether he or she is rich or poor, of one caste or another, etc. The classical Indian vision would not subscribe to this—in spite of the failures of the system in the praxis and even the degeneration in time—but it would start from a wholistic conception and then define a portion of Reality by function of its situation in the totality. In a certain sense, the knot is nothing—because it is the whole net.

6. Both systems (the Western and Hindu) make sense from and within a given and accepted myth. Both systems imply a certain kind of consensus. When that consensus is challenged, a new myth must be found. The broken myth is the situation in India today, as it is in the world at large. That the rights of individuals be conditioned only by their position in the net of Reality can no longer be admitted by the contemporary mentality. Nor does it seem to be admissible that the rights of individuals be so absolute as not to depend at all on the particular situation of the individual.

In short, there is at present no endogenous theory capable of unifying contemporary societies and no imposed or imported ideology can be simply substituted for it. A mutual fecundation of cultures is a human imperative of our times.

The Declaration defends the individual from the abuses of the State or Society. The Indian view would say that we are part of a harmonious whole on pilgrimage toward a non-historical goal. Interactions are the very warp and woof of the universe. Cultural and religious traditions offer a whole that cannot easily be dismembered without doing violence to their insights. Hindu karma outside its context may become fatalistic. Christian charity outside its system may turn oppressive. The universalization of Human Rights is a very delicate question indeed.

By Way of Conclusion

Is the concept of Human Rights a Western conception?
Yes.
Should the world then renounce declaring or enforcing Human Rights?
No.
Three qualifications, however, are necessary:

1. For an authentic human life to be possible within the *megamachine* of the modern technological world, Human Rights are imperative. This is because the development of the notion of Human Rights is bound up with and given its meaning by the slow development of that megamachine. How far individuals or groups or nations should collaborate with this present-day system is another question altogether. But in the contemporary political arena as defined by current socio-economic and ideological trends, the defense of Human Rights is a sacred duty. Yet it should be remembered that to introduce Human Rights (in the definite Western sense, of course) into other cultures before the introduction of *techniculture* would amount not only to putting the cart before the horse, but also to preparing the way for the technological invasion—as if by a Trojan horse, as we have already said. And yet a technological civilization without Human Rights amounts to the most inhuman situation imaginable. The dilemma is excruciating. This makes the two following points all the more important and urgent.

2. Room should be made for other world traditions to develop and formulate their own homeomorphic views corresponding to or opposing Western "rights." Or rather, these other world traditions should make room for themselves, since no one else is likely to make it for them. This is an urgent task; otherwise it will be impossible for non-Western cultures to survive, let alone to offer viable alternatives or even a sensible complement. Here the role of a cross-cultural philosophical approach is paramount. The need for human pluralism is often recognized in principle, but not often practiced, not only because of the dynamism which drives the paneconomic ideology, linked with the megamachine, to expand all over the world, but also because viable alternatives are not yet theoretically worked out.

3. An intermediary space should be found for mutual criticism that strives for mutual fecundation and enrichment. Perhaps such an interchange may help bring forth a new myth and eventually a more humane civilization. The dialogical dialogue appears as the unavoidable method.

Perhaps a suggestion here may prove helpful. Playing on the metaphor of the knots (individuality) and the net (personhood) we could probably affirm that traditional cultures have stressed the net (kinship, hierarchical structure of society, the function to be performed, the role of each part in relation to the whole), so that often the knot has been suffocated and not allowed sufficient free-space for its own self-identity. On the other hand, Modernity stresses the knots (individual free will to choose any option, the idiosyncrasies of everyone, the atomization of society) so that often the knot has been lost in loneliness, alienated by its own social mobility, and wounded (or killed) in competition with other more powerful knots. Perhaps the notion of personhood as the interplay between the knots and the net, as well as the realization that freedom is not just the capacity to choose between given options but also the power to create options, could provide a starting point for the proposed mutual fecundation.

If many traditional cultures are centered on God, and some other cultures basically cosmocentric, the culture which has come up with the notion of Human Rights is decisively anthropocentric. Perhaps we may now be prepared for a cosmotheandric vision of reality in which the Divine, the Human and the Cosmic are integrated into a Whole, more or less harmonious according to the performance of our truly human rights.

Chapter 8

Is History the Measure of Man?

Three Kairological Moments
of Human Consciousness

Between the cosmic yardstick of a Teilhard de Chardin, measured in hundreds of thousands of years, and the sociological perspective of decades or even the historical studies of some centuries, lies the astrological meter of the solar rhythm. This is the natural equinoctial rhythm of the Earth, which takes 25,000 years for its axis to precess round to the same alignment. Each astrological month would then be 2,100 years. If we have entered the Aquarian period around 1950, ending the Piscean month which began about 150 B.C., my perspective would be to situate the following reflections over against the backdrop of the beginnings of what we call human history, which coincides with the two previous periods, i.e., Aries, from 2,250 B.C., and Taurus, which began around 4,350 years B.C. Human memory has then a span of roughly 6,500 years. Can we meaningfully say something on this scale?

I would like to venture some ideas, based not on astrological considerations, but on my diachronical and diatopical experience of cultures and peoples. This leads me to think that we are at the end not only of *an* historical period, but of *the* historical period of mankind, which is to say that we are witnessing the collapse of the Myth of History. The main elements of the Transhistorical Myth are already present—or else we could not speak of it intelligibly—but a critical consciousness of what this may mean has not yet emerged for most people. Therefore I shall try to describe these characteristics in

This essay is a modified and abridged version of "The End of History," the author's presentation at the Centenary Symposium *"Teilhard and the Unity of Knowledge"* held at Georgetown University, Washington, D.C., May 1–3, 1981. It was previously published under the same title in *Teilhard Review* 16 (1981): 39–45.

relation to pre-historical and historical consciousness. I shall speak of three *kairological* moments of human consciousness. These moments should not be interpreted chronologically, i.e., as though they follow one after the other. They are qualitatively different, and yet intertwined, aspects of human awareness which certainly co-exist in the unfolding of individual and (especially) collective life.

Pre-historical Consciousness

Pre-historical consciousness informs the prevalent worldview and self-understanding of so-called prehistoric Man from time immemorial up until the universally accepted historical period of humankind. The decisive moment is the invention and spread of writing scripture. That old Egyptian legend reported by Plato, of the king berating his fellow-god for having invented writing, represents this mutation. After this event, everything changes: the past acquires a consistency of its own. The past can be kept, frozen, fossilized in special devices of stone, leaves, or whatever. The past is no longer accumulated in Man's memory, nor does it permeate the present in every pattern of daily life. Scripture represents the beginning of the end of pre-historical consciousness.

Now pre-historical Man lives mainly in *space*. Time is subsidiary to space, and an autonomous (human) time does not appear strongly in Man's consciousness. Time is natural, not cultural. The human beings are agriculturists and/or hunters, settlers and/or nomads. The biological or vital functions, in the noblest but also most elementary sense of the word, occupy their minds and hearts. Work is done in order to eat, drink, and be protected by clothing and a house. Work is done primarily for the living, for life to go on from the ancestors to the descendants, for the world to continue. Living, say the Navajo, means "to walk in beauty," to enjoy life, to be open to the beauty of nature, the joy of human intercourse on all levels, the ecstasy of self-discovery and the complex numinous relationships with supernatural and superhuman powers. Men go to war to wreak vengeance, or to rescue someone, or to obtain better hunting or fields, or even eventually to conquer an empty space, but they do not make war to march into the *future*. That is left for the Alexanders, Akbars, and Napoleons of the following period.

The World of pre-historical Man, his environment, is the *theocosmos* or theocosm, the divinized universe. It is not a "World of Man," but it is also not the world of the Gods as a separate and superior realm hovering over the humans. The Gods do not yet form a clan of their own, as they do at the beginning of history: and it is viewed only from the historical realm that the pre-historical milieu seems "full of Gods." In the pre-historical mentality, it is the *World* that is divinized (to use historical language). The divine permeates the cosmos. The forces of nature are all divine. Nature is supernatural. Or rather, nature is that which is "natured," born, from the divine. Pre-historical Man's milieu is a *cosmotheological* one. *Harmony* is the supreme principle—which does not mean that it has been achieved.

Historical Consciousness

In the second moment, the previous kairological phase is not discarded, but progressively superseded. Man passes from *agri*-culture to *civi*-lization, from the forests, fields and villages to the city. City time is not cosmic time, but human and social temporality. It is *historical* time, which may best be understood as the thrust toward the future—where it is supposed one reaches the fullness of one's existence, be this of the individual, the tribe, a race, or even all humanity.

Esau was a pre-historical man; Jacob had historical consciousness. Esau cared nothing for his historical destiny, and found in the exquisite taste of a potful of lentils the fulfillment of the present, and thus of life. Jacob was concerned with what has come to be the dominant feature of Semitic civilization: the coming of the Kingdom—variously called promised land, nation, church, paradise, justice, or whatever. Jacob understood his grandfather's move out of Ur and into the future. He was eager to be the heir. Esau cared nothing for history, i.e., historical destiny or vocation: the future. Christ irritated the children of Jacob when he told them to let the day take care of itself and not to worry over the morrow. Historical time is under the spell of the future and the guidance of reason. Only the historical is real. What Esau did was not reasonable, nor was what Christ preached, for that matter.

People and peoples are set whirling into motion; their movement accelerates not because they wish to subjugate space, but because they want to conquer *time*. Wars are waged to make their victors great and their children powerful. Man works under the mirage of a historical future: a great empire to be built, a better future to be conquered. The sense of purpose becomes the essence of education. Science means the ability to foresee the future, so that you may control where the ball is going to fall, or predict when the eclipse is going to occur. We need only substitute atoms, bombs, chromosomes, and epidemics for balls; and upheavals, inflations, crystallizations, amalgams, and synthetic products for eclipses; and we have spanned 6,000 years of human "science:" the knowledge and control of those parameters that can be expressed in terms of space and time. It is important to bear in mind that the first name for Science, as the control over empirical causality, was Magic. The paramount question is to know how things will happen in space and time, because then you can control them. Space and time are the paradigms of reality. Something is real when it is historical, i.e., when you can locate it in space and time. Jesus is real only if he is a historical figure. On the other hand, Krishna would lose his reality were he to be described as only a historical figure.

The entire world economy today, and with it the world of politics as well, is geared to the future under the name of growth and the power of credit. No wonder that cancer is the modern epidemic par excellence: here the trouble begins. The Modern world has begun to surmise that there may be limits to growth. In the world of the Spirit, growth has no limits; growth does not mean more, but better. Not so in the world of quantifiable Matter, where better has to mean *more:* more accumulation of more finite entities into a finite receptacle or recipient. Another theological idea—the infinity of God wrongly translated into the infinity of Matter—gone berserk. It has to come to an end, but it cannot stop itself—unless a qualitative change takes place. Otherwise, a catastrophe or a dictator is welcomed, if only to contain the runaway growth. History cannot come to a halt of itself. He who rides the tiger cannot dismount. And this seems to be the very precarious predicament of our Modern world.

The world of historical Man, his environment, is the *anthropocosmos* or anthropocosm, the human world, the universe of Man. He is not inserted in the evolution of the cosmos; his destiny has little to do with the fate of the stars or the phases of the moon, or even the seasons and the rivers. He lives in a superior world, the human one; cold and heat, day and night, rain and drought have been overcome. He is not dependent on the seasons, and as little as possible on the climate. Nature has been tamed and subjugated. It has been demythicized and there is nothing "mysterious" about it. Historical Man has overcome the fear of nature. His backdrop is *cosmosociological.* The meaning of his life is not to be found in the cosmic cycles, but in the human sphere, the society. *Justice* is the supreme principle—which does not mean that it has been achieved.

By the same token, the World of historical Man is not the world of the spirits. Angels, *apsaras,* devils, dwarves, elves, *devatas,* sirens, goblins, genii, seraphim, *būhtas* and the like have all, if not completely disappeared, been rendered impotent and subservient to human reason. At any rate, all these ghosts have no history, and Man's life no longer unfolds in such a theater. The only scene is the historical arena. With the DDT of his reason, Man has rendered all these "forces" innocuous—or sent them to the psychiatrists and parapsychologists. Man's life in this second moment is an unfolding of his possibilities in front of his fellow beings. He stands alone in the world-theater. If some still accept God, this God is transcendent, impassive, perhaps good for another life, but certainly not about to meddle in human affairs. God has left the world to the strivings of Men; historical Man controls and forges his own destiny, or likes to think he does. The present human predicament, however, seems utterly to have escaped his control. And it is precisely this loss of control that has produced the current crisis of historical consciousness.

Transhistorical Consciousness

A third degree of consciousness is coming more and more to the fore. The two others are far from having disappeared and, indeed, this third degree—in the form of metaphysical insights and mystical experiences—has always been in the air, but today it gains momentum and changes its character.

The *Myth* of Progress has practically collapsed; the symptoms of disintegration are legion. The *historical* situation of the world today is nothing less than desperate. There really is no issue of "development" for the famine-plagued masses, over half the world's population, just as there is no consolation for those mentally and physically handicapped for life by malnutrition. What is worse, people have also lost any vestige of hope that the lot of their children is somehow going to be better. They are already in the third generation of being "evangelized" by the hope of an earthly paradise, and they have reached the end of this tether. Today the heavenly paradise, or the collective Utopia, or the glittering "good life," have all lost their grip on the people. A life of privation here, a vale of tears now, a bad karma in this life so that I may be rewarded later on with a heavenly Garden, a city of Brahman, a vision of God or a more comfortable rebirth—all these are rapidly receding myths. Election discourses and traditional religious preachings may stir the masses for an emotional moment, but the human race is becoming more and more immune to such social viruses. The goods have to be delivered *now,* and not when God or the Party is going to win. And despair is not limited to the poor. There is equally disenchantment among the rich. The poor of the world still retain a certain pre-historical religiosity that gives them something to hold on to. Those who live in scientific and technological comfort have discarded the Gods and now find that their practical supreme value shows signs of radical impotence. But no solution is at hand, and we have lost innocence.

If the discovery of Script could be said to have been the decisive break between the pre-historical and the historical consciousness, the corresponding event here—which opens up the new horizon of the post-historic period—is the discovery or invention of the internal power of the *atom.* So powerful is its nature that it has ceased to be what it was purported to be: *akṣaram,* indestructible. It has ceased to be *atomos,* indivisible, thus simple, and in a certain way, everlasting. The splitting of the *atomos* has also exploded historical consciousness.

Modern Man is not yet fully aware of the anthropological (and not only political and sociological) consequences of that fact. This change is qualitative, not only in weaponry and technology, not only in the nature of war and the mechanisms of the economy, but also in the newly emerging understanding of Man in an increasingly universal way. This change may well represent the end of the Western period of humankind. There is no doubt that history is tied not only to the Judaeo-Christian-Islamic tradition, but also to Western dominance of the entire planet, even if the Modern name for such dominance is today Science and Technology. It all comes to an end. The Historical Imperative has failed. All messianisms lose their *raison d'être.*

Post-industrial society is becoming more and more conscious that the trend of the present world cannot just be stopped. Standstill would amount to chaos. Armaments proliferate to maddening proportions—and have to, or else the present economic system would collapse tomorrow. The paneconomic ideology is bound to explode sooner or later. If you quantify everything and put a price tag on every human value, the *humanum* vanishes and gives way to the *oeconomicum.* Every "human" good becomes subservient to its economic value. And there is still more to it: An economy based on profits is bound to burst the day you have no more markets by which to make the operation profitable, because all the "others" are living at a lower standard. Still today among the tribes of Nagaland in Northeast India, rice is not *sold;* i.e., you do not speculate with the elementary needs of life. They do not have market value, but human value. Fundamental human needs should be out of the economic bounds. We do not eat human flesh, not because it is not good or nutritious, but because it is human. We do not kill our fellow beings to eat their flesh, yet we arrange things so that they must sell their rice and starve in consequence.

Again, it is not convincing to say that technology in *itself* is not bad, or that money *as such* is a handy invention; because there is no such *in itself* or *as such*. Abstraction is a good scientific method, but inapplicable to human questions. Nothing human can be subtracted from Man without changing the very variables of the problem.

My contention here is that the contemporary technologico-paneconomical ideology is intrinsically connected both with the historical consciousness and with the specific character that consciousness has taken in the Western world. The Western roots of Modern Science have been sufficiently studied, and this is equally the case with technology, which could only become what it has turned out to be with the collaboration of the present economic system of the West.

Let us put it in very crude terms. Many people are afraid of the Third World War and a major atomic catastrophe. (Another example of projecting into the future our fears as well as our joys and triumphs.) Those who feel such panic are generally the well-to-do citizens of the First and Second Worlds. But for two-thirds of the people of the world, that cataclysm has *already* come. Please ask not only those living in sub-animal conditions (over one-third of the world's population), please ask those living in sub-human conditions (again much over one-third of Mankind); please ask also the millions of displaced persons and have a look at the geopolitical chart of the world (since one can hardly call it a human map). Gulags, concentration camps, persecution and real wars on every continent. *The Third World War has already come,* and the atomic phase of it may be only the predictable outcome and final act of a drama which is now not only Myrdal's Asian Drama, but a World Drama of massive proportions and devastating implications.

Here the wisdom of pre-historical Man, as well as the teachings of the great masters of the historical period, come to our aid without our having to escape into superhuman or metacosmic Utopias. If it is true that we are beginning to witness the end of history, this does not have to mean the end of Man. Yet the ordeal is going to have historical repercussions, precisely in order to bring history to a close.

In this crucible of the Modern world, only the mystic will survive. All the others are going to disintegrate: they will be unable to resist either the physical strictures or the psychical strain. And this disintegration will include the so-called middle class, which for the moment can eat sufficiently, and doesn't need to take a stand on any slippery decision-making platforms. The bourgeois, i.e., the inhabitants of the burghs, are today citizens of the megalopolis: bombarded by noise, haunted by fear, drowned in information overload, propagandized into stupefaction; people anonymous to one another, without clean air to breathe, or open space for human—not just animal—intimacy; with no real *scholé*, leisure, because no time is free.

Nature was fearful for pre-historical Man, but he managed in his own way to come to terms with Mother Earth or the Earth Goddess. Big Brother and his twin, Technology, are frightening historical Man, who now tries desperately to cope with them. Pre-historical Man had to keep his distance from nature, so to speak, in order to survive as Man. It is this alienation from nature that made him Man and differentiated him from animals—for better or for worse. Modern, i.e., historical Man has in turn to separate himself from *the System* in order to live as Man. It is this salutary alienation, a genuine segregation from the System, that will differentiate those who succeed in preserving their humanness from the robots, the victims of the System: ants, work-addicts, cogs in the megamachine, "bits" identified by number in the ubiquitous computers' memory banks. Withdrawal from the System does not necessarily mean a flight into the mountains or just escapism from history. It does mean, certainly, a pilgrimage unto the "high places" of the human spirit and the human Earth, as well as an overcoming of the historical dimension and its shortcomings. But it also means keeping one's hands and heart free to help fellow beings on their way to the next higher level of consciousness. Perhaps we could call this moment *Realization*.

Here are some characteristics of this Realization: If pre-historical consciousness is geared to the present, and historical consciousness to the future, *trans*historical consciousness attempts to integrate the future into the present and transcend both. The mystic, or the contemplative, or the true intellectual, has often attested to a transhistorical experience. Human existence is more than just extension in time and space. It is both (and together) the *ex* and the *sistence* which constitute our being; only by in-sisting on the ex-sistence are we saved. This is the experience of the contemplatives. They live the present in all its intensity, and in this tension discover the intentionality and integrity of life, the tempiternal, ineffable core which is full in every authentic moment.

The novelty of the phenomenon today—although the word novelty is improperly used, for it belongs to historical consciousness—is the increasingly collective or societal aspect of transhistorical consciousness as it appears on the contemporary scene. It is no longer some few individuals who may reach salvation, i.e., true happiness, the fulfillment of life or whatever, by crossing to the other shore, experiencing the transtemporal, the tempiternal. It is Humankind itself which is now making this breakthrough in its consciousness—out of sheer survival necessity—because of the stifling closeness of the System. It is precisely the instinct for survival that today throws us toward the other shore of time and space, because the spatiotemporal framework of this Earth has been polluted and prostituted beyond measure by the mechanical robots of the megamachine, all victims of the technological cancer.

Summing up: The background of pre-historical Man is the *theocosmos*. He finds himself in friendship and confrontation with the *numina:* the natural and divine forces. His scenario is the divinized cosmos.

The horizon of historical Man is *history.* He finds himself in collaboration and struggle with human society of the past, present and future. His world is the human world.

The emerging myth of transhistorical Man is situated in the *theanthropocosmos.* He finds himself in harmony and tension with a cosmotheandric *reality* in which all the forces of the universe—electromagnetic to divine, angelic to human—are intertwined.

Pre-historical Man has *fate.* He is part and parcel of the universe. Historical Man has *destiny.* He predestines where he stands. He arranges his own life. Transhistorical Man has his *lot.* He is involved in the total adventure of reality, by participating freely in the portion allotted to him.

The pre-historical mentality does not have to justify Man's existence. The human being simply lives, like any other living being. Historical consciousness has to justify, i.e., prove, the value of Man's existence by his *doing*—doing what is right, what fosters society (Modern Man is a worker). Transhistorical Man has lost both the pre-historical naivete and the historical optimism. He feels the urge *to be* what he is supposed to be, occupying his proper place in the universe.

The World of transhistorical Man, his environment or ecosystem, is the cosmotheandric universe. The renewed interest in astrology, for instance, is due not merely to a desire to know what will happen, or how a marriage or a business will develop, but to the increasing awareness that personal identity is linked both with the fate of society and with the adventure of the entire cosmos, where humans are not the only conditioning forces. The destiny of Man is not just a historical existence. It is linked with the life of the Earth and with the entire fate of reality, the divine not excluded. God or the Gods are again incarnated and share in the destiny of the universe at large. We are all in the same boat, which is not just this planet Earth, but the whole mystery of Life, Consciousness, Existence. *Love* is the supreme principle—which, again, does not mean that it has been achieved.

In sum, transhistorical consciousness is not worried about the future because time is not experienced as linear, or as an accumulation and enrichment of moments past, but as the symbol of something which, while it does not exist without Man, cannot be identified with him either. It is neither the City of God nor the City of Man that transhistorical Man is about to build. He or she would rather concentrate on building, or bringing to completion, the microcosm that is Man—both individually and collectively: mirroring and transforming the macrocosm altogether.

My essay here has been to render plausible the thesis that the exclusive dominance of historical consciousness is coming to an end. Man is embarking upon a new venture...about which we know only that we shall act the more freely the more we allow the internal dynamism of our deepest being to express itself, without projecting beforehand what we are about to do and to be. We are consciously participating in the very existence of the cosmotheandric reality.

We may now ask: What does it mean to be human? It is the perennial question: What is Man?

A qualified tautology says that it means to be real. Man has to realize itself. This realization or becoming real entails to become what one really is. But we have to acquire our human identity in the technocratic society where we live.

It is disputable whether techno-science can enhance or weaken this realization. But the *humanum* (human realization) cannot depend on techno-science, unless we affirm that only Modern Man is really human. The humanness of Man lies deeper than in the "achievements" of one particular culture.

We touch here the ultimate constitution of Man, usually called the religious factor or the faith dimension. Faith is a constitutive human dimension. It should not be confused with belief. Beliefs are generally intellectual articulations of faith. They are cultural and historical expressions of Man's self-understanding. And they are in crisis today due mainly to the spreading technocratic civilization.

Our problem could be formulated thus: How to reach the fullness of the *humanum* in a technocratic society?

We should examine, at least, the following options:

Reformation. Acknowledging the dehumanizing aspects of technocracy we should figure out ways and means to reform the System by redefining the very idea of Progress. *"Extra scientiam nulla salus."*

Deformation. We should recognize that Mankind has suffered an essential drawback, dissimulated by fragmentary achievements, and dismantle the present System which represents a regression from *homo sapiens* to *homo habilis.*

Transformation. While recognizing the diagnosis above we should take into account the fact that we cannot begin *ab ovo,* and that not is all wrong in the quantification of knowledge. This metamorphosis requires an active cross-cultural approach, the collaboration of other cultures in determining the *humanum.* This *metamorphosis* is more than *metanoia,* this latter understood as a change of mind. It implies an overcoming of the intellect. The *humanum* cannot be dealt with the *logos* alone. It demands the *mythos* also.

We should not skip this challenge nor eschew our responsibility.

Chapter 9

The Invisible Harmony

A Universal Theory of Religion
or a Cosmic Confidence in Reality?

> *Harmonia aphanēs phanerēs kreittōn.*
> Invisible harmony is stronger than the visible.
> —Heraclitus, Fragm. 54

Introduction

My presentation is going to be succinct, dialectical, and basic. *Succinct,* because, based on previous studies, published and unpublished, it will allow me to refer to them for the justification of my assertions.[1] *Dialectical,* because, I fear, I may represent a minority view and can put forward my opinion only in confrontation with the predominant trends among the experts in this field. *Basic,* because it tackles the problem at the very fundamental structure of the human being, from the perspective of a metaphysical anthropology, one could say, and not from a sociological or pragmatic viewpoint.

In a first part I shall examine the reasons that direct modern Western scholarship to search in the direction of a universal theory of religion. In a second part I shall submit the "universal theory" to a critique. In the third, I shall attempt to offer an alternative.

A general remark at the very outset is called for. I am fully aware that there is no East and no West, no monolithic Christianity, nor standard Hinduism, that human traditions and even human beings themselves are much more holistic than most of our intellectual disquisitions tend to assume. In every one of us looms an East and a West, a believer and an unbeliever, a male and a female, and so on.

This chapter appeared previously in Leonard Swidler, ed., *Toward a Universal Theology of Religion* (Maryknoll, N.Y.: Orbis, 1987), 118–53.

Every human being is a microcosm and every human culture represents the whole of humanity. The true *ātman* of (in) every one of us is Brahman. Buddha-nature lies at the bottom of every being. We all are called upon to share divine nature. Hence, the level of my discourse is directed at detecting predominant winds, leading threads, the dominating *Zeitgeist,* on the one hand, and the deeper structures of the human being and of Reality on the other.

I encompass under the notion of "universal theory" all those efforts at reaching a global intellectual understanding, be it called "ecumenical Esperanto," "world theology," "unified field theory," or even a certain type of "comparative religion" and "ecumenism." The common trait here is the noble effort at reducing the immense variety of human experiences to one single and common language, which may well respect the different dialectical forms of expression and of life, but which somewhat subsumes them all and allows for communication and understanding on a universal scale. The universal theory assumes that a certain type of rationality is the general heritage of humankind and even more, that it is the one specifically human trait. It assumes we are human beings because we are rational creatures, reason being our last appeal; thus the same reason theoretically has to be capable of solving all the problems that plague our human race.

The gist of this study is a challenge to all this. And yet, the alternative is not solipsism on the one hand or irrationalism on the other, being respectively victim of a depressive individualism or of a shallow sentimentalism. I have already hinted that a whole anthropology and metaphysics are here called into question. The raising of such problems should be the concern of cross-cultural studies if they want to be really cross-cultural and not simply window dressing with more or less exotic or less known ways of thinking.

The reader will have noticed that I do not mention the usual names of sociologists, anthropologists, and philosophers dealing with the traditional problems of evolutionism, structuralism, synchronicity, and the like. Is there a common human nature, does evolution or, on the other hand, structuralism, offer a basis to understand our phenomenon? Although it would have been very instructive to take a position in the contemporary discussions, I have opted for not entering into the scholarly debates for two main reasons. The one is that to do it properly would require an almost independent study as long as the present one—and it has been done several times.[2] The other and more important reason is that my perspective claims to be more cross-cultural and "metaphysical" than such studies usually

are, for they by and large remain within the problematic of today's
(and yesterday's) Western scholarship.
   I am not now criticizing a particular theory of an individual
scholar or a school. I am submitting to analysis the sense of the enterprise itself. However, because of the very holistic character of our
being, our theories also are more comprehensive than we generally
imagine. Thus, if my criticism is answered by showing me that what
I am saying is precisely what others wanted to say, because it was
already implicit or taken for granted in their minds, I shall then be
glad to have elicited this clarification.

Analysis of the Intent

Continuation of the Western Syndrome

The thrust toward universalization has undoubtedly been a feature of
Western civilization since the Greeks. If something is not universal, it
looms as not really valid. The ideal of humanity of the Greeks, the
inner dynamism of Christianity, the feats of the Western empires, the
emancipation of philosophy from theology in order not to be tied to
a particular confession, the definition of morality by Kant, the modern cosmological worldview, and so forth, all are explicit examples
claiming universality. *Plus ultra* was the motto of imperial Spain, and
following it the Spaniards could reach America. Would government,
global village and global perspective, planetarian culture, universal
net of information, world market, the alleged universal value of technology, democracy, human rights, nation-states, and so on—all point
to the same principle: universal means catholic, and catholic means
true. What is true and good (for us) is (also) true and good for everybody. No other human civilization has reached the universality that
the Western has. The way was prepared since the Phoenicians, pre-
figured by the Christian empires, and made actually geographically
possible by the technocratic complex of present-day civilization.
   To be sure, this feature is not totally absent in other civilizations,
but it is not so prominent, so developed, and so powerful. The belief
in being the best, which the Chinese culture had, is different from the
belief in being universal—and thus *universalizable,* exportable to any
place and time.
   Further, this feature is not altogether negative. Yet it is ambivalent
and often ambiguous. The destiny of the West rises and falls with this
basic thrust. It is visible in the Abrahamic religions, without excluding Marxism and liberalism, as well as in the universal dominion of

technology, the modern scientific cosmology, and the universal economic system. Proselytism as well as messianisms and expansionisms of all kinds also imply a conviction of representing universal values, which thus impels those who are charged with this burden to share, communicate, convince—and ultimately conquer (for the benefit of the conquered). This feature is also visible in the psychological make-up of *homo occidentalis* and is clearly detectable in the very spirit of Western philosophy. The "once and for all" of the Christian event (see Heb. 7:27) and its claim to universality are perhaps the clearest manifestation of this spirit. From the point of view of the history of religions we may say that only the Western Gods (Yahweh, Allāh, Mammon,...), which like most divinities were tribal deities, became the universal God—and this to the extent that Christianity even renounced a proper name for God—or accepted the Jewish one. Most religions have a proper name or proper names for God or the Gods. Christianity uses the common name "God," although the New Testament makes a distinction between *Theos* and *ho Theos*. In a word, the power of the West is linked with this thrust toward universalization. It has produced glorious results and also deleterious effects. But this is not my point now. My only point is to detect this specific trait.

To be sure, the Chinese Son of Heaven or the Indian *cakravartin,* the Buddhist *dharma* or the Confucian *li* have an inbuilt claim to unbound validity, and Nâgârjuna's philosophy has an equivalent pretension when it criticizes all possible *dṛṣtis* or worldviews. But in most cases that universality was more of a metaphor and an expression of power and grandeur than an a priori. It was often a sense of superiority, not of universality. There is something democratic in the belief of being universalizable. Which monarch in history, to give another example, has claimed to have universal jurisdiction over the world, without even the intention of conquest, as did the Renaissance popes? What philosopher begins thinking by inquiring about the very conditions of absolute possibility, as did Kant? Heretics have been butchered in Asia and Africa because they were judged to be harmful and had to be punished, but not because truth was considered to be one and they had to be saved, as in the Inquisition. In short, there is here something special in Western civilization. "Everything that exists, exists therefore because it is one" (*Omne quod est, idcirco est, quia unum est*), said the synthetic mind of Boethius (PL 64, 83 b) speaking for the West. The *unum* is not the vedic *ekam* and much less upanishadic *ekam evâdvitîyam* (CU VI, 2, 1), which are surrounded by *asat,* nonbeing (RV X, 129, 2). This thirst for universality forms part of the Western myth. Yet it is difficult to argue, because we discover only the myth of the others, not the myth in which we live.

A long story (of thirty centuries!) in short: the very trend of looking for a "universal theory," even if expressed with all the respect and openness possible, betrays, in my opinion, the same *forma mentis,* the continuation of the same thrust—the will to understand, which is also a form of a will to power, and thus the felt need to have everything under control (intellectual, in this case).

I have not said that this feature is wrong. I have only situated it within a particular context and submitted it to an initial analysis by sociology of knowledge. It is not accidental that this need for universalization is felt precisely in the West and more especially *today.*

The *today* should be clearer than the preceding general reflection on the character of the Western mind. Probably in no other time of human history have we had so much information available regarding the ways in which our fellow human beings live and have lived. The time is gone when the *oikumene* could be the *mare nostrum,* when the languages of the human race were believed to be seventy-two, and true religions only those of the "peoples of the book," when we could speak of Christianity on the one hand and all the other religions lumped together. We are now submerged in an avalanche of data. How to proceed in this jungle of information? The need for intelligibility becomes imperative. We cannot live as if we were self-sufficient in our own corner. "The Spirit of the Lord *filled* the whole earth" (*Spiritus Domini replevit orbem terrarum;* Wis. 1:7), sang the Christian liturgy at Pentecost. Now radio and television waves fill the whole world.

I am saying that in the present situation of the world we cannot have the innocence of the Amerindian tribes, assuming that the others worship more or less the same Great Spirit and are governed by similar cosmic feelings. We need knowledge, and knowledge of the other, for survival and for self-identity. The thrust toward a universal theory is very comprehensive indeed. Join to this the desire to understand the other (and even ourselves better) without committing the past blunders of intolerance and fanaticism—and we all rejoice in this mood. The intention is more than justified. My doubt is whether it offers the proper remedy.

Inasmuch as we generally learn more from other areas when the subjects are too touchy for our own skin, I may cite simply as an example the ideal of the physical sciences. It was Einstein's dream—and drama—to work toward a "unified field theory," as he called it.

In it the set of laws governing gravitation and the other set governing electricity should find a common mathematical formula. Faraday had succeeded in "converting magnetism into electricity," thus unifying those two groups of phenomena. Einstein later unified gravitation, time, and space. No wonder that the next step should appear to be the total unification. Yet we are still waiting for the formula. Perhaps not even in mathematics and physics can all be reduced to unity (think of Gödel and Heisenberg). We should be alert to this warning.

In short, my suspicion is that the drive toward a "universal theory," be it in physics, religion, or politics, belongs to the same Western thrust. And I repeat that this trait, in spite of its often bitter results and today its menacing danger, is not altogether negative, and that at any rate we have to reckon with it as probably the most powerful force in the world today. But I also insist that this thrust is not universal—and thus not a proper method (to deal with human problems), both because it is not truly a universal *theory* (rationality is of many kinds) and, more importantly, because no theory is *universal* (rationality does not exhaustively define the human being). Moreover, the phenomenon of religion is certainly not exclusively theoretical. May I recall that I am trying to be succinct, dialectical, and basic?

The Unavoidable Search

The important thing for us is not whether Einstein's lifelong search will fail or not, or whether a universal theology of religion convinces or not. The important thing is to realize that Western culture apparently has no other way to reach peace of mind and heart—called, more academically, intelligibility—than by reducing everything to one single pattern with the claim to universal validity.

I could, to put it facetiously, be describing the plight of the drunk coming home in the early hours of the morning and looking for his lost house key under a particular streetlamp. Asked by the police whether he was sure he lost the key there, he answered: "No, but there is more light here." We look under the only light we have.

Now, my whole enterprise here consists in showing that there are other streetlamps in the city of humanity and that the Western lamp is not the only one we have. Obviously, the response is to say that it is not a question of a Western lamp, but that it is the human lamp of reason, the sole source of intelligibility, and that unless we wish to break off all human intercourse, commerce, and communication we have to accept that single light. Pushing the example further, I would suggest that to find the key to the house of wisdom we had better rely on the daylight and that only the superhuman light of the sun may be the common lamp for the entire universe, and not the artificial streetlamps, be they of the gas of reason, the electricity of intuition, the neo-gases of feeling, or whatever. Yet, what if it is at night that we lose our key? But I am not now pushing a theological argument.

Without identifying Descartes with our drunk I may recall the logical fallacy of the father of modern Western philosophy: everything that I see with clarity and distinction (remember, under the lamp)— that is, all evidence—must be true. I may concede here, for the sake of the argument, that it may be the truth. But from this it does not follow that truth is *only* what I see with clarity and distinction. Evidence may be our criterion of truth, but, first, I cannot a priori assume that what I see with clarity and distinction, you also will see in the same way. Secondly, truth may be wider, deeper, or even elsewhere than what I, or even we, see with clarity and distinction. Here we must recall the Western philosophical paradigm that was present since the beginning: "Humanity is the measure of all things, how those which exist do exist and those which do not exist, do not exist" (*Pantōn chrēmatōn metron anthrōpon einai. Tōn men ontōn hōs esti, tōn de nē ontōn hōs ouk estin*), as Protagoras said (reported by Plato, *Theat.* 151e–152a.)

This is not necessarily sheer humanism, as it is often said. It can also be traditional theology, for even if God speaks, God will have to use human language and be ultimately dependent on our understanding of the divine words. My quarrel here is not with *anthrōpos,* with humanity, or even anthropocentrism—although I would contest this; my quarrel is with *metron,* with the drive to measure everything— and extrapolating, with the thrust to want to know everything, because it is assumed that everything is knowable. Ontologically said: thinking does not need to exhaust Being. Now, under those Western assumptions, the move toward a "universal theory" is a welcome move to put a certain order among the many worldviews. Within that framework it may be the best way of expressing it. But Reality is richer. The "divine darkness" of Gregory of Nyssa has not had a follow-up in the West. It became the "dark night of the soul" in St. John of the Cross, and faded into the unconscious of modern psychology—after the lightning of Meister Eckhart.

This is my point. Granting that a hypothetical universal theology of religion were possible, it would be a very positive contribution to understanding the phenomenon of religion *only* for those who live within the cultural process in which all those words make sense— that is, for those who in one form or another subscribe to the myth of history, who accept the *intellectus agens* (*nous poiētikos*) of Aristotle and the Arab philosophers, the Cartesian intuition, the Kantian critical revolution, the Marxist analysis, or an absolute monotheism. This is a very impressive and powerful club, but it is not for everybody. To be sure, nobody now consciously wants to circumcise the others to their own ways of thinking in order to reach universality. In short, the striving for a universal theory is *one way* of expressing the manifoldness of the human religious experience, but it is just one way of doing it. It has a formal value. It expresses the genius of the West. However, we do not any longer want intellectual colonialisms.

I should not be misinterpreted. The effort at a universal theory is a noble enterprise. It is also a fruitful one. So many misunderstandings are overcome when we search for a common language; so many unclarities are dispelled; collaboration is made possible and religions are purified of so many excrescences, so much narrowmindedness and fanaticism. It would be totally mistaken to interpret my critique as not being a constructive one, as not aiming at the same goals and going in the same direction of mutual "understanding," tolerance, and appreciation. It may appear that I am also searching for a universal myth—although it would not be the same. Myth emerges and cannot be concocted; myth is polysemic and irreducible to one interpretation; myth does nor support any particular theory.

What I am against ultimately is the total dominion of the *logos* and a subordinationism of the Spirit—to put it in Christian trinitarian words—or against any form of monism, in philosophical parlance. And yet I am against all this, I repeat, without ignoring the function and power of the *logos,* this fellow-traveler of all reality, coextensive with it, but not exhaustively identifiable with it.

Let me sum up my misgivings before I engage in a more positive critique. The search for a "universal theory" indeed fosters dialogue, but runs the great danger of imposing its own language or the frame within which the *dia-logos* has to take place. It claims to be a *lingua universalis,* which amounts to reductionism, to say the least. Secondly, it assumes that religion—or in a broader sense, human traditions—are, if not reducible, at least translatable into *logos* (and probably one kind of *logos*), and thus gives a supremacy to the *logos* over against the Spirit. But why should all be put into words? Why is not acceptance without understanding—as I read the Christian symbol of Mary (Luke 2:19, 51)—also an equally human attitude?

Critique

The Question of Pluralism

I have the impression that most of those who speak about pluralism and fill it with a positive meaning are not sufficiently aware of the far-reaching consequences that pluralism entails: the dethronement of reason and the abandonment of the monotheistic paradigm. It is like those who speak grandly of tolerance of others without taking into consideration that the real problem of tolerance begins with why and how to tolerate the intolerant. "The tolerance you have is directly proportional to the myth you live and inversely proportional to the ideology you follow."[3] This could be the Law of Tolerance.

Pluralism in its ultimate sense is not the tolerance of a diversity of systems under a larger umbrella; it does not allow for any superstructure. It is not a supersystem. Who or what principles would manage it? The problem of pluralism arises when we are confronted with mutually irreconcilable worldviews or ultimate systems of thought and life. Pluralism has to do with final, unbridgeable human attitudes. If two views allow for a synthesis, we cannot speak of pluralism. We speak then of two different, mutually complementary, although apparently opposite, attitudes, beliefs, or whatever. We do not take seriously the claim of ultimacy of religions, philosophies, theologies, and final human attitudes if we seem to allow for a pluralistic supersystem. In that case, obviously, we all would like to be pluralistic and not so narrow-minded as the Muslims, Catholics, Marxists, or whoever, who still think that their analyses or views are ultimate—at least within their respective horizons. It is easy to be pluralistic if the others abandon their claim to absoluteness, primacy, universality, and the like: "We pluralists have allotted each system its niche; we then are truly universal." This, I submit, is not pluralism. This is another system, perhaps a better one, but it would make pluralism unnecessary. We have a situation of pluralism only when we are confronted with mutually exclusive and respectively contradictory ultimate systems. We cannot, by definition, logically overcome a pluralistic situation without breaking the very principle of non-contradiction and denying our own set of codes: intellectual, moral, esthetic, and so forth.

In other words, to assume that Hindus or Catholics are so dull as to be either fanatics or blind to the fact that the other also has the same or similar ultimate claims is to do an injustice to the self-understanding of the best minds of those religions. They know well that the claim of absoluteness, for instance, is a scandal to the human mind and that it does not entail disrespect of the other or straight condemnation of other views. There exist in the world even today well-balanced and thought-out absolutistic and mutually irreconcilable positions. And when we have to deal with sufficiently long-standing traditions, we cannot reasonably be satisfied with the proleptic attitude of a vague "hope"—I would rather call it expectation—that in the future our dissensions will fade away or find a solution. They have lived too long for us to believe that one fine day the *Vaishnavas* finally are going to recognize that the *Shaivaites* are right. The pious hope (without irony) is a very healthy attitude, as far as it goes.

Christian ecumenism offers a good example: what was considered impossible at one time became a fact a couple of decades later. But this model cannot so easily be extrapolated, for not everyone necessarily shares the conviction that history is the locus of Reality or has a central point of reference, like Christ. In other words, an interdisciplinary study is not yet cross-cultural.

There is even more. A pluralistic system as such could not be understood. Pluralism is only a formal concept. Sensible persons cannot understand how on earth there are many who think that all is matter, or that there is a God, or that the inferior races or less intelligent persons should not serve the superior ones, and so on, if they happen to have firm convictions in the opposite direction. And yet we are forced by circumstances to coexist with such worldviews or systems. No overarching is possible. Either there is God or there is no God, either the individual does have ultimate value or does not, either the cosmos is a living organism or it is not. Despite all our sympathy and effort to understand, we disagree with the other; we cannot even understand how the contrary opinion may be reasonably held. We may have our person interpretation and interpret the given examples, for instance, as false dilemmas. It remains, nevertheless, a fact that the others may not share our belief in a *coincidentia oppositorum*.

In short, there are a few fundamental human attitudes at the very basis of different human traditions that are mutually irreconcilable. I am an animist and you are a positivist scientist. Our two visions of the world cannot be both true. Or can they? The question of pluralism belongs to that ultimate level. And we should not take this lightly. Is it allowed to torture one individual, who otherwise will not speak, in order to save fifty thousand persons who are going to be blown up in the next few hours? We cannot say yes and no, or withhold an answer, for that would already imply giving one.

What this example contains in a time capsule is the situation of the world today. My hypothesis may be right or wrong, but I am not off the track. Such is the seriousness of the problem of pluralism. We cannot postpone to an eschatological happy ending the solution of all antinomies, nor can we rely on the last scientific or theological discovery of some guru telling us what they do. By that time, not the fifty thousand of my example, but millions of our fellow beings will have already starved to death or been killed in fratricidal warfare.

The problem of pluralism is paramount and has many facets. One of them is the question of good and evil. For my purpose I shall concentrate on the central issue of truth. What happens to it in face of so many disparate ultimate convictions? Let us assume that we have exhausted all the provisos and cautions at our disposal. We know that the context is essential, that different perspectives yield different visions, that temperament, culture, and the like, vouch for bewildering diversities. As long as the lines of dialogue are open, as long as the other does not draw the ultimate conclusion, there is no need to speak of pluralism. We are still struggling to find a common truth. We speak, then, of dialogue, of tolerance, of difference of opinions, and even of competition of worldviews in the human arena. We all recognize a legitimate multiperspectivism. The question of pluralism appears only when all those doors have been shut, when we return to ourselves and then have to take the decision to *écraser l'infâme,* or to allow ourselves to be overrun by evil, either to tolerate ultimate error and evil, or to fight it, even succumbing to it.

If the history of humankind is a succession of wars, and if war today appears so terrible, our issue of pluralism is not alien to this human predicament. What is the place of the philosophies underlying the Hitlers and Stalins in a "pluralistic worldview"? There is no "pluralistic worldview"; there are simply incompatible worldviews.

One of the presuppositions of the universal theory is that all problems are theoretically soluble. I am in complete agreement with the effort to try to solve the problems, and with patience, good will, and intelligence much can be achieved. We should go on trying again and again, untiringly. But we have to recognize two facts. One is that the partner may break off relations, stop the dialogue, become dangerous, oblige me to make decisions. And this is not necessarily because of some evil design, but because of the inner logic of the system. Not all who waged wars were criminals, not all who preached crusades were corrupt, not all those who believed in the inquisitions and slaveries of various types were subhuman—although now in our age we could not justify such acts or attitudes, which today should be condemned as out-and-out aberrations.

Now, there is no guarantee whatsoever that all human problems are (should be) theoretically soluble. This is probably not the case, even in mathematics, let alone in the complex existential situations in which contradictory human views are embedded. The universe may not have the logical coherence assumed by the spirit of Laplace or even by the belief in a monotheistic Deity for which nothing is unintelligible. These are already religious presuppositions not shared by every human tradition. Would those who think differently from us have to be excluded from a universal theory?

A second fact we have to take cognizance of is of another nature altogether. It is the unexamined presupposition—it has been taken for granted, "pre-subposed"—that truth is one rather than pluralistic.

The pluralism of truth is a much more serious and disturbing hypothesis than the obvious recognition of *perspectivism* and *relativity.* To admit that truth is perspectival should not offer any difficulty, although on that ultimate level the problem emerges as the question of what is the most adequate perspective in order to have the most accurate vision of things. And this obviously cannot be again another perspective without a *regressus ad infinitum.*

The *relativity* of truth, once it is distinguished from *relativism,* should also not be difficult to accept. Relativism destroys itself when affirming that all is relative and thus also the very affirmation of relativism. Relativity, on the other hand, asserts that any human affirmation, and thus any truth, is relative to its very own parameters and that there can be no absolute truth, for truth is essentially relational. The latter case is the reverse of the former. Relativism destroys itself if we affirm it. Relativity on the other hand is presupposed in the act of denying it. Any truth actually relates to an intellect. The concept of absolute truth has to relate to an infinite intellect.

The pluralism of truth goes a step further. It asserts that truth itself is pluralistic, and thus not one—nor many, for that matter. Pluralism is not plurality. To affirm that truth itself is pluralistic amounts to averring that there is no one all-encompassing or absolute truth.

The pluralism of truth is based on two fundamental assumptions: (1) the *first* is anthropological; (2) the *second* theological— or philosophical. I should prefer to stay in communion with all those traditions that do not make the split between philosophy and theology.

The *first* assumption is the recognition that each person is a source of understanding. Person here means not only any subject of rights, as an individual or a juridical person; it also includes collective units, and especially cultures as historical entities.

I am not necessarily resurrecting the Augustinian illumination theory of knowledge, or subscribing to any subject/object epistemology. I am saying only this: each person is a source of self-understanding. What a person is has to take into account the self-description and definition of the person in question. I am another person and have no right to superimpose my parameters and categories of understanding on others. Or, rather, if I do, the understanding I impose would be my understanding of the others, not the understanding of the others as they understand themselves—that is, as the understanding of their self-understanding. When the Hindu tells you or the Bantu tells me something that to us sounds preposterous, we have no way of passing any other judgment than that to us it sounds unacceptable for such and such reasons, apparently not accepted—or seen—by the other. However, we cannot reduce it all to objective statements. We are dealing with personal convictions, not with objectifiable events.

This almost obvious fact has been often dimmed by the influence of the natural sciences, which deal mainly with objectifiable phenomena and even more precisely with measurable entities. There is, for instance, a relative universality, at least in elementary mathematics, so that $2 + 3 = 5$ may appear as a universal truth independent of any source of understanding besides the objective intelligibility of the statement. Without discussing the nature of mathematics, suffice it to say that this is not the case when dealing with human affairs. And this happens even in applied mathematics. If $3 + 2 = 5$, everybody should agree in exchanging three canoes plus two women for five pounds sterling. And if it is replied that the quantities have to be homogeneous, we should then be inclined to agree to exchange two acres of land plus three houses for some other two acres and three houses (of the same price) outside the tribal country—and wonder why those "savages" of Papua, New Guinea, make such a fuss at being relocated, or why the Israelis could not go elsewhere, or the Palestinians for that matter. The fact is that neither land nor house are measurable entities. Each being is unique—that is, incommensurable.

Be this as it may—although it is not off the track—we may easily agree that the self-understanding of a particular culture is in a certain sense an ultimate and has to be taken as such without a reductionist twist to our ways of judging things. This is an epistemological statement. I am in no way saying that the Aztecs did well in performing the human sacrifices they did, just as I am not saying that some countries today do well in trading arms or in building atomic arsenals. I am saying that unless we understand the inner logic of a person and consider that person to be a source of self-understanding, we shall not understand that person and this will remain a permanent irritant among us.

Just as each human being qua human is endowed with self-understanding, each culture is also, because it possesses a specific vision of reality, a certain myth as the horizon within which things and events are discerned. Now, to privilege our understanding of reality and reduce all other perspectives to our own, even if we accept the data of the others, does not seem a proper method of dealing with what humans think about themselves and the universe, unless we reduce the human being to a set of data scientifically detectable.

If each person is a source of self-understanding, if humans are beings endowed with self-understanding, then we shall not be able to understand humans without sharing the self-understanding of the person(s) concerned. In that sense, an objective anthropology makes no sense. Human beings are not objects, but subjects. It would be methodologically wrong to treat humans as scientific objects.

All religions deal principally with the collective ultimate self-understanding of a human group. The truth of religion can be gauged only within the unifying myth that makes the self-understanding possible. If we want to cross boundaries, we will have to share in some common truths brought forth in common endeavor. But we should not project the truths of one religion over against an objective screen of truth in itself. Even if such an objective truth were to exist, we could not apply its canons in order to understand the self-understanding of a tradition that does not recognize them without distorting the issue. We may eventually condemn a religion as a human aberration, but always judging with our standards.

If the first assumption is anthropological, the *second* is theological, or rather, metaphysical. It contests one of the most widespread beliefs in the West as well as in the East—namely, that Reality is totally intelligible, that the *noēsis noēseōs* of Aristotle, the *svayam-prakāsha* of the Vedantins, the self-intelligible and omniscient God of the Christians, the total reflection of many spiritualist philosophers, is really the case. It contests the ultimate belief of every idealistic monism—that there is a Being or a Reality that encompasses all that there is and that this Reality is pure consciousness, absolutely self-intelligible, because all is transparent to the light of the intellect, all is pervaded by *cit, nous,* mind. I am not contesting that *logos, nous, cit,* or by whatever name we may call this dimension of the real, is a fellow traveler of reality or coextensive with Being. I am only contesting that Being is totally reducible to it. What I am saying is that Reality has other dimensions—Matter, for instance, or Spirit—which cannot be reduced to *logos,* word, *vāc, nous,* mind, consciousness, *cit.* Consciousness is Being, but Being does not need to be only Consciousness.

One of the philosophical implications of this view is that there is no being absolutely identical to itself. Self-identity would imply absolute (total) reflection (an *a* identical to *a*). Each being, not excluding a possible Supreme Being, presents an opaque remnant, as it were, a mysterious aspect that defies transparency. This is precisely the locus of freedom—and the basis of pluralism. Thinking, or the intelligence, covers the totality of Being only from the exterior, so to say. Being has an untapped reservoir, a dynamism, an inner side not illuminated by self-knowledge, reflection, or the like. Spontaneity is located in this corner of each being—its own mystery. It is unthought, unpremeditated, free, even from the structures of thinking. The mystery of Reality cannot be equated with the nature of consciousness. There "is" also *sat* (being) and *ānanda* (joy), the Father and the Spirit. They may be correlative and even coextensive with consciousness, probably because we cannot speak (think) of the one without the other, but certainly they cannot be all lumped together as ultimately one single "thing." This is one of the consequences of what I call the theanthrocosmic or cosmotheandric insight. From all this follows that there is no absolute truth, not only because we mortals have no access to it, but because reality itself cannot be said to be self-intelligible—unless we a priori totally identify Reality with Consciousness. The Absolute is in the Relative. Something can be absolutely true, but this is not absolute Truth. Truth is always a relationship, and one of the poles of the relationship is the intellect that understands what is the case (intelligible, coherent, and so on).

Even assuming a divine or perfect Intellect, it could know only what is intelligible. To aver that it can know All amounts to gratuitously affirming that All is intelligible, that Being is intelligible—in other words, that Being is Consciousness.

In this scheme, to know is to become the known. In the process of a real understanding the identity between the subject and the object is total. Vedāntic and Christian Scholastic philosophies, for instance, defend the ontological significance of the epistemological act. Ultimately Being is reduced to Consciousness. The (epistemological) principle of non-contra-diction becomes here the ontic principle of identity. Only a noncontradictory thing is identical to itself. It *is* itself (identity) because it is noncontradictory. Thinking, governed by the principle of noncontradiction, amounts ultimately to Being, which is governed by the principle of identity. Thinking and Being form the ultimate paradigm.

The application to our case is easy to detect. There can be a universal theory of religion, or of anything, only under the assumption that Theory covers Reality, that Thinking can (theoretically, in principle) exhaust Being—can know Being without any (unknown) remnant. In a word Being is intelligible (*quoad se*). This is the ultimate presupposition of any universal theory. But it is this ultimate presupposition that is here called into question. To affirm that Consciousness is Being is a postulate of intelligibility, but not of Being. Truth is the result of some equation between Consciousness and Being. But Being may transcend its equation with Consciousness.

Furthermore, de facto, the actual pole for all our truth utterances is not a divine or perfect intellect but human consciousness, individual or collective, situated in space, time, matter, culture, and so forth. We have to take our own contingency very seriously; and our grandeur lies precisely in the awareness of our limitations. Anything we touch, think, speak—including all our ideas about any Supreme Deity—is permeated by the contingency of our being. I am not excluding the possible existence of the supreme consciousness of a realized soul, a *jīvanmukta*. I am saying that even *that* language is a relative language and suffused in polysemy. The moment that we come into the picture, all is tinged by our creatureliness, humanness, or whatever we may call it.

To sum up, the pluralistic character of truth does not mean that there are many truths. "Many truths" is either a contradiction in terms if we admit the possibility of many true and mutually incompatible answers to a particular judgment, or it is a displacement of the problem to a meta-truth that would be the conceptual truth of the many truths, as our single concept of sardine allows us to recognize many sardines. Truths would then be many exemplars of the meta-truth and the problem would begin with the meta-truth all over again.

The pluralism of truth means fundamentally two things. First, that truth cannot be abstracted from its relationship with a particular mind inserted in a particular context. "There is bread on this table" cannot be criticized outside the perspective of the author of the sentence, although "the city of Madras is on this table" cannot be literally true, for lack of internal coherence. We cannot abstract from every context and proclaim the oneness of truth. We have to recognize perspectivism and contextualization. Truth is relationship, and quantification does not occur.

Secondly, and more importantly, the pluralistic character of truth shows that the notion of truth is not identical, say, with the notion of goodness. Ultimately Truth and Goodness may coalesce, but even then they are not the same. History shows us what an amount of evil (nongoodness) has been perpetrated in the name of Truth. Truth *alone* in this sense is not enough—that is, does not fulfill the function that truth is supposed to perform. It also explicitly requires goodness. Truth is pluralistic; hence, truth alone, disincarnated truth, cannot be an absolute, and ultimately it is not true. It needs other elements, at the same level of truth, as it were. Goodness is a case in point. Truth is not goodness and yet truth without goodness is maimed, is not truth. I shall not discuss whether one of the weaknesses of the dominant Western philosophy is that it desired to be merely *sophia* (converted into *epistēmē*) and reduced the *philia* to desire (of wisdom), forgetting that it has equally to be (wisdom of) love.

Be this as it may, the pluralistic character of truth denounces the monism of thought and reveals the existential aspect of truth. Each truth is one, certainly, but a universal truth in general is just an extrapolation of our mind.

This does not mean that within one particular period in history or within one given culture—I should prefer to say within one living myth—there are no unanimously accepted standards and, in that sense, relatively universal truths. There are such truths, because they are seen as such by that particular group of humans. Slavery as an institution, to give just one example, may today elicit a general consensus as being something to be abolished, so that even those who still practice it do so with bad conscience. God was for a long time and in a great part of the world such a myth or recognized truth. It now no longer is. Anticapitalism and democracy could be adduced as examples of absolute political truths for some and yet contested by others.

My thesis is clear: a universal theory of whatever kind denies pluralism. Any alleged universal theory is one particular theory, besides many others, that claims universal validity, thus trespassing the limits of its own legitimacy. Further, no theory can be absolutely universal, because theory, the contemplation of truth, is neither a universal contemplation, nor is (theoretical) "truth" all that there is to Reality.

The Inner Limits of the *Logos*

We have indicated, so far, the impotency of the *logos* to unify (identify) itself completely with itself, thus showing a dimension of Reality "incommensurable" with the *logos*, or rather "incommensured" by it. We have implicitly mentioned the Unspeakable and also the Unspoken, as well as the Unthinkable and the Unthought. We have obliquely realized that there is a place for the Unthought and the Unspoken. The Unspeakable and the Unthinkable are in a way within the realm of speech and thought inasmuch as we are still aware of them. With the Unthought it is different. We are not aware of it. We recall only later that something remained unthought for a while, and from there we assume that there still may be more, and that perhaps something always remains unthought—but we can neither speak of it nor prove it. We speak about the Unspeakable as that *x* about which nothing *else* can be said. If we were to speak about the Unspoken, we would destroy it; it would be a contradiction in terms.

I here want to deal with the inner boundaries of the word. Language is neither singular nor plural. Like the notion of the personal person, it defies number. A person is not just a single individual. An I entails a thou and both imply he/she/it/they/we. An isolated I is a contradiction in terms. It is an I only because of a thou—and vice versa.

Similarly, language entails not only more than one speaker (a single individual would not speak—there would be neither any need of nor meaning in speaking), it also entails more than language. Language in the singular makes no sense. There is no private language, nor is there a single language. First, de facto, there is not just a single language. There are languages in the world. Secondly, de jure, no language could exist alone. A single language (and this implies a single speaker) would coincide with the things it speaks about, and words would be the things.

The distance between word and thing would be zero. There would be no need to express the thing other than by itself if there were a single language.

By language I do not mean now, say, English. English inasmuch as it is spoken by a number of persons, each one of them having a different perspective in the use of each word, is already a polyphonic and even polysemic language.

English is a set of speeches with certain common sounds and structures. What we now call language, or *a* language, is the homogeneous integral of a group of speeches. I made reference to a single language in the sense of a single speech by a single speaker (or a plurality of speakers using the identically same speech). Words are not things: things can be worded differently. Otherwise the word would be the thing or no-thing. No word exhausts the thing; no word expresses the thing completely; no name is the real name, the name that could totally cover the thing. Language is language because it speaks, it says, it unfolds things and reveals them, it unveils them, to the persons for whom they are precisely things. This fundamental reflection on language seems all too often overlooked, and it is relevant for our topic.

The phrase, "In the beginning was the Word," means in so many traditions from Asia and Africa that in the beginning there was a Speaker, a Spoken To, a Spoken With, and a Spoken About. Without this *quaternitas perfecta* there is no Word. If "Word was at the beginning," now after the beginning there are words, languages, and a plurality of those *quaternitates*. The temptation to make sense of it all by returning to the beginning is comprehensible, but it is also understandable that to "want to be *like* God" was condemned by God as a hybris that led to human alienation. Let me close this reference by saying that what that tradition tells us is to become Christ himself—*ipse Christus,* not *alter Christus.*

In a simpler manner: we do not speak language. We speak a language, a language that has relationships with other languages and each of which represents a new perspective on the world, a new window and often a new panorama. We cannot understand all the languages of the world. We can cross the boundaries of, say, a dozen languages, and become aware of the multidimensionality of the things we word so differently. Other persons can also cross some other boundaries, and so the net can spread all over the world—but with a center nowhere. This is what happens in predominantly oral cultures.

Illiterates in many countries of the so-called Middle East and India, and I suppose Africa as well, are not persons who do not know how to read and write (this is a Western fixation), but individuals who know only a single language, who understand only the dialect of their own village. As a matter of fact, what we call languages are certain dialects that have gained some power and been endorsed by Royal Academies and Learned Societies, and been printed as the official or correct way of saying things. This is a phenomenon unheard of a few centuries ago in Europe, and still today in most of the world. The real languages are the dialects.

Illiterates are those persons who cannot distinguish a particular locution from what it means, because they know only that locution and are not aware that the "same" thing can be said in different ways so that nothing is absolute. In point of fact each village develops its own language, but the villagers know perfectly well that some miles away the "same" thing is given another name, which they also know. In this way they do not confuse the name with the thing. (The importance of this is not to know how to name utensils—so we can buy and sell in the neighboring bazaar—but how to understand living words like beauty, justice, propriety, politeness.) They know that no one word, no one language, can exhaust the immense variety of the human experience. So it is only together, in *colloquium,* that we touch the universality of human life.

A universal theory claims to be a universal language, a language in which all languages find themselves reproduced, reflected, or into which they can be translated. Yet a universal language does not exist. And if it would, it would represent an impoverishment of the riches of the many languages.

Certainly we can and should stretch the meaning of words as much as we can, so as to make them say what until then they did not mean. I have cited the example of "grace" elsewhere, which for a long period of Christian theology was almost by definition the exclusive property of Christianity. Today we have rescued that word from meaning only the saving grace as a share in the divine nature, as the apostle Peter understood it. There are also Indian religions of grace, and Christian theology does not deny it, although it will have to find theological explanations for this fact. But words, in spite of their elasticity, have their limits.

Theology is a case in point. We can say that by *theos* we understand the Christian concept; but can we include in the meaning of this word what a Buddhist means with no proper word and a Marxist by denying the existence of such a being? If we mean just transcendence, let us say it and not speak about the Transcendent.

In order to properly approach cross-cultural problems I have developed a theory of *homeomorphic equivalents* as analogies of a third degree. "Brahman" is not the translation of "God," for instance, but both perform the equivalent functions required in their respective systems. We may perhaps find the homeomorphic equivalents of the word "theology," but we cannot assume that this word encompasses all those equivalents, just as God does not cover what Brahman stands for. It may even be that on the doctrinal level they are incompatible notions. Either there is a creator God, or an inactive noncreator Brahman, but not both, in spite of the fact that in the respective systems both are not only legitimate but necessary. Or we need to modify the meaning of the two words so as to make them compatible within one single system. It is very proper to have our language and to want to express all that we can in our own language, but it will remain only one possible language, which should not pretend to supplant the others.

As I have argued elsewhere, terms, as signs for scientific information—as labels in a nominalistic world—can certainly be all translated more or less artificially into any language. We can say entropy or weight in any language. They all have a measurable point of reference. Not so with words whose points of reference are the historical and cultural crystallizations of human experiences, which can be verified only by sharing in those experiences. How do we translate French *esprit*, Catalan *seny*, Navajo *hosho*, Sanskrit *rayi*, English *countenance*, German *Stimmung*? Poets know something about this. A universal theology of religion would not want to deal only with the equivalent of mathematical infractures common to most religions.

There have been in our days efforts at highly formalized theories of religion. They are useful attempts at finding some common structures and formal gestalts of religion. I myself define religion as something fulfilling the equation $y = f(x)$, where x is the human condition as seen by any culture or religion at any given moment; y is the goal, aim, end, solution, meaning, result, or whatever of x, the human condition of life; and f is the function that transforms x into y.

All religions, I submit, claim to fulfill this condition and satisfy this structure. This is a formalized language that helps us to understand religious phenomena by finding an ultimate common structure, so that if something fulfills that equation, like a certain type of humanism, for instance, it should—or could—be called religion, although the label "religion" may not be customary. But all this is far from providing us a universal theory by which to understand religion. It provides us, certainly, a kind of algebra about which I have elsewhere also commented on its limitations.

A truly universal theory of religions should be a sort of theory of theories, for every religion has its thinkers and systematizers spinning out theories of their respective religions, calling them theologies, philosophies, or whatever. A theory of theories amounts to a language of languages, a meta-language, a meta-theory. By now we should know the dialectic of such attempts. Either the theory of theories is another theory, and then it falls into the class of which it claims to be the set (which is a contradiction), or it is a meta-theory—that is, not a theory at all but something else. What can that "else" be if not another more sophisticated theory of a second degree, as it were? But then we may need another theory of a third degree to explain the other possible meta-theories that may emerge, *et sic ad infinitum.* If the "else" is of another order, we can no longer call it "theory"; it ceases to be of the order of the *logos.* This insight will open a door for us (see "The Alternative," below). But there is still another point to consider.

The Outer Boundaries of Any Theory

We have seen the inner limits of a universal theory. But there is still more. No need to be a Marxist or to follow any particular sociology of knowledge in order to subscribe to the philosophical insight that any theory stems from a praxis and is nurtured by it, even if often standing in dialectical opposition to it. Any theory not only attempts to explain the status quo (of the physical sciences, for instance); it also springs from that very status quo (of the post-Einsteinian physics, in our example). It would suffice to change the praxis (in our case it would be the appearance of an unaccounted for physical fact) to upset all existing theories. What would become of a universal theory of religion if suddenly (or less abruptly) a new religion would appear or even a new notion of religion? The universal theory would either have to be given up or it would have to deny a priori the character of religion to the newcomer. Let us not forget that for a long time Confucianism and Buddhism were not considered religions, because they did not fit into a neat theory of religion. I am afraid that something similar happens with regard to Marxism and Humanism, to which many would deny the name (and not just the label) religion.

I have already made allusion to the (colonialistic) cultural mono-formism from which most of the universal theories come. They assume that we are today in a better position than ever to know the essence of religion. In that we are free from any desire to dominate, all we need to do is to evaluate and understand the present (religious) situation—without being aware that this very attitude both consecrates, as it were, the status quo, and transforms it in one very particular direction. In other words, a universal theory of religion is loaded with political overtones. A telling example today is the so-called theology of liberation within the Catholic Church. It raises waves within the institution because it does not tally with a "universal theory of Christian religions" sponsored by the Supreme Pontifex of that church.

Any theory is only an intellectual explanation of a given datum, but it is all too often blind to the fact that the datum appears first as such when seen under the light of a particular theory. The relationship between theory and praxis is that of a vital circle—not a vicious circle. Any human praxis entails a theory and any human theory entails a praxis, not because the one is *based* on the other and presupposes it, and vice versa—which would constitute a vicious circle—but because the two are intrinsic components of one and the same human factor. Both are interdependent, though not through a causal link, and probably not even by means of a logical dialectic. It is rather a ying-yang dialogical relationship. There is no synthesis possible, but only a constituent and mutually dependent polarity.

The problem has been sufficiently studied so as to spare us the task of spelling it out. It suffices to have mentioned it. In a word: any alleged universal theory is dependent upon a praxis that is far from being universal. It is an iron colossus with earthen feet!

The Alternative

What, then, is to be done if we reject any grandiose universal theory and even detect in this intent a latent will to dominate and a fear that if we do not make sense of everything we will lose our bearings and become vulnerable? I repeat that I do not minimize the importance of the noble desire to overcome exclusivistic doctrines and to open up ways of communication between compartmentalized and often frozen traditions. Yet, I discover a change in a fundamental human attitude that may have begun very early in human history. It is a shifting from a natural confidence in Reality to a cultural mistrust, even of ourselves. We may recall Descartes's existential doubt: even our mind may cheat us, were it not for a veracious and trustworthy God. It begins a culture of mistrust (which is different from critique) and it ends a civilization of (in) security (which has to do with the obsession for certainty). But then, should we give up any critical stance or, on the other hand, any hope at understanding each other? Should we resign ourselves to provincial explanations and eventually to more rivalries and further wars of "theologies," and religions? Far from it. I need not repeat that my entire life is directed toward mutual understanding and cooperation among religious traditions.

After having criticized a universal theory I obviously cannot fall into the trap of proposing one of my own. What I espouse could be summarized in the three headings of this third part. First, we must put our house in order, as it were. Secondly, we must open ourselves to the others; and thirdly, we both, or if need be, we alone, must rely on the overall thrust of the human experience.

I should add here that these three moments are intertwined and require each other. They are three moments of one and the same fundamental religious attitude. This fundamental religious attitude, I submit, is a basic human attitude. It is an attitude of trust in Reality. *Apistia* is a cause of ignorance, said Heraclitus (Frag. 86). Without a certain confidence somewhere, the human being cannot live. I have to trust my parents, my friends, the grocer, language, the world, God, my own evidence, my consciousness, or whatever.

The fundamental error of Descartes, as the father of modernity, along with the founders of the "new science," which since then has dominated Western civilization, it that once the method of doubting of everything is consciously started, there is no end to it, and yet it has a beginning, a foundation that is taken for granted. God, for Descartes, is the "object" that will put an end to the *regressus ad infinitum,* but what he does not see is his taking for granted the *ego* of his doubt as well as of his *cogito.* Even if he doubts that he doubts or thinks, it is always his *ego* that is presupposed.

This is the birth of modern individualism. And once we identify ourselves with our singularity we have to look frantically for a foundation. Singularity needs support, a foundation. I am no longer a constitutive element in the universe. I am no longer a communion with the whole, no longer the whole. I no longer am, for I could *not* be. *Angst* is the companion of an isolated singularity. I have to justify my existence and conquer my being; I have become a stranger to Reality, a mere spectator who suddenly discovers I have no ticket (no reason) to see (share) the spectacle of the real. The estrangement begins. We may say, this is what the loss of innocence means. It *may* be. We discover ourselves naked—that is, alone, alienated from the rest of the universe.

Whatever this may be, the fact is that the old innocence cannot be recovered. A second innocence is a contradiction in terms. The moment that I become aware that it is second, it ceases to be a real innocence. It is not for nothing there was an angel at the gate of paradise with a sword of fire to prevent return. There is no point in going back. But there can be a new innocence, so new that it does not even remember the previous one, or rather that it does not believe in the first innocence. The essence of paradise is to be lost—always and ever lost. It is the necessary mental hypothesis for the myth of the fall, be it of Eve or of Galileo/Descartes and Co. The resurrection myth looms on the horizon.

Having discovered the precariousness of the individual—that is, having practically exhausted all the arguments of reason for a better world, or a good life, for total security, or a real foundation of thinking, behavior, and what not—having discovered in the entire explanation of ourselves and of the universe at least one weak spot that makes the whole thing foundationless, we may as well make a jump, a *metanoia*, a conversion, and discover that, in spite of all our efforts, we were all the time assuming an unconscious trust in Reality, a confidence perhaps in life, certainly in "that" which makes the entire human enterprise an adventure, either with sense or meaningless. We discover, in short, that it all may be a game, even a bad game at that, an illusory one, or whatever, but ultimately it is our game, our entertainment, our adventure. In a word, we recognize, we believe that we are created, born, thrown out, existing, dreaming, living, or even imagining it all, but nevertheless doing it. It is to that fundamental human trust that I appeal—and personally confessing that I do not find the human adventure so dull, uninteresting, or negative.

The Harmony from Within

If we speak of religious traditions or of religion in general, we should not remain at the surface of the human religious experience. We should begin by living, knowing, and experiencing our own tradition, or particular subtradition, as intensively and deeply as possible. Religion has been probably the place where the worst human passions and the most dangerous human attitudes have occurred. At the same time, religion is the locus where the highest peaks of the human experience have been reached and where the most sublime quality of human life has been unfolded.

I shall not linger here at defining religion as the quest for the ultimate, as the set of symbols and practices of the human being when confronted with the most definitive questions as to the meaning of life and the universe, not just on an intellectual plane, but on an existential and vital level. Religion is, in the last instance, a dimension of human life.

My first point is this: when trying to understand the religious phenomena of the human race, we cannot neglect our own personal religious dimension, developed with more or less force in one particular tradition. Otherwise, we distort the entire enterprise. Only those who knew "number" were allowed to enter Plato's Academia, only those endowed with "faith" could duly practice Christian theological reflection. Only those with a medical title are allowed to practice

170 / *The Invisible Harmony*

medicine. Only those who know how to rule themselves are the true rulers of others, declared Lao-tzu, Plato, and sages from practically all traditions. Only those who cultivate the religious dimension in their own lives can really dare to enter upon the excruciating task of trying to understand what religion is all about. The study of religion is not the classification of "religious" data, but the study of the religious dimension of human being. I am not saying that scholars should belong to any particular religious persuasion or that they should be outwardly "religious" in the almost hypocritical sense that the word is used in many circles today. I am affirming that without both an intellectual and an experiential knowledge (which implies love, involvement, and a certain pathos) there is little hope of succeeding in this enterprise. All too often individuals who seem to pose as exponents of some other religion know fairly little about the riches of their own tradition.

But I am saying still more, and it is a delicate matter to formulate it without being misunderstood. I am not preaching that one has to belong to any religious institution. I am propounding that one has to have reached a certain religious insight, poise, maturity, wisdom, and even inner peace and harmony within one's own being, without which intellectual discourse about religions will be marred at the very outset. I am saying that knowledge requires connaturality and even implies a certain identification with the things known.

The classic Western word for this gnosis is wisdom (*sapientia: sapida scientia*). Religion is not like geology, which may be cultivated provided we have enough information of the objective facts and the scientific theories. But the study of religion demands a special kind of empathy with the subject matter, which cannot be dissociated from one's own life. We can write about the symbolic meaning and extraordinary beauty of dance as an expression of the sacred and compare Greek with Amerindian rituals, for instance. But if we have not had at least a glimpse both of the transforming effects of the dance and of the inner relationship between dance and the rest of life, we shall not be able to make much headway in the interpretation of the religious phenomenon of the dance. Religion is a certain wholeness. A good oboe player is not automatically a good conductor of a symphony orchestra. One needs something more than the sum total of the skills of the individual instruments. Religion, I submit, is the symphony, not the solo player or singer.

The inner harmony I am referring to is manifested in the spontaneous and creative way in which we may be able to deal with one particular religion because we are really at home there and able to simplify, to relate disparate things, or put practices together. I am speaking about a certain identification with that tradition, which does not preclude, of course, critical opinions and even harsh judgments, but which are always somewhat from within. When dealing with a religion at that level we should speak *ex abundantia cordis et mentis* more than from a catalogue of propositions. The existential reason is obvious. Any authentic religious dialogue dispels misunderstandings from both sides and calls for rectifications and new interpretations. If one of the partners is not at home in the process, because of not knowing almost spontaneously and by an instinctive sense (what the Scholastics, following Plato and Aristotle, called *per connaturalitatem*) the living sources of his or her tradition, discussion will stick to mere formulations and become rigid. No encounter, no dialogue, will take place.

If scholars gain this insight into their own tradition, they will be able to become aware of what I call the *pars pro toto* effect. In order to be brief I may exemplify it with the attitude we find in so many truly spiritual masters. I am aware that I see reality, although through the perspective of my own window. I may believe that I see the entire panorama of the world and the meaning of human life, although through the color, shape, and glass of my particular window. I may further believe that it is the best window, at least for me, and that the vision it allows is not distorted. I may at this moment withhold judgment regarding the validity of the vision through other windows, but I cannot hide the fact that I believe that through my window I see the entire panorama—the *totum*.

Nobody is ultimately satisfied with partialities. A Christian, for instance, will say that Christ represents the totality or is the universal savior or the center of the universe, to utilize different metaphors, the interpretation of which does not enter now into the picture. We may well demythicize them. Nevertheless the Christian will not be satisfied with a partial view, that Christ is just one *avatāra* among many, and be content with it as the Christian's lot (or *karma?*). In short, Christians will have to say that in Christ they find the truth—and with qualifications, the whole truth.

But there is a third experience still to pass through. We should, further, be aware that we see the *totum per partem,* the whole through a part. We will have to concede that the other, the non-Christian, for instance, may have a similar experience and that the non-Christian will have to say that the Christian takes the *pars pro toto,* for from the outside one only sees the *pars,* not the *totum*—the window, not the panorama. How to combine these apparently contradictory statements? We will have to say that the other is right in discovering that we take the *pars pro toto* (because the outsider sees the window), but that we are also right in seeing the *totum per partem* (because we see the panorama). It is a *totum* for us, but *per partem*, limited to our vision through the one window. We see the *totum*, but not *totaliter* one may say (because we do not see through other windows). We see all that we can see. The other may see equally the *totum* through another window, and thus describe it differently, but both see the *totum*, although not *in toto*, but *per partem*. *Rota in rotae* (*trochos en trochō*) said Christian mystics commenting on Ezekiel 1:16.

This means that we do not need a universal theory as if we could enjoy a global perspective—which is a contradiction in terms. It means that each one of us may be aware of the whole under one particular aspect—and not just that we see only a part of it. Both the subjective and objective models break down. There is neither subjective nor objective universality. We see all that *we* can see—one may grant—but only *all* that we can see, our *totum*. The whole is what is wholesome for us (and healthy—following the wisdom of the words). Something is complete when it has an inner harmony—as we shall still emphasize. Let us recall that the root *kail* (*koil*), from which the word "whole" derives, suggests both beauty and goodness.

Dialogical Openness

Once internal dialogue has begun, once we are engaged in a genuine intra-religious scrutiny, we are ready for what I call the *imparative* method—that is, the effort at learning from the other and the attitude of allowing our own convictions to be fecundated by the insights of the other. I argue that, strictly speaking, comparative religion, on its ultimate level, is not possible, because we do not have any neutral platform outside every tradition whence comparisons may be drawn. How can there a no-man's land in the land of Man? In particular fields this is indeed possible, but not when what is at stake is the ultimate foundations of human life. We cannot compare (*comparare*—that is, to treat on an equal—*par*—basis), for there is no fulcrum outside. We can only *imparare*—that is, learn from the other, opening ourselves from our standpoint to a dialogical dialogue that does not seek to win or to convince, but to search together from our different vantage points. It is in this dialogue, which cannot be multitudinous, but only between a few traditions in each case, where we forge the appropriate language to deal with the questions that emerge in encounter. Each encounter creates a new language.

In these dialogues we do not come up with great universal theories, but with a deepened mutual understanding among, say, Catholic Christianity and Śaivasiddhānta, or between Lutheranism and Shī'ah Islām, or between modern Western philosophical categories and traditional Bantu religiousness. Once a net of relationships has been developed, it is relatively easy to establish new and more general links and even venture common categories. The great religions of Africa should be mentioned here, for they offer a peculiar difficulty on the one hand, and a grand facility on the other, to dialogue. It is difficult because often dialogue becomes doctrinal, abstract, metaphysical, and the genius of many an African religion lies elsewhere. We have difficulty in finding common categories. It is easy, on the other hand, because of the charge of humanity and concreteness of such exchanges. The common language is the simplest one.

These mutual studies, relationships, and dialogues change both the opinion of the one partner and the interpretation of the other. Religions change through these contacts; they borrow from each other and also reinforce their respective standpoints, but with less naivete. This type of dialogue is not only a religious endeavor for the participants, it is a genuine *locus theologicus,* to speak in Christian Scholastic parlance, a source in itself of religious (theological) understanding. A theory of a particular religion today has also to deal with other religions. We can no longer ignore the other. The religions of others—our neighbors—become a religious question for us, for our religion.

In a way, there is many a theory of religion claiming to be a universal theory of religion. But then we are, although on a second and much more fruitful higher spiral, at the same initial point—namely, having to confront a series of universal theories of religion. We will have to deal with, say, how Islam sees itself in the religious mosaic of our times, or how Marxism confronts the Hindu interpretation of Reality.

This process of mutual learning has no end. Imparative religion is an open process. A universal theory attempts to clarify everything as neatly as possible in one single place and ends eventually by stifling any ultimate dialogue. In my alternative the polarities remain and the ideal is not seen in a universal theory, but in an ever-emerging and ever-elusive myth that makes communication, and thus mutual fecundation, possible without reducing everything to a single source of intelligibility or to mere intelligibility. The very theory is dialogical. In a word, the dialogical character of being is a constitutive trait of Reality. Agreement means convergence of hearts, not just coalescence of minds. There is always place for diversity of opinions and multiplicity of mental schemes of intelligibility.

Human Cosmic Trust

What I am trying to put forward is not a counter-theory, but a new innocence. We should beware of so many reform systems that began with a greater universalistic impulse than the original systems and became new philosophies, new sects, or new religions. Often they do not subsume or even enhance the others but simply multiply their number. This may be not bad—except they do not achieve what they started to do. Any universal theory will soon become another theory.

We should beware of claiming to understand religions better than they have understood themselves. I do not deny this possibility, but it should carry along some contemporary representatives of such a religion, and at least partially transform that religion, lest our interpretation become a new religion. Religious traditions have more existential than doctrinal continuity. There are not many doctrines in common between a Christian of the first century and a present-day one, for instance. The case of Hinduism is still clearer. Hinduism is an existence, not an essence. The decisive factor is the existential confession, not the doctrinal interpretation.

The study of religion, I repeat, is not like the scientific approach to physical phenomena, which even in the sciences is becoming obsolete. We are not dealing with objective facts—supposing they existed. Even in the case of allegedly revealed facts, we are still dealing with human constructs, which house, as it were, a group of human beings, giving them the housing of a more or less coherent and protective universe.

In our days we feel, perhaps more acutely than at other times, that we do not know each other, that we still mistrust one another, that in fact we are at loggerheads in many fundamental insights of immediate importance for the praxis of our lives. We are painfully aware of our differences because we are more conscious of our mutual existence and the need to intermingle—brought about by the techniculture of our times. But we cannot chop off our divergences to remain only with what we have in common: we all want to eat and to be happy. This is fundamental, but hunger has many causes and the ways to happiness, and even its concept, differ.

Religions can no longer live in isolation, let alone in animosity and war. Traditional religions nowadays are not, by and large, very powerful and thus do not present a major threat, except of course in some countries. More secular religious ideologies today have greater virulence and fight each other. They cannot be left out of the picture in a discourse about the encounter of religions. The last two world wars were not strictly religious, and yet they were "theological." Where do we turn for harmony and understanding?

The political and economic situation of the world today compels us to radical changes in our conception of humanity and the place of humanity in the cosmos. The present system seems to be running toward major catastrophes of all kinds. This situation brings near the thought that if the change has to be radical and lasting, it also has to transform our ways of thinking and experiencing Reality. The point in case of the religious traditions could not be more pertinent. I am prepared to argue that if there is any solution to the present predicament, it cannot come out of one single religion or tradition, but has to be brought about by collaboration among the different traditions of the world. No single human or religious tradition is today self-sufficient and capable of rescuing humanity from its present predicament. We can no longer say "that's your problem!" Hinduism will not survive if it does not face modernity. Christianity will disappear if it does not meet Marxism. Technocratic religion will destroy itself if it does not pay heed to, say, the Amerindian tradition, and so on. Humanity will collapse if we do not gather together all the fragments of the scattered cultures and religions. But togetherness does not necessarily mean unity, nor is understanding absolutely required.

What is needed is trust, a certain trust that sustains a common struggle for an ever better shaping of Reality. I mean something like this. As the very word suggests (especially in Latin—*fiducia*), this "trust" entails a certain "fidelity" to oneself, "con-fidence" in the world as cosmos, "loyalty" in the struggle itself, and even (as perhaps etymologically hinted at) an attitude rooted in the soil of Reality like a "tree," a basic "belief" in the human project, or rather in the worthwhile collaboration of humans in the overall adventure of being. It excludes only the suicidal and negative desire of self-destruction and annihilation of everything. It does not eliminate the passionate thrust toward the victory of one's own ideals—reprehensible as this may appear to many of us if this is striven for as an absolute.

Elsewhere I have proposed the distinction between the basic and constitutive human *aspiration* by which the human being is constituted precisely as a human being, and the *desires* that plague concrete human existence when not walking on the path toward realization. This, I would submit, takes into account the Buddhist criticism of *tanha, tṛṣṇa,* thirst, desire, the one-pointedly Hindu concern for realization, and the Christian preoccupation with dynamism and creativity. There is a primordial human aspiration, but there are equally hasty desires. The trust I am speaking of is related to human aspiration by which humans believe that life is worth living, because Reality can—must—be trusted.

The danger in this aspiration—in our case, we may say, toward truth—is that it can become a desire for our own understanding. In other words, the danger lies in the possible confusion between our *desire* to understand everything, because we assume (a priori) that Reality is (should be) intelligible, and the *aspiration* of making sense of our life and all reality. This latter is the trust that there is some sense (direction, "meaningful" dynamism) in the universe.

This assumption is not a universal theory, not even a universal praxis. It is only so far a relative cultural invariant inasmuch as exceptions are seen precisely as aberrant deviations by the vast majority of mortals. This trust is an impulse simply not to give up in the task of being what we are (or should be), which some may say is that of being human, others divine.

Half a century ago I called this cosmic trust the cosmological principle, and millennia before it was called *ṛta, tao, ordo.* Even when we formulate the ultimate metaphysical question, "Why is there something rather than nothing?" we are assuming that the question is meaningful—that it is a real question—even if we do not find an answer, or only a nihilistic one. It may be said of this ultimate ground that there is something somewhere asking whether it all makes sense at all, or that it is all the dream of a dreamer and has never existed outside the dream, or that it is a very weak ground indeed for the unfolding of the universe and our participation in it. Yet it may be enough, for in one way or another we have to stop somewhere. Traditionally this ultimate ground has been called God, Man, or World. We have further interpreted those words as meaning consciousness, goodness, power, intelligence, nothingness, absurdity, matter, energy, and the like. We may change words and interpretations, but some fundamental trust indeed persists.

The ultimate ground for this cosmic confidence lies in the almost universal conviction that Reality is ordered—in other words, is good, beautiful, and true. It is a divine Reality, say most of the human traditions. There is no need to blow up a wretched universe, because Reality is not evil ultimately. We have to bring it to completion, to achieve it, as the fundamental principle of alchemy puts it, and eventually correct it, but not create an artificial-mechanical universe that we must have under control because we cannot trust Reality. Underlying this felt need for control there is a certain Protestant climate that "creation" is a fiasco, combined with some "humanistic" interpretation that the redeemer is Man. But Christian theology will tell us that redemption entails an inner dynamism that ultimately belongs to the "economic Trinity."

Cultural Excursus

> *To hen ... diapheromenon auto autō xumpheresthai,*
> *hōsper harmonian toxou te kai luras.*
>
> The one ... is brought together by opposition with itself,
> like the harmony of the bow and the lyre.
> —Heraclitus, in Plato, *Symposion*, 187a[4]

What I am trying to demythicize is the deeply anchored belief that the true and the one are convertible: *vernum et unum convertuntur* was the traditional formulation.[5] It reaches even as far as the curious etymology of Theodoricus of Chartres: *unitas quasi ontitas ab on graeco, id est entitas* (un-ity amounts to *on-ity* [be-ingness] from *ōn* [be-ing] in Greek—that is, en-tity [be-ingness]).[6] To understand, then, is to reduce everything to unity and this unity is the oneness of Being. This almost universal insight begins to go astray when interpreted quantitatively. The One is not the counterpart of the Many. *Tò métron* is the first endowment of Reality, according to Socrates.[7] The Bible states that God arranged everything according to measure, number, and weight (but not according to meters, quantities, and gravitation).[8]

In attempting to criticize a utopian single theology of religions, or theology of religion, and at the same time trying to awaken a new awareness, I would ally myself here with one of the most incisive leitmotifs of one branch of the Western tradition[9]—and, obviously, predominant in the East.[10] I would even suggest that this has been the prevalent human vision of Reality and that the belief in a possible exhaustive rational explanation of everything is the exception. The alternative is neither anarchy nor irrationalism (even under the cloak of *Gefühlsphilosophien*). The alternative is a dynamic notion of freedom, of Being, and the radical relativity of everything with everything, so that all our explanations are not only for the time being, because ours is being in time, but also because no Absolute can encompass the complexity of the Real, which is radically free. The Absolute is only absolutely incarnated in the Relative.

It is not enough to say *multa et unum convertuntur,*[11] or to introduce a *coincidentia oppositorum.* It is not convincing to revert to a new individualistic monadology either.[12] These attempts do not assume a dialogical relationship between the One and the Many *(hen kai polla).*[13] With the concepts of quantity and individuation we fail to do justice to the problem. We should introduce other symbols. The one I would choose here is the widespread symbol of *concord,* which as such defies quantification.[14] Neither multiplicity as such nor sheer unity brings about, or even allows, harmony.[15] Harmony implies a constitutive polarity, which cannot be superseded dialectically. It would be destroyed.

Concord is neither oneness nor plurality. It is the dynamism of the Many toward the One without ceasing to be different and without becoming one, and without reaching a higher synthesis. Music is here the paradigm. There is no harmonical accord if there is no plurality of sounds, or if those sounds coalesce in one single note. Neither many nor one, but concord, harmony.

We find this root metaphor almost everywhere from the last mantra of the Ṛg Veda[16] to Chuang Tzu.[17] It is the thought repeated differently by Heraclitus and taken up by Filolaus,[18] commented upon by Ramon Llull,[19] Pico della Mirandola,[20] Cusanus,[21] and so many others,[22] up to St. François de Sales,[23] and lately taken as title for a book by R. C. Zaehner.[24] This leitmotif has been often submerged by the predominant trend of victory and unity.[25] The Christian symbol is the Trinity.

"Yield and overcome," says Lao-tzu.[26] Fight and overcome, echoes the predominant spirit of Western culture: *Veni, vidi, vici,* said Caesar.[27] Make everything *inclusive,* India would say.[28] Make everything *universal,* responds the West. Strive to make everything complete by realizing harmony is what this third tradition is saying.

My motto would then be *concordia discors,* "discordant concord," and it could have as underplay the opposite, "concordant discord," for as the always paradoxical Heraclitus liked to put it: "The mysterious harmony is stronger than the evident one"; or again, "The unspoken harmony is superior to the verbalized one."[29]
But we may still quote:

> *Kai ek tōn diapherontōn*
> *Kallistēn harmonian*
> *Kai panta kath erin ginesthai.*[30]
> (And from divergences
> the most beautiful harmony [arises],
> and all happens through struggle.)[31]

It is the same Heraclitus who praises harmony as the result of polarity.[32] He formulates it in the most general way: "Nature aspires to the opposite. It is from there and not from the equal that harmony is produced."[33]

This is insight into the agonic character of Reality.[34] In point of fact this experience is not as uncommon as one might assume.[35] It lasted until our times.[36] It was with Descartes that divergency of opinions created philosophical anguish. It was the beginning of the modern age. I should like to insist on this. Diversity of opinions becomes disturbing once we direct our attention to mere orthodoxy severed from orthopraxis, and the former is thought to express the essence of being human. Once we take individualism for granted, we find it scandalous that there is diversity of opinions—forgetting the beautiful metaphor of Fernando de Rojas.[37] It is the estrangement of the human mind from nature that leads to the assumption that univocity is the ideal. Thinking begins to be understood as measuring, calculating.

I have quoted these texts in order to suggest the spirit and the method in which I would like to situate the entire enterprise. I have on purpose quoted mainly from the Western tradition, because I have been criticizing mainly a Western theory and attempting to enter into dialogue with it. I am far from wanting to reduce all to any unity.

We hear of a friendly enmity, of a polarity between concord and discord, and a link between the two; we hear of a discordant concord, of the fundamental thrust of nature toward diversity, and we try to understand that true concord is not unity of opinion or equality of intellectual views, but of an order higher than the intellect, for it entails precisely struggle, strife, antagonic dynamisms—*agōn* the Greeks would say, as already indicated.

Discordia is disagreement—literally, setting our hearts at variance, and yet not asunder. Why? Obviously because we do not absolutize our opinions, or identify our being with our "thoughts," because we realize that, by my pushing in one direction and your pushing in the opposite, world order is maintained and given the impulse of its proper dynamism.

The very words by which we often express what we are striving for—"unanimity," "consensus," "agreement," "concord"—all have a cordial or an existential core. One *animus* does not mean one single theory, one single opinion, but one aspiration (in the literal sense of one breath) and one inspiration (as one spirit).[38] Consensus ultimately means to walk in the same direction, not to have just one rational view.[39] And again, to reach agreement suggests to be agreeable, to be pleasant, to find pleasure in being together.[40] Concord is to put our hearts together.

Another word for harmony may be *sympathy,* which does not primarily mean individual, sentimental compassion, but the common *pathos* among all the constituents of Reality. Universal sympathy is another way of overcoming the split between individual and collective interests, the one and the many. And the word here suggests not only a more "feminine" receptivity for a predominantly "masculine" culture, but also a greater awareness of the mystery of suffering (pathos, *duḥkha*) in a civilization that shuns facing this most elemental factor, which awakens us to transcendence and interiority.

This is the discordant concord: a kind of human harmony perceived in and through the many discordant voices of human traditions. We do not want to reduce them to one voice. We may yet want to eliminate cacophonies. But this again depends very much on the education and generosity of our ears.

All this should not be taken as a mere metaphor. If we live only or even mainly on the values of the eye, the intellect, truth, and we neglect—on that ultimate level—the other senses, the heart, beauty— in a word, the concrete over against the general—we shall live a crippled life. Academia, scholarship, and modern education in general, let alone *techniculture,* seem to have almost forgotten all those other values that we find still so prominent and effective in other cultures. No need for me to understand what the animist or the Hindu or the Christian ultimately mean when they voice their respective worldviews. We may somewhat enjoy the beauty of the symphony, the inexplicable concord out of so many dissenting voices. Pluralism tells us here that one should not assume for oneself (person or culture) the role of being the conductor of the human and much less of the cosmic orchestra. It is enough with the music (divine), the musicians (the human), and their instruments (the cosmos). Let us play by ear!

Conclusion

I have tried to spell out some of the implications of that attitude. I may sum it up with the word "confidence." I mean by this a certain fundamental trust in Reality, which impels us to trust even what we do not understand or approve of—unless there are positive and concrete reasons to fight what we discover to be evil or

error. To understand that we do not understand is the beginning
of transcending knowledge, as most of the spiritual traditions of
the world will tell us.[41] Further, to understand that the other is
an equal source of understanding, and not only an object of it,
is again what many a school has called the beginning of enlightenment.[42]

It all boils down to the experience of our personal and collective
limitations, including the very limits of the intellect, not only in us,
but in itself. The last function of the intellect is to transcend itself.
And this is possible only by becoming aware of its own limitations—
and this, I submit, not only in every one of us, but in itself. If we
want to reduce everything to consciousness, we are forced to admit
that pure consciousness is not conscious of itself. It would then not
be pure. Brahman does not know that it is Brahman, says Vedānta
coherently. Īśvara knows that "he" is Brahman. The knowledge of
the Father is the Son, the *Logos,* says the Christian Trinity. This
is not irrationalism. It is the highest and intransferable mission of
the intellect, to become aware of its own boundaries. In becoming
conscious(ness) of itself, consciousness becomes conscious(ness) of its
own limits, and by this very fact transcends them. If pure Consciousness is aware of its limits, this amounts to conceding that not All can
be reduced to Consciousness.

Humankind is held together not because we have the same opinions, a common language, the same religion, or even the same respect
for others, but for the same reason that the entire universe is held
together. We mortals strive not only among ourselves, but we also
struggle with the Gods for the order of the universe. And yet this *eris*
(*kāma* and *tapas,* the Vedas would say)[43] is also our responsibility,
our answer to the very challenge. To maintain the world together,
the *lokasaṁgrah* of the *Gītā,*[44] is precisely the function of primordial
dharma, of which humans are active factors.[45]

At Pentecost the peoples did not all speak the same language, nor
did they have simultaneous translation, nor did they understand the
mutual refinements of the respective liturgies. Yet, they were convinced, they felt, they sensed, that all were *hearing* the great deeds
of God, the *megaleia tou Theou.*[46]

This cosmic confidence certainly has an intellectual dimension; I
have been speaking about it on the intellectual level. Yet, it does
not need to be put into words. And it is this cosmic confidence that
stands at the very basis of the dialogical dialogue and makes it possible. The dialogue—we all agree on this—is not a trick, a stratagem
to get to the other, to defeat the partner. There is a basic confidence

that, although we neither understand nor often approve of what others think and do, we still have not given up all hope (which is a virtue of the tempiternal present and not about the temporal future) that human conviviality makes sense, that we belong together, and that together we must strive. Some thinkers may be tempted to say that this is an option. I would prefer to suggest that this is an instinct, the work of the Spirit.[47]

Notes

Introduction

1. Raimundo Panikkar, *Myth, Faith and Hermeneutics* (New York: Paulist Press, 1979), 2.

2. Idem, *Blessed Simplicity* (New York: Seabury Press, 1982), 10.

3. Jawaharlal Nehru invited Mr. Panikkar to join his government in a "cabinet level" position, his son told me, but the elder Panikkar refused.

4. In several instances, Panikkar explains his use of the masculine pronoun to refer to the general. See, for examples, *Myth*, 12–13, and *Simplicity*, 10–11. See, e.g., n. 3 in chapters 1, 2, and 4 below.

5. Said in our dialogue.

6. Panikkar, now retired, splits his time between Spain and India.

7. *Myth*, 10.

8. Said in our dialogue.

9. Raimundo Panikkar, "Religious Pluralism: The Metaphysical Challenge," in *Religious Pluralism*, ed. Leroy S. Rouner (Notre Dame, Ind.: University of Notre Dame Press, 1984), 110.

10. Ibid., 98.

11. *Myth*, 242.

12. Ibid.

13. Raimundo Panikkar, "The Mirage of the Future," *Teilhard Review* 8 (1973): 42.

14. Ibid.

15. *Myth*, 105.

16. Ibid., 232.

17. Ibid., 362–63.

18. "Mirage," 45.

19. Perhaps the distinction is best presented by Panikkar in *Simplicity*, 69–71.

20. *Simplicity*, 12–13.

21. Raimundo Panikkar, *Worship and Secular Man* (Maryknoll, N.Y.: Orbis, 1973), 1.

22. *Myth*, 334 and our dialogue.

23. Cf. particularly: Raimundo Panikkar, *The Trinity and World Religions* (Madras, India: Christian Literature Society, 1970).

24. In *The God Experience,* ed. Joseph P. Whelan, S.J. (New York: Newman Press), 1971.

25. Ibid., 83.

26. Ibid., 87. See also *Myth,* 6, where Panikkar says that the question "Do You Believe in God?" is meaningless.

27. Ibid., 89.

28. Ibid., 91.

29. *Simplicity,* 128.

30. *Myth,* 137.

31. *Trinity,* 17.

32. Ibid., 21–22.

33. Ibid., 24ff.

34. *Myth,* 288.

35. Raimundo Panikkar, "The Myth of Pluralism: The Tower of Babel— A Meditation on Non-Violence," *Cross Currents* 29 (Summer 1979): 205, reproduced here as chapter 4.

36. Ibid., 206.

37. Ibid., 205.

38. See especially chapter 5 in this volume.

39. "Religious Pluralism," 111.

40. In *Teilhard and the Unity of Knowledge,* ed. Thomas M. King and James F. Salmon (New York: Paulist Press, 1983), 83–141. See chapter 8 in this volume.

41. Ibid., 85.

42. Ibid., 85–86.

43. Harry James Cargas, *Harry James Cargas in Conversation with Elie Wiesel* (New York, 1976).

44. Cf. Raimundo Panikkar, "Letter from the Holy Mount Athos," *Sobornost* 4 (1965).

45. *Simplicity,* 45.

46. See, for example, *Simplicity,* 123.

47. Ibid.

48. *Myth,* 72.

49. Ibid., 82.

50. *Worship,* 34.

51. *Myth,* 373.

52. See Viktor Frankl, *The Unconscious God* (New York: Simon and Schuster, 1975). He writes on page 29: "As long as we speak only of body, and psyche, wholeness has not yet come in."

53. He says this in many ways including in *The Divine Milieu* (New York: Harper Brothers, 1960), 29: "...we bring to Christ a little fulfillment."

54. Nikos Kazantzakis, *The Saviors of God* (New York: Simon and Schuster, 1960), 74.

55. Par Lagerkvist, *Evening Land* (Detroit: Wayne State University Press, 1975), 117.

56. *Myth,* 147.
57. Ibid.
58. Ibid., 379.
59. *Simplicity,* 131.
60. *Myth,* 436.
61. Ibid., 437.
62. Ibid., 448.
63. Ibid., 447.
64. Ibid., 440.

Chapter 1. The Contemplative Mood

1. Cf. Blessed Callistus of Xanthopoulos, Patriarch and monk of Mount Athos, in his texts on prayer. See *Writings from the Philokalia on Prayer of the Heart,* trans. from the Russian text, "Dobrotolubiye," by E. Kadloubovsky and G. E. H. Palmer (London: Faber, 1951, 1977), 272.

2. Luke 23:43.

3. *Man* with a capital *M* will stand for the human being as such (*anthropos, puruṣa,* person, *Mensch*), for I would like to prevent that male monopoly which makes women second-rate humans by calling them women. The plural adjectives and pronouns used to avoid the gender will not do, and to split Man into male and female, he and she, is also not convincing because the sex differentiation is not the only possible division of Man, perhaps not even the most important one. Certainly the whole (Man) is more than its parts (male and female).

4. Cf. v.g. Predigt 26 (*Deutsche Werk* II, 26–27), Predigt 41 (*DW* II, 249) and *passim* as given in the critical edition, ed. Quint (Stuttgart: Kohlhammer, 1936).

5. Quoted by the monks Callistus and Ignatius, "Directions to Hesychasts," in *Writings from the Philokalia,* 220. Cf. also Chrysostom: "Thus abide constantly with the name of our Lord Jesus Christ, so that the heart swallows the Lord and the Lord the heart, and the two become one." Ibid., 223.

6. Ramana Maharshi.

7. John 14:9.

8. "The Ultimate Reality is this world and this world is the Ultimate Reality: there is not the slightest difference between the two." The astonishing insight of Nāgārjuna in the *Mādhyamika-kārikā* XXV, 19–20. Cf. also, for similar insights, the rich tradition of Kashmir Śaivism, and its principal figure, the post and philosopher Abhinavagupta. There the formula is to see *vikalpa* (the world of differentiation) in *nirvikalpa* (the undifferentiated, Ultimate Reality) and *nirvikalpa* in *vikalpa.* Cf. Silburn translation and commentary, *Hymnes de Abhinavagupta* (Paris: L'Institut de Civilisation Indienne, 1970), 36.

9. And also Bistami. Cf. other references in G. C. Anawati, L. Gardet, *Mistica islamica* (Turin: S.E.I., 1960), 173, etc. Cf. also the chapter "Rābi a, chantre du pur amour" in L. Gardet, *Expériences mystiques en terres non-chretiennes* (Paris: Alnatia, 1953), 101–14.

10. TU II, 9.

11. Cf. v.g. BG II, 50.

12. TU II, 9, Cf. also BU IV, 3, 22 and MaitU VI, 18.

13. Cf. Panikkar, "The New Innocence," in *Cross Currents* 27, no. 1 (Spring 1977): 7–15.

14. St. Isaac, quoted by Callistus and Ignatius, in *Writings from the Philokalia*, 219.

15. Cf. Matt. 6:10.

16. Fuṣūṣ al-hikam XVI.

17. Cf. Taishö 45, 500b. The saying is attributed to Nāgārjuna.

18. Dogma (in Latin *placita*) comes from the Greek word *dokéo*, which signifies "that which appears to be," and whose first translation is "opinion." Cf. my discussion in *Religión y Religiones* (Madrid: Gredos, 1965), 76–77. *Contemplāre* is Cicero's translation of the Greek *theoria*, "to see."

19. *De Deo abscondito*, 3.

20. The Spanish text was anonymous for fear of the Inquisition. It has been attributed to St. Teresa, among others. Cf. BG III, 4; IV, 20; XVIII, 49; *Dīgha-nikāya* III, 275.

21. Ritual phrase of the *Brāhmaṇás*.

22. Matt. 5:3.

23. Cf. R. Panikkar, "Is There Place for the *Temple* in the Modern City?" in *Changing Perception of Developmental Problems*, vol. 1 of United Nations Center for Regional Development, *Regional Development Series*, ed. R. P. Misra and M. Honjo (Singapore: Maruzen Pte. Ltd., 1981), 275–88.

24. Cf. Panikkar, "El presente tempiterno: Una apostilla a la historia de la salvación y a la teología de la liberación," in *Teología y mundo contemporáneo*, ed. A. Vargas Machuca (Madrid: Cristiandad, 1975), 133–75; and, for a more general study of time and the mysticism of time, my "Time and Sacrifice: The Sacrifice of Time and the Ritual of Modernity" in *The Study of Time III*, ed. J. T. Fraser (New York: Springer, 1978), 683–727.

25. Cf. Ch. Vaudville, *Kabīr* (Oxford: Oxford University Press, 1974), 267.

26. Cf. Matt. 6:34.

27. *Llibre de contemplacio* I, 2: "*molt se deu alegrar l'home per ço com es en ésser.*" The first chapter, of course, deals with the human joy that God is; and the third because the neighbor is. "*Philosophus semper est laetus*" (the philosopher is always happy) he adds in his *Liber Proverbiorum* (*editio moguntina* VI, int. V, 122 in Sala-Moliris, 1974, 113. He begins his *Llibre dels mil proverbis* with a proverb on joy: "*Haja's u alegre, per ço car Deus es tot bo e complit.*" (Be happy for this, that God is good and perfect.) Cf. also my *La gioia pasquale* (Vicenza: la Locusta, 1968).

28. *Exposition Sancti Evangelii sec. Iohannem*, no. 8 (Owit and Koch, 1936,L.W. III, 9). For a recent selection of English translations of some astonishing Latin texts (including commentary on the Prologue to St. John, see the recent *Meister Eckhart: The Essential Sermons, Commentaries, Treatises, and Defense*, trans. and intro. Edmund Colledge and Bernard McGinn, Classics of Western Spirituality (New York: Paulist Press, 1981).

29. Quoted in H. H. Brinton, *The Mystic Will* (New York: Macmillan, 1930), 252.

30. Cf. a remarkable text of Kashmir Śaivism, the *Spandanirṇaya* of Kṣemarāja, I, 21: *"Vastutas tu na kiṃcid udeti vyayate vā kevalaṃ spandaśaktir eva bhagavaty akramāpi tathāthatābhāsarupatayā sphuranty udetīva vyayataiva ca."* ("In reality, nothing comes forth [into existence], nothing disappears; there is nothing [in this universe] but the illustrious vibrating energy [*spanda*] which, even though free of all temporal succession, reveals itself in diverse appearances. To say that it comes forth and disappears is pure metaphor.") Quoted in Silburn, *Hymnes*, 29.

31. Matt. 26:10.

32. Cf. in the collection Classics of Western Spirituality *Francis and Clare*, Regis J. Armstrong and Ignatius C. Brady, eds. (New York: Paulist Press, 1982), 165–66. For another account of the Perfect Joy discourse of St. Francis: see Johannes Jorgensen, *St. Francis of Assisi: A Biography*, trans. from the Danish by T. O'Conor Sloane (New York: Image Books, 1955), 108–10.

33. *Proverbios y Cantares*, V.

34. *Duineser Elegien: Die Siebente Elegie*, 1. 51.

35. *Dhammapada*, 315.

36. *Svadharma* is one's professional duty fulfilled with skill (Cf. BG II, 31) and in harmony with one's own personal nature (BG XVIII, 47); being faithful to one's own being.

37. 2 Thess. 3:10—although the context here is different.

38. Thomas Merton, *New Seeds of Contemplation* (New York: New Directions, 1961), 29.

39. *Llibre d'amic e amat*, 56: *"—E qui es ton maestre?—. Respos, e dix que les significances que les creatures donen de son amat."* Cf. also St. Bonaventure, *Breviloquium*. I, 5, 2.

40. TU III, 1–2; 6–10. For my commentary on these remarkable texts cf. Panikkar, *The Vedic Experience: Mantramañjarī* (Berkeley and Los Angeles: University of California Press, 1977), 224–37.

41. BG III, 4; IV, 20; XVIII, 49.

42. Christians should remember that they have been sent to a world which is not the fruit of their labor (John 4:38). They have been presented the lilies as ideal for their lives, and reminded that lilies neither work nor weave (Matt. 6:28; Luke 12:27). Those who have labored the entire day receive the same pay as those who have toiled only for an hour (Matt. 20:1ff). It is for this reason that I have elsewhere elaborated the distinction between labor and work. Labor would be an activity for producing some external

good: *poiêsis.* Work is rather similar to *praxis,* that activity which enhances the very quality of the doer. Labor is to put my skills at the service of something (or someone) with which (or whom) I am not really concerned (except for the money or other benefits I receive, of course). Work is creativity. But in this chapter I have mostly followed the current use of the words.

43. Cf., for this problematic treated with regard to "Human Rights," Panikkar, "Is the Notion of Human Rights a Western Concept?" in *Diogenes* (Florence, Casalini Libri), 120 (Winter 1982): 75–102, reproduced as chapter 7 in this volume.

44. A young man once wrote to a famous columnist of a North American newspaper: "I have refused a promotion, I am happy with what I have." "You bastard!" was the reply, "do you think that this is the way we have made this country great?"

45. Cf. R. Panikkar, *Blessed Simplicity* (New York: Seabury Press, 1982).

46. Laudi LX. Cf. also Angelus Silesius, *Der cherubinische Wandersmann,* I, 289: *"Die Ros ist ohn warum, sie blühet, weil sie blühet."* And cf. Meister Eckhart, already cited.

47. It is not for me now to delimit the boundaries or to stress the difficulties of such an attitude. Rather, my concern has been to underscore the threat it represents to the present-day modern ideology (and even psychology). It is here that we meet the "hidden enemies..."

48. We may see the peculiar tension between the activity of the mind and discursive reason (Logos) and the ineffable experience of the divine light, had by so many mystics, in the following text of Philotheus of Sinai. After speaking of the "tasting" of divine light, he goes on: "This light, which draws the mind as the sun draws the eyes, this light, inexplicable in itself, which however becomes explicable, only not in words but by experience of him who receives its influence, or rather who is wounded by it—this light commands me to be silent, although the mind would still have enjoyed conversing on the subject." *Writings from the Philokalia,* 334. Cf. the classical notion of *svādhyāya* in Jainism and Hinduism. Cf. v.g. TU I, 9, 1, and in the Western monastic tradition, *lectio divina.*

49. Cf. the Sanskrit word *gati,* which denotes both the way and the goal.

50. Augustine, *Confessions,* XIII, 9.

51. Samuel Butler as quoted in S. J. Gould's *The Panda's Thumb* and approved by P. B. Medawar, *New York Review of Books* 28, no. 4 (March 19, 1981): 53.

Chapter 2. Action and Contemplation as Categories of Religious Understanding

1. *"Perdam sapientiam sapientium, et prudentiam prudentium reprobabo."* Cf. Isa. 29:14; Ps. 33:10. Practically all traditional Scriptures as well as oral traditions of Mankind are full of such statements, which have so often been interpreted hyperbolically by scribes and pandits.

2. *"...nisi circumcidamini..., non potestis salvari."*

3. When I write *Man* I also mean *woman*, just as when I use the masculine "he" I also mean "she." I would not like to split the androgenous character of the human being, and so do not use the grammatical masculine as a sign for male or neuter, but as a human, androgenous symbol—which was, incidentally, the original meaning of most "masculine" words. Grammatical gender refers to function and not to sex.

4. Cf. also "He who knows (sees) the supreme Brahman becomes Brahman." in MundU III, 2, 9. Interestingly enough, it was this passage which Anquetil Duperron, the first translator of the Upanishads into Latin in 1801, put as the motto of the whole work: *"Quisquis Deum intelligit, Deus fit."*

5. *"Quam dabit homo commutationem pro anima sua?"* Cf. the previous sentence: "What will a man gain by winning the whole world, at the cost of his true self?" (NEB).

6. Cf. my study "Verstehen als Uberzeugtsein" in *Neue Anthropologie*, ed. H. G. Gadamer and P. Vogler (Stuttgart, 1974), 132–67.

7. Cf. my studies, Panikkar, *Kultmysterium in Hinduismus und Christentum* (Freiburg, Munich: Alber, 1964), and a French revised translation, *Le mystère du culte dans l'hinduisme et le christianisme* (Paris: Cerf, 1970); "Aktion und Kontemplation im indischen Kultmysterium," *Una Sancta* (Freising) 2 (1966): 145–50, and "The Supreme Experience: The Ways of East and West" in *Myth, Faith and Hermeneutics* (New York: Paulist Press, 1979), 292–317.

8. Cf. my article "Faith and Belief: A Multireligious Experience," in Panikkar, *The Intrareligious Dialogue* (New York: Paulist Press, 1978), 1–23.

9. Cf. my essay *L'homme qui devient Dieu* (Paris: Aubier, 1970), and in abridged form "Faith as a Constitutive Human Dimension" in Panikkar, *Myth, Faith and Heremeneutics*, 188–229.

10. It may be noted that the Christian view, which believes in the Resurrection, is more that of a *postmortal life* than that of an immortal soul.

11. I may be allowed to draw the materials of the following paragraphs, as well as the supporting authorities, from my studies "Algunos aspectos de la spiritualidad hindú," in *Historia de la Espiritualidad*, ed. L. Sala Balust and B. Jimenez Duque (Barcelona: Flors, 1969), 433–542; "La loi du Karma et la dimension historique de l'Homme," in *La théologie de l'histoire: Herméneutique et eschatologie*, ed. E. Castelli (Paris: Aubier, 1971), 205–30; "Comparative Philosophy and the Theory of Karma," *Journal of the Ganganatha Jha Kendriya Sanskrit Vidyapeetha* 28 (January–April 1972), Parts 1–2 (1972): 475–85; and the English translation and revision of the Castelli paper, "The Law of *Karman* and the Historical Dimension of Man," in *Myth, Faith and Hermeneutics*, 361–68.

12. Cf. Richard of St. Victor in his *De Trinitate*, IV, 12: *"Qui est enim existere, nisi ex aliquo sistere, hoc est, substantialiter ex aliquo esse?"* (Migne, PL 196, 937).

13. Cf. BU III, 2, 1.

14. Cf. 1 Cor. 15:22: "As in Adam all die, so in Christ all will be made alive."

15. Cf. my studies on this subject: *Die Vielen Götter und der eine Herr: Beiträge zum Ökumenischen Gespräch der Weltreligionen* (Weilheim: Barth, 1963). *The Unknown Christ of Hinduism*, subtitled "Toward an Ecumenical Christophany" (London: Darton, Longman and Todd; and Maryknoll, N.Y.: Orbis, 1981). *Mâyâ e Apocalisse, L'incontro dell'Induismo e del Cristianismo* (Rome: Abete, 1966); *Kerygma und Indien: Zur heilsgeschichtlichen Problematik der christlichen Begegnung mit Indien* (Hamburg: Reich Verlag, 1967); *Offenbarung und Verkündigung: Indische Briefe* (Freiburg: Herder, 1976); "Christianity and World Religions," in *Christianity* (Patiala: Punjabi University, 1969), 78–127; "The Relation of the Gospels to Hindu Culture and Religion," in *Jesus and Man's Hope*, vol. 2 (Pittsburgh: Pittsburgh Theological Seminary, 1971), 247–61; "The Meaning of Christ's Name in the Universal Economy of Salvation," in *Evangelization, Dialogue and Development* (Rome:,1972), 195–218; "Christians and So-called 'Non-Christians,'" *Cross Currents* 22, no. 3 (Summer–Fall 1972): 281–308; "Ṛtatattva: A Preface to a Hindu-Christian Theology," *Jeevadhara* (Kottayam) 9, no. 49 (January–February 1979): 6–63, and "Man and Religion: A Dialogue with Panikkar," 11, no. 61 (1981): 5–32.

16. Cf. my forthcoming *Christophany* published as *Cristofania* (Bologna: EDB, 1994), where these main ideas are expanded and also given the necessary support of tradition and philosophy.

17. Gal. 2:20. Cf. also Col. 3:3; etc.

18. Cf. John 1:13–14.

19. John 14:9.

20. Cf. my *El Silencio del Dios: Un mensaje del Buddha al mundo actual—Contribución al estudio del ateismo religioso* (Madrid: Guadiana, 1970), 179–87, 213–28.

21. *ouk estin ōde, ēgerthē gar; non est hic. surexit enim!* Matt. 28:6; cf. Luke 24:6. In Mark 16:6, it is said in a more forceful and shorter way: "He is risen, he is not here"; *ēgerthē, ouk estin ōde; surexit, non est hic.* We should say in English either "He is risen" (AV and RV) or "He has been raised" or "was raised," but it is more difficult to admit "He has been raised again" (NEB).

22. Cf. John 16:7.

23. Cf. Matt. 24:23–27.

24. Cf. Matt. 15:31ff.

25. *Resurrexi, et adhuc tecum.* Introit to the Easter Liturgy of the Latin rite. Cf. Ps. 138 (139):18.

26. Cf. Luke 24:31.

27. *Non omnis, qui dicit mihi, Domine, Domine intrabit in regnum caelorum; sed qui facit voluntatem Patris mei...*

28. Only Begotten: *Monogenēs;* cf. John 1:14; 1:18; 3:16; Heb. 11:17;

1 John 4:9. Firstborn: *Prōtotokos;* cf. Rom. 8:29; Col. 1:15: 1:18; Heb. 1:6; Rev. 1:5.

29. Cf. the *prathamajā ṛtasya* in RV I, 164, 37; AV II, 1, 4.

30. Cf., for a general treatment of the problem, my essay "The Rules of the Game in the Religious Encounter," *Intrareligious Dialogue* (New York: Paulist, 1978), 25–37.

31. Cf. my early treatment of this problematic in my Indian letters, *Offenbarung und Verkündigung,* 48–55.

32. Cf. my essay "The Dream of an Indian Ecclesiology," *Searching for an Indian Ecclesiology,* ed. G. van Leuwen (The Statement, Papers and the Proceedings of the Seventh Annual Meeting of the Indian Theological Association, Nagpur, October 21–23, 1983; Bangalore: ATC, 1984), 24–54.

33. Cf. Matt. 6:34.

34. Cf. BU II, 4, 14.

35. Cf. 1 Cor. 1:18 sq.

36. This contemplative vision of the radical interdependence of all things is the central intuition of Buddhism. See my discussion of this in *The Silence of God: The Answer of the Buddha* (Maryknoll, N.Y.: Orbis, 1989).

Chapter 3. Word of Silence

1. TB II, 8, 8, 5. Cf. Raimundo Panikkar, trans. and ed., *Vedic Experience* (Berkeley: University of California Press, 1977), 88–94.

2. TMB XX, 14, 2.

3. BU I, 3, 21.

4. Cf. BU IV, 1, 2.

5. RV VIII, 75, 6.

6. AV IV, I, 1. The "Sacred Word" is here *brahman.*

7. AB II, 38.

8. SB X, 6, 5, 5. Cf. BU I, 2, 5.

9. TB II, 8, 8, 4.

10. Cf. Panikkar, *The Silence of God: The Answer of the Buddha* (Maryknoll, N.Y.: Orbis, 1989), which will exonerate us from further quotations.

11. With apologies to semantics.

12. Cf. Panikkar, "Words and Terms" in *Esistenza, Mito, Ermeneutica* (Scritti per Enrico Castelli), ed. M. M. Olivetti, Archivio di Filosofia 2 (Padova: CEDAM, 1980), 117–33.

13. Cf. Panikkar, "Per una lettura transculturale del simbolo," *Quaderni di psicoterapia infantile* (Rome: Borla, 1981): 53–91.

14. Cf. J. Bierhorst, *In the Trial of the Wind: American Indian Poems and Ritual Orations* (New York: Farrar, Straus and Giroux, 1971), 3.

15. Cf. The Hymn of Origins, RV X, 129, and commentary in *Vedic Experience,* 54–59.

16. SB I, 4, 5, 8–12.

17. Cf. Panikkar, *The Trinity and the Religious Experience of Man*, 2d ed. (London: Darton, Longman and Todd, 1973; reprint Maryknoll, N.Y.: Orbis, 1975).

18. BU I, 4, 1 sq.; cf. Kaus U I, 6, for the right place of the *He:* "What you are that am I" (*vas tvam asi so'ham asmi*).

19. Cf. CU VIII, 7, 1 sq.

20. *Ardhanārīśvara:* a tantric and purāṇic androgynous conception: the Lord as half woman and half male.

21. Cf. Panikkar, "Changer la vie ensemble," *Monchanin information* 2, no. 2 (Montreal, 1969): 4–5. Cf. the biblical theme of Yahweh and Israel and the Christian dogma of the Incarnation.

22. Cf. Panikkar, *Kultmysterium in Hinduismus und Christentum: Ein Beitrag zur vergleichenden Religionstheologie* (Freiburg, Munich: Alber, 1964), 124–42.

Chapter 4. The Myth of Pluralism

1. The three names are connected: Babel means *megalē polis,* the Great City; Babylon is *Bab-ilim,* the Gate of God with the connotations of "confusion" and "stranger"; Barbara is *Barbaru* from the Indo-European root *balbal* (*babal*), to stammer.

2. Following the usual English norm of capitalizing concrete and proper names, I include also those names which no longer appear as common from a cross-cultural viewpoint, like Modern, Atheist, Technocrat, or Humanist.

3. I shall be using the word "Man" guardedly to refer to the entire human being, irrespective of gender. Calling women *wīf-mann* is more derogatory than calling the whole species "Man" and recognizing that males have no monopoly on being human. When I say "Man," therefore, or use the masculine pronoun as the case requires it, I mean *anthropos*— the human being as distinct from the Gods—shortcomings of grammar notwithstanding.

Chapter 6. Philosophy and Revolution

1. Contemporary literature on the subject is overwhelming. The notes throughout this article are intended as a cursory and elementary bibliographical survey. L. Mendieta y Nuñez, *Teoría de la Revolución* (Mexico City: Biblioteca de Ensayos Sociológicos, Universidad Nacional, 1958), 10 and passim; C. Brinkmann, *Soziologische Theorie der Revolution* (Göttingen: Vandenhoeck und Ruprecht, 1948); Chalmers A. Johnson, *Revolution and the Social System* (Palo Alto, Calif.: The Hoover Institution, Stanford University, 1964); Chalmers A. Johnson, *Revolutionary Change* (Boston: Little, Brown and Co., 1966); B. Mazlish, Arthur D. Kaledin, and David B. Ralston, eds., *Revolution: A Reader* (New York: Macmillan,

1971); M. A. Kaplan, ed. *The Revolution in World Politics* (New York: John Wiley and Sons, 1962).

2. Antoine C. Condorcet: "The word 'revolutionary' can be applied only to revolutions whose aim is freedom," "Sur le sens du mot révolutionnaire," in *Oeuvres* 12 (Paris: 1847–1849): 21.

3. Cf. the contemporary trends of Latin American theology, for instance, the journal *Cristianismo y Sociedad* (Montevideo) in most of its recent issues, and also J. Pablo, *Mística, desarrollo y revolución* (Montevideo: Mundo Nuevo, 1969); J. Petras and M. Zeitlin, eds., *Latin America— Reform or Revolution?* (New York: Fawcett, 1968); and the many writings of G. Gutiérrez Merino and J. Míguez Bonino. Cf. also the 159 bibliographical items compiled by Fidel González V., "Revolución en América Latina" (Cuernavaca, 1968), the following recent contributions:

Alfaro, Juan. *Cristología y anthroplogía.* Madrid: Cristiandad, 1973.

———. *Esperanza cristiana y liberación del hombre.* Barcelona: Herder and Herder, 1972.

Assmann, Hugo. *Opresión-liberación: Desafío a los cristianos.* Montevideo: Tierra Nueva, 1971.

———. *Theology for a Nomad Church.* Maryknoll, N.Y.: Orbis, 1976.

Balasuriya, Tissa. *The Eucharist and Human Liberation.* Maryknoll, N.Y.: Orbis, 1979.

Boff, Leonardo. *Jesus Christ Liberator.* Maryknoll, N.Y.: Orbis, 1978.

———. *O evangelho do Cristo cósmico.* Petropolis, 1970.

———. *Vida religiosa e a Igreja no processo de liberatação.* Petropolis, 1975.

Comblin, José. *Théologie de la révolution.* Paris: Editions Universitaires, 1970.

Dussel, Enrique. *Caminos de liberación latinoamericana: Interpretación histórica de nuestro continente latinoamericano.* 2 vols. Buenos Aires: Latino-américa Libros, 1972–73.

———. *History and the Theology of Liberation.* Maryknoll, N.Y.: Orbis, 1976.

———. *Filosofía de la Liberación.* Mexico: Editorial Edicol, S.A., 1977.

———. *Para una ética de la liberación latinoamericana.* 3 vols. Mexico City: Siglo Veintiuno, 1973.

Eagleson, John, ed. *Christians and Socialism: Documentation of the Christians for Socialism Movement in Latin America.* Maryknoll, N.Y.: Orbis, 1975.

Ellacuría, Ignacio. *Freedom Made Flesh: The Mission of Christ and His Church.* Maryknoll, N.Y.: Orbis, 1976.

Gibellini, Rosino, ed. *Frontiers of Theology in Latin America.* Maryknoll, N.Y.: Orbis, 1979.

Gutiérrez, Gustavo. *Praxis de liberación y fe cristiana.* Madrid: ZYX, 1974.

———. *Teología de la liberación: Perspectivas.* Lima: CEP, 1971. Cf. also *A Theology of Liberation: History, Politics and Salvation.* Maryknoll, N.Y.: Orbis, 1973.

Gutiérrez, G., J. L. Segundo, S. Croatto, B. Catâo, and J. Comblin. *Salvación y construcción del mundo.* Santiago: Nova Terra, 1968.

Míguez Bonino, José. *Christians and Marxists: The Mutual Challenge to Revolution.* Grand Rapids, Mich.: Wm. B. Eerdmans, 1976.

Miranda, José Porfirio. *Marx y la biblia: Crítica a la filosofía de la opresión.* Salamanca: Sígueme, 1971. Cf. also *Marx and the Bible: A Critique of the Philosophy of Oppression.* Maryknoll, N.Y.: Orbis, 1974.

Sobrino, Jon. *Cristología desde América Latina: Esbozo a partir del seguimiento del Jésus histórico.* Mexico City: CRT, 1976. Cf. also *Christology at the Crossroads* Maryknoll, N.Y.: Orbis, 1978.

Segundo, J. L. *Masas y minorías en la dialéctica divina de la liberación.* Buenos Aires: La Aurora, 1973.

———. *Liberación de la teología.* Buenos Aires: Carlos Lohlé, 1975. Cf. also *The Liberation of Theology.* Maryknoll, N.Y.: Orbis, 1976.

For an application of the above Latin American problematic to the Asian context see the excellent book by Aloysius Pieris, S.J., *An Asian Theology of Liberation* (Maryknoll, N.Y.: Orbis, 1988).

4. Cf. G. F. Lucini, "Teologia della Rivoluzione," *Contributi dell'Istituto di Filosofia,* Series 3, Philosophy 15, vol. 2 (Milan: Vita e Pensiero, 1972): 195–221.

5. *"El revolucionario, en cambio, no se rebela contra los abusos, sino contra los usos,"* J. Ortega y Gasset, *El tema de nuestro tiempo* (2d ed. of the 4th original edition) (Buenos Aires: Espasa-Calpe Argentina, 1939), 102.

6. If "the ends which Buddhism seeks to realize are outside of any social or historical contexts" [R. Puligandla and K. Puhakka, "Buddhism and Revolution," *Philosophy East and West* 20, no. 4 (October 1970): 354], we have hardly to do with a theory of revolution but with a worldview which makes modern Western revolutions meaningless.

7. Contemporary studies are more precise in applying the word "revolution" than a few decades ago. Cf., for example, the difference from "revolt" by J. Ellul, *Autopsie de la Révolution* (Paris: Calmann-Lévy, 1969), 129: "*Pour que la révolution se dégage de sa confusion avec la révolte, pour qu'elle cesse d'être le tremendum mysterium, pour qu'elle apparaisse comme une action raisonnable, il fallait que l'homme cessât de vivre sa misère et l'injustice comme un destin, et qu'il apprenne qu'elle est une 'condition,' sa condition que, par conséquent il ne dépend pas de puissances, mais du jeu objectif, explicable, d'un certain nombre de facteurs sociologiques, de décisions purement humaines de rapports politiques, de structures économiques: à ce moment, les possibilités de changer sa condition sont (en apparence) à sa hauteur, à son niveau, a portée de sa main.*"

"The modern concept of revolution, intrinsically bound up with the notion that the course of history suddenly begins anew, that an entirely new story, a story never known or told before, is about to unfold, was unknown prior to the two great revolutions at the end of the eighteenth century." H. Arendt, *On Revolution*, 3d ed. (New York: Viking Compass Edition, 1965), 21.

8. Only with an introductory chapter on "A Role for History" can Thomas S. Kuhn write on *The Structure of Scientific Revolutions*, 2d ed. (Chicago: University of Chicago Press, 1970). Cf. also V. Mathieu, "La sécularisation profane" in *Herméneutique de la sécularisation*, ed. E. Castelli (Paris: Aubier, 1976), 20: "*A ce point-là, la* conditio sine qua non *de la sécularisation est la révolution.*" For Mathieu "sécularisation" is what I call *secularism* (as opposed to *secularity*), i.e., the "degradation" of the absolute to our level. From this viewpoint, because the just society or the perfect human order is not "here" at our fingertips, we have no other option than that of reversing it, "turning it on its head," to use Marx's phrase. Secularism has no "patience."

9. Cf. R. Panikkar, "Die Philosophie in der geistigen Situation der Zeit," *Akten des XIV. Internationalen Kongresses für Philosophie*, Vienna, 2–9 September 1968 (Vienna: Herder, 1968): 75–87.

10. Cf. my chapter "Necesidad de una nueva orientación de la filosofía india" in *Misterio y Revelación* (Madrid: Marova, 1971), for further elaboration.

11. Cf., for example, the many institutions today and projects dedicated to religion and social change.

12. For the concept of *ontonomy* over against heteronomy and autonomy, cf. R. Panikkar, "Le concept d'ontonomie," in *Actes de XIe. Congrès International de Philosophie* 3 (Louvain: Nauwelaerts, 1953): 182–88.

13. Cf. the autobiography of the "Frontier Gandhi," Badshan Khan, *My Life and Struggle*, Delhi (Hind Pocket Books, Orient without date): "A revolution is like a flood, it can bring blessings, but it can also bring devastation; it can bring fertility and prosperity, but it can also bring ruin. Only a nation that is awake, whose people are aware of themselves as a nation, where all live together as brothers, in harmony and love, only that nation, I tell you, will benefit by the revolution.

"A revolution is like a flood. If the people are vigilant they will be ready for the flood and when it comes the whole nation will move along with it. And like the flood, when it subsides, it leaves fertile fields behind, so the revolution, when it is over, leaves the ground clear for the reconstruction of the nation. But if the people are asleep, indifferent to each other and indifferent to the country, the whole nation will be swept away by the flood, by the revolution when it comes" (p. 94). Then again: "I have been told that Amanullah Khan used to call himself the revolutionary King of the Pakhtuns. And indeed it was he who inspired us with the idea of the revolution. But the Afghans did not take as much advantage of it as we did, because they were asleep and we were beginning to wake up" (p. 95).

14. Cf. Gabriel Marcel, "L'homme révolté," a philosophical study of Camus's *L'homme révolté*, in *Homo Viator* (Paris: Aubier, 1944).

15. As far back as 1921, Ortega y Gasset said, "*La revolución no es la barricada, sino un estado de espíritu. Este estado de espíritu no se produce en cualquier tiempo...*" (*El tema de nuestro tiempo*, 101).

16. The following Sanskrit words are given under *revolution*, but not all refer to a political revolution: *parivartana*: causing to turn around, revolved, end of a period of time (cyclic conception); *parivṛtti*: turning, rolling; end, termination; *āvartana*: circular motion, stirring; *āvṛtti*: turning back, reversion, retreat; *āvarta*: turning round; *vivarta*: modification, transformation (and significantly enough the vedāntic meaning of illusion); *vivartana*: turn, change, causing to turn or to change, overturning; *parāvṛtti*: turning back, change, exchange.

All the words refer first to a circular conception of cosmos and history (most of these "revolutions" refer to the movement of the planets etc.). They have hardly been used in the sense of a political revolution or total change of society. For the latter, the following rather artificial terms have been created (maybe only by Monier Williams): *rājyaparivartana*, *rājyarītiparivartana*, all meaning more or less, the same, that is, a change in government.

The most appropriate word for revolution would be *krānti*, which is used in Hindi in the modern political context. The root is *kram*, to step, to go. *Krānti* originally means going, proceeding, step, overcoming, surpassing. Whereas *krama* means the regular process, succession, order, etc., *krānti* is the intensified form.

17. The modern Anglo-Indian expression "what to do?," a direct translation of the Hindi "*kyā kare*," exasperating as it is felt by so many Westerners (who do not "get things done"), may serve as a popular example of our case in study. What is the use or worth of so much effort to change structures that are ultimately irrelevant? Cf. also my early study of India, *La India: Gente, cultura, creencias* (Madrid: Rialp, 1960), translated into French as *Lettre sur L'Inde* (Tournai: Casterman, 1963) and Italian as *L'India* (Brescia: Morcelliana, 1964), and my forthcoming study *Indra's Cunning*.

18. This is what the *Naxalites* are attempting, perhaps unconsciously, in India today. It is a movement which broke from the Communist Party of India (C.P.I.) in 1967 in quest of a more just answer to the cry of the oppressed. Due to the rooted feudalism of the Indian society and the ruthless repression of the government, they took to violence.

19. One could stretch the meaning of the sentence by S. Jankélévitch, *Révolution et Tradition* (Paris: J. B. Janin, 1947), 13: "*Au point de départ de toute action révolutionnaire il y a ce qu'on peut appeler le 'mythe des origines.'*"

20. Cf. R. Panikkar, "The Law of *Karman* and the Historical Dimension of Man," *Philosophy East and West* 22, no. 1 (January 1972): 25–43.

21. "From the Christian standpoint there is no absolute criterion of liberation within history." P. Abrecht "The Revolution beyond Revolutions," *Anticipation* 9 (October 1971): 39.

22. The contemporary example of Jaya Prakash Narayan is a case in point. In order to strike a note with universal Indian appeal, he could not base his movement on any futuristic ideal, but only on the facts of the present situation. Consequently he would stress the eradication of corruption and call for a radical change in the system of education. The Congress some years ago had a slogan that belonged to this same pattern of emphasis on present facts and not future ideals: *garibi hatao*—"eradicate poverty." But, of course, the Indian scene is immensely complex, and this study does not pretend to be exhaustive of the pluralistic nature of Indian politics. Western categories have taken root in many indigenous movements. It is no wonder, for instance, that Kerala (with its Christian elements) and Bengal (with its "Renaissance" stimulated by the Western impact) are two of the more "revolutionary" of states. Both with a strong Communist Party, a longstanding Communist government in Bengal, a sporadic one in Kerala. And both states have a high degree of literacy. It is also no wonder that the youth—particularly the college youth—should be the most open in all the society to revolution. Cf. "Youth in Revolt," *Jeevadhara*, Kottayam, no. 19 (January–February 1974). But I would like to stress the provisional character of these Western-influenced movements and tackle the question at the deeper level of comparative philosophy and cross-cultural studies.

23. In India, a great section of society strives also to get rid of the overall monopoly of brahmanism. There is a strong movement of the Dalits (downtrodden). They feel they have no place and role in the country at all levels, sociological, political, religious. There is an increasing awakening among them which manifests itself under different forms, for instance of a new political party. At a deeper level, there is a search for their identity leading to a breaking with the Hindu society at large, with institutionalized churches for the Christians—as both never fully integrated them—and the discovery of a new culture and religiousness springing from their roots. Cf., e.g., Prabhakar, ed., *Towards a Dalit Theology* (Delhi: ISPCK, 1989); Ayrookuzhiel, ed., *The Dalit Desiyata* (Delhi: ISPCK, 1990).

Further Bibliography

Abrecht, P. "The Revolution beyond the Revolution." In *Anticipation* (Geneva, W.C.C.) 9 (October 1971): 28–39.

Arendt, H. *On Revolution*. 3d ed. New York: Viking Press, 1966.

Beals, C. *The Nature of Revolution*. New York: Thomas Y. Crowell, 1970.

Brinkmann, C. *Soziologische Theorie der Revolution*. Göttingen: Vandenhoeck and Ruprecht, 1948.

Brinton, C. *The Anatomy of Revolution.* New ed. New York: Random House, Vintage Books, 1965.

Brogan, D. W. *The Price of Revolution.* New York: Grosset and Dunlap, 1966.

Buchanan, S. *On Revolution: A Conversation with J. Lyford.* Santa Barbara, Calif.: Center for the Study of Democratic Institutions, 1962.

Dewart, L. *Christianity and Revolution: The Lesson of Cuba.* New York: Herder and Herder, 1963.

Drimmel, H. *Der konservative Mensch und die Revolution.* Vienna, Munich: Herold, 1970.

Ellul, J. *Autopsie de la révolution.* Paris: Calmann-Lévy, 1969.

Freire, P. *Pedagogy of the Oppressed.* New York: Seabury, 1970.

González, V. F. "Revolución en América Latina." Cuernavaca, 1968. (pro manuscripto).

Griewank, K. *Der neuzeitliche Revolutionsbegriff.* 2d ed. Frankfurt am Main: Europäische Verlagsanstalt, 1969.

Hunter, R. *Revolution: Why, How, When?* New York and London: Harper and Brothers, 1940.

Jankélévitch, S. *Révolution et Tradition.* Paris: J. B. Janin, 1947.

Johnson, Ch. *Revolution and the Social System.* Palo Alto, Calif.: The Hoover Institution, Stanford University, 1964.

———. *Revolutionary Change.* Boston: Little, Brown and Co., 1966.

Kaplan, A. M., ed. *The Revolution in World Politics.* New York, London, Sydney: John Wiley and Sons, 1962.

Keyserling, C. H. *La révolution mondiale et la responsabilité de l'Esprit.* Paris: Delamain et Boutelleau, 1934.

Kuhn, S. *The Structure of Scientific Revolution.* 2d ed. Chicago: University of Chicago Press, 1970.

Kurtz, P., and S. Stojanovic. *Tolerance and Revolution: A Marxist—Non-Marxist Humanist Dialogue.* Beograd: Philosophical Society of Serbia, 1970.

Leeuwen, A. Th. *Desarrollo y revolución.* Buenos Aires: La Aurora, 1967.

Lobkowicz, N. *Theory and Practice: History and Concept from Aristotle to Marx.* London.

Lowy, M. *La théorie de la révolution chez le jeune Marx.* Paris: F. Maspero, 1970.

Lucini, G. F. "Teologia della Rivoluzione." In *Contributi dell'Istituto di Filosofia.* Filosofia 15, Serie III, vol. 2, 195–221. Milan: Vita e Pensiero, 1972.

Lutz, Wm., and H. Brent. *On Revolution.* Cambridge, Mass.: Winthrop Publishers, 1971.

Mazlish, B., ed. *Revolution: A Reader.* New York: Macmillan, 1971.

Mendieta y Nuñez, L. *Teoría de la revolución.* Mexico City: Biblioteca de Ensayos Sociológicos, Universidad Nacional, 1958.

Ortega y Gasset, J. *El tema de nuestro tiempo.* 2d ed. Buenos Aires, Mexico City: Espasa-Calpe Argentina, 1939.

Panikkar, R. "Die Philosophie in der geistigen Situation der Zeit." In *Akten des XIV Internationalen Kongresses für Philosophie,* vol. 6, September 2–9. Vienna: Herder, 1968.

———. "Le concept d'ontonomie." In *Actes du Xiè. Congrès International de Philosophie, Bruxelles 20–26, August 1953.* Vol. 3, 182–88. Louvain: Nauwelaerts, 1953.

———. "The Law of *Karman* and the Historical Dimension of Man." In *Philosophy East and West* 22, no. 1 (January 1972): 25–43.

Pablo, J. *Mística, desarrollo y revolución.* Montevideo: Mundo Nuevo, 1969.

Petras, J., and M. Zeitlin, eds. *Latin America—Reform or Revolution?* New York: Fawcett, 1968.

Puligandla, R., and K. Puhakka. "Buddhism and Revolution." In *Philosophy East and West* 20, no. 4 (October 1970): 345–68.

Raines, J., and Th. Dean, eds. *Marxism and Radical Religion: Essays Toward a Revolutionary Humanism.* Philadelphia: Temple University Press, 1970.

Roszak, Th. *The Making of a Counterculture.* New York: Doubleday, 1967.

Seifert, R. *El Sí de la no-violencia.* Montevideo: Editorial Movimiento de Reconciliación, 1965.

Shaull, R. "The End of the Road of a New Beginning." In J. D. Raines and Th. Dean, eds. *Marxism and Radical Religion: Essays Toward a Revolutionary Humanism.* Philadelphia: Temple University Press, 1970.

Trotsky, L. *The Permanent Revolution (and) Results and Prospects.* New York: Pioneer Publisher, 1965.

Urdaneta, I. *Polémica en la revolución.* Caracas: Editorial Nueva Izquierda: 1969.

Chapter 7. Is The Notion of Human Rights a Western Concept?

1. Cf. probably the first Symposium of its kind convened by UNESCO at Bangkok in December 1979, *Meeting of Experts on the Place of Human Rights in Cultural and Religious Traditions,* where nine major schools of religious thought discussed the issue and recognized "that many of them have not paid sufficient attention to human rights... (and that) it is a task of the different religions of the world to deepen and eventually to enlarge and/or reformulate the urgent and important issue of human rights." 116, g of the Final Report SS-79/CONF, 607/10 of February 6, 1980. The entire report is worth reading.

2. By diatopical hermeneutics I understand a thematic reflection on the fact that the loci (*topoi*) of historically unrelated cultures make it prob-

lematic to understand one tradition with the tools of another, and the hermeneutical attempt to bridge such gulfs. Cf. R. Panikkar, *Myth, Faith and Hermeneutics* (New York: Paulist Press, 1979), 8ff.

3. Cf. R. Panikkar, *The Intrareligious Dialogue* (New York: Paulist Press, 1978), xii. The two words *Brahman* and *God,* for instance, are neither analogous nor merely equivocal (nor univocal, of course). They are not exactly equivalent either. They are *homeomorphic.* They perform a certain type of respectively corresponding function in the two different traditions where these words are alive.

4. I shall capitalize Human Rights when these words have the particular meaning derived from this "Universal Declaration."

5. The dates to recall are: December 10, 1948: Universal Declaration of San Francisco; November 4, 1950: Mandatory International Law; March 20, 1952: Paris Clause; December 16, 1966: Covenant on Economic, Social and Cultural Rights; Covenant on Civil and Political Rights Optional Protocol (to the latter—not passed unanimously).

6. For the astounding documents of the first nine Christian centuries, cf. the collection and translation with insightful introduction by H. Rahner, *Kirche und Staat* (Munich: Kosel, 1961). The first edition, published in 1943 during the Second World War with the title *Abendlandische Kirchenfreiheit,* is in itself a document for Human Rights.

Because it is less known than the *Magna Carta* of King John of England in 1215, let us mention King Alfonso IX of Leon in 1188 with his rights to life, honor, home and property.

Interesting also is the statement and justification of Francisco de Vitoria in 1538: "*Cuando los súbditos tengan conciencia de la injusticia de la guerra, no les es lícito ir a ella,* sea que se equivoquen o no" (emphasis mine). *De los indios o del derecho de la guerra,* 2, 23 (Madrid: Ed. BAC, 1960), 831. ("When its subjects are aware of the injustice of a war, it is not lawful for them to go to it, *whether they are in error or not.*") And the reason he gives is to quote Rom. 14:23: "*omne quod non est ex fide peccatum est,*" which he translates "*todo lo que no es según* conciencia *es pecado*" (ibid., emphasis added). The Pauline passage is usually rendered: "Whatever does not come from faith is sin." Vitoria's variation reads: "Whatever is not in accordance with one's *conscience* is a sin." Cf. the Thomistic principle that the rational being that is Man has to follow his or her personal conscience in order to act morally.

7. Just as a memorandum, we may recall: 1689: Bill of Rights (England); 1776: Virginia Bill of Rights; 1789 (August 26): Déclaration des droits de l'homme et des citoyens; 1798: American Bill of Rights.

8. The San Francisco document is a *declaration,* a manifest statement making clear what is already there, an explicitation (*dēclarare,* to make clear—from de-clarāre. Cf. *clarus,* clear, but also loud [*clamor*]). It is not a law, a superimposition, a human creation, but the recognition or discovery of something intrinsic to the nature of the thing; in this case "the inherent

dignity and equal and inalienable rights of all the members of the human family," as the Preamble to the 1948 Declaration says.

9. This practical a-theism and even practical ignorance of any ulterior philosophical issue or religious factor became patent in the presentation and discussion of the Bangkok Conference mentioned above, let alone in the more official meetings where Philosophy and Religion have hardly a voice.

10. Cf. R. Panikkar, "Singularity and Individuality: The Double Principle of Individuation," in *Revue Internationale de Philosophie,* 19, 1–2, nos. 111–12 (1975): 141–66, where it is argued that the ontic status of human individuals is basically different from that of all other individual entities; in short, that we cannot treat human individuals as we could peanuts or cattle, by a merely numerical individuality.

11. "The will of the people shall be the basis of the authority of government" (Art. 21, 2 of the Declaration).

12. "In the exercise of his rights and freedoms, everyone shall be subject only to such limitations as are determined by law *solely* for the purpose of securing due recognition and respect for the rights and freedoms of others and of meeting the *just* requirements of *morality, public order* and the general *welfare* in a democratic society." Art. 29, 2 (emphasis of the problematic words added).

13. We do not include here a fourth source of dissent, namely the *political,* because the argument in such cases bears mainly on different interpretations of facts, emphases, and factors other than those related to the nature of Human Rights. Cf. as a single example: *Colloques de Riyad, de Paris, du Vatican, de Genève et de Strasbourg sur le dogme musulman et les droits de l'homme en Islam* (Riyad: Ministère de la Justice; Beyrouth: Dar al Kitab Allubhani, 1974); and D. Sidorsky, ed., *Essays on Human Rights, Contemporary Issues and Jewish Perspective* (Philadelphia: Jewish Publication Society, 1979).

14. "Human rights, in short, are statements of basic needs and interests." S. I. Benn, *The Encyclopedia of Philosophy* (New York: Macmillan, 1967), s.v. Rights, speaking about the U.N. Declaration.

15. Cf. K. Marx, *Zur Judenfrage* 1, 352.

16. "*Keine Rechte ohne Pflichten, keine Pflichten ohne Rechte,*" Marx-Engels, *Werke* 17, 521; in G. Klaus, M. Buhr, *Philosophisches Worterbuch* (Leipzig: VEB, 1976), s.v. "Menschenrechte."

17. Cf. R. Panikkar, "Aporias in the Comparative Philosophy of Religion," *Man and World* 13, 3–4 (The Hague: Martinus Nijhoff, 1980): 357–83.

18. *Tao Te Ching,* 18.

19. The *Mananadharmasastra* (2–4) puts the same idea in a more sophisticated way: To act from a desire for reward is reprehensible. Yet without that desire, no action is possible. Laws are needed to put order into those human actions.

20. A recent example: A Catholic missionary, after over a year of really

living together with an Asian tribe and sharing with the people their respective beliefs, thinks that the moment has come for some formal conversions, since they are already practically Christians. He talks matters over with the enthusiasts about Christianity: "Would you like to become officially and publicly Christians? You are already convinced..." et cetera. Answer: "No, because some other people in the tribe are not ready." "But it is your *right!*" says the missionary. "You have the *right* to decide by yourselves—all the more since you neither harm nor despise the others." The answer is cutting: "We only have the right to take this step if the whole tribe does it."

21. From the root *dhr,* to hold, to maintain, keep together. Cf. Latin *tenere* and English *tenet.*

22. Manu, I, 31 and I, 87.

23. Cf. the famous *lokasamgraha* of the *Gītā,* and the well-known definition of the *Mahābhārata:* "that which maintains and sustains the peoples" (*Karnaparvam,* LXIX, 59).

24. A recent example may illuminate the issue: In July 1981 the Indian nation is in an uproar because some 352 outcastes of the small village of Minakshipuram in Tamilnadu converted to Islam, probably in protest and reaction against their ostracism (to say the least) from the Hindu caste-communities. For our point it is interesting to remark that H. H. Sri Vishvesva Tirtha Swamiji of Pejavar Mutt along with many other Hindu religious leaders can now—for obviously political and opportunistic reasons—raise their voices against untouchability and discrimination without paying attention to the *Manaradharmaśastra* (III, 150; 157; III, 92; IV, 79, 213; IX, 238–39; etc.) and other sacred Laws sanctioning the system. Cf. the Indian press from May to August 1981; e.g., *The Hindu* from Madras, May 26; July 15, 18, 28, 29, 20; August 2; etc.

Chapter 9. The Invisible Harmony

1. See, e.g., "Die existentielle Phänomenologie der Wahrheit," *Philosophisches Jahrbuch der Göttesgesellschaft,* 1964 (Munich, 1965), 27–54; *Religionen und die Religion* (Munich: Max Hueber, 1965); "La philosophie de la religion devant le pluralisme philosophique et la pluralité des religions," in *Pluralisme philosophique et pluralité des religions,* ed. E. Castelli (Paris: Aubier, 1977), 193–201; "*Colligite Fragmenta:* For an Integration of Reality," in *From Alienation to At-Oneness: Proceedings of the Theology Institute of Villanova University,* ed. F. A. Eigo (Villanova University Press, 1977), 19–91; "Ṛtatattva: A Preface to a Hindu-Christian Theology," *Jeevadhara* 49 (January–February 1977): 6–63; *The Intrareligious Dialogue* (New York: Paulist Press, 1978); "The Myth of Pluralism: The Tower of Babel—A Meditation on Non-Violence; Panikkar in Santa Barbara," *Cross Currents* 29, no. 2 (Summer 1979): 197–230; "Hermeneutics of Comparative Religion: Paradigms and Models," *Journal of Dharma* 5, no. 1 (January–March 1980): 38–51; "Aporias in the Comparative Philos-

ophy of Religion," in *Man and World*, 13, nos. 3–4 (The Hague: Martinus Nijhoff, 1980): 357–83; "Words and Terms," in *Esistenza, Mito, Ermeneutica (Scritti per Enrico Castelli)* 2, ed. M. Olivetti (Padua: CEDAM, 1980): 117–33; "Is the Notion of Human Rights a Western Concept?" *Diogenes* 120 (Winter 1982): 75–102; "The Dialogical Dialogue," in *The World's Religious Traditions*, ed. F. Whaling (Edinburgh: Clark, 1984), 201–21.

2. As a single example useful not only for its contents but also for its rich bibliographical references (mainly German, English, and French) see Llufs Duch, *Religió i món modern*. *Introducció a l'estudi dels fenòmens religiosos* (Montserrat: Abadia, 1984), which I wish could soon be translated from its original Catalan into some major European language.

3. R. Panikkar, *Myth, Faith and Hermeneutics* (New York: Paulist Press, 1979), 20.

4. See below, n. 32.

5. See Aristotle, *Met.*, II, 1 (993 b 30) as the *locus classicus* from which the Scholastic principle derived—although Aristotle's dictum is somewhat more subtle: *ekaston hōs échei tou einai outō kai tēs alētheías*. Compare the traditional Latin version: *unumquodque sicut se habet ad hoc quod sit, ita etiam se habet ad hoc quod habeat veritatem*. Or more literally: *Quare unumquodque sicut se habet ut sit, ita et ad veritatem*. Cf. Thomas Aquinas, *Summa Theol.*, I, q. 2, a. 3: *Quae sunt maxime vera sunt maxime entia*.

6. Jansen, ed., *Commentarium in Boethia De trinitate*, p. 11, in P. Gaia, *Opere religiose di Nicolò Cusano*, Classici delle religioni (Turin: UTET, 1971), 636.

7. Cf. the astounding text of Plato, *Philebus*, 66a, where, after measure as the first value, comes proportion, and only thirdly reason, followed by *techné*, and fifthly pleasure.

8. Wis. 11:21: *Omnia in mensura (metrō), et numero (arithmō), et pondere (stathmō) disposuisti*.

9. The two modern symbols could be the two seventeenth-century figures of Descartes (*cogito ergo sum*) and Pascal (*le coeur a ses raisons que la raison ne connaît point*).

10. Suffice it to quote the famous *Brahma-sūtra* text, I, 1, 4: *Tat tu samanvayāt* ("But that [because of] the harmony") of all texts of all the sacred scriptures—in spite of the fact that they write, teach, and even command different and prima facie diverging things. Harmony is not uniformity. Even today in India religious understanding is rendered as *dharma samanvaya*. See *Prabuddha Bharata* 90 (April 1985): 190.

11. As P. Gaia, *Opere*, interprets the *unum* as *complicatio multorum* of Nicholas of Cusa.

12. See the insightful study of Maurice Boutin, "L'Un dispersif," in *Neoplatonismo e religione (Archivo di filosofia)* 51, nos. 1–3 (1983): 253–79, commenting on François Larvelle, *Le principe de minorité* (Paris: Aubier, 1981). There are *"des monades absolument dispersées et dépourvues de*

monadologie, de raison ou d'universel," says Larvelle, for individuals are the *"constituants ultimes de la réalité"* (ibid., 261).

13. Plato, *Phileb.*, 15 D, as *locus classicus.*

14. This is the rich concept of *homóuoia*, concord, unanimity, sameness of mind (*homó-uoia;* just as *homó-nomos* means of the same order, law) in the Hellenic tradition since Demosthenes. This concord is defined as *epistēmē koinōn agathōn* in the *Stoicum Veterum Fragmenta* 3, ed. H. von Arnim (Leipzig, 1903), 160; as the science of the common goods (in Liddell-Scott, *A Greek-English Lexicon,* Oxford, 1973). See the bibliographical references in Liddell-Scott and in N. G. L. Hammond and H. H. Scullard, eds., *The Oxford Classical Dictionary* (Oxford, 1973).

15. "Sameness (*ta homoia*) and the similar (*homóphyla*) do not need harmony; but the different (*anómoia*), the not-similar, and that which is not ordered need to be brought together through harmony," wrote the Pythagorean Philolaus of Kroton, Fragm. 6, in H. Diels-W. Kranz, *Die Fragmente der Vorsokratiker,* 9th ed. (Berlin: Weidmann, 1960). The entire text is fundamental.

16. *Samānī va ākūtiḥ / samānā hṛdayāni vaḥ / samānam astu vo mano / yathā vaḥ susāhāsati.* (Harmonious be your intention, / harmonious your hearts, / may your spirit be in harmony, / that you may be together in concord!) RV X, 191, 4. I give here a different translation from that in my anthology *The Vedic Experience* (Berkeley: University of California Press, 1977), 863.

17. Passim. See, e.g., *Innder Chapters* 2, in the translation of G. F. Feng and J. English (New York: Vintage Books, Random House, 1974), 46.

18. Fragm. 10. See Diels-Kranz, *Fragmente,* I, 410.

19. *"Per ço que enans nos puscam concordar"* are practically the last words of one of the three sages (Jewish, Christian, Muslim) after they left the gentile (who would choose the right *lig* [religion] without the knowledge of the three): Ramon Llull, *Libre del gentil e los tres savis,* in *Obres essencials* (Barcelona: Selecta, 1957), I, 1138. However, Llull is perhaps too much in favor of unity. See the dissertation by François Medeiros, "Judaïsme, Islam et Gentilité dans l'oeuvre de Raymond Lulle" (Munich: Evangelisch-theologische Fakultät, 1976).

20. *Dopo [Dio] comincia la belleza, perchè comincia la contrarietà, senze la quale non può essere cosa alcuna creata, ma sarebbe solo esse Dio: nè basta questa contrarietà e discordia di diverse nature a constituire la creatura, se per debito temperamento non diventa e la contrarietá unita e la discordia concorde, il che si può per vera deffinizione assignare di essa bellezza, cioèche non sia altro che una amica inimicizia e una concorde discordia. Per questo diceva Eraclito la guerra e la contenzione essere padre e genetrice delle cose; e, appresso Omero, chi maladisce la contenzione è detto avere bestemmiato la natura. Ma più perfettamente parlò Empedocle, ponendo, no la discordia per sè, ma insieme con la concordia essere principio de le cose, intendendo per la discordia la varietà delle nature di che*

si compongono, e per la concordia l'unione di quelle; e pero disse solo in Dio non essere discordia perchè in lui non è unione di diverse nature, anziè essa unità semplice sanza composizione alcuna (*Commento*, II, 9, in H. de Lubac, *Pic de la Mirandole* [Paris: Aubier Montaigne, 1974], 296, emphasis added). In *Heptaplus (aliud proemium)* he again writes about a discordant concord: *Quoniam sc. astricti vinculis concordiae uti naturas ita etiam appellationes hi omnes mundi mutua sibi liberalitate condonant: . . . occultas, ut ita dixerim, totius naturae et amicitias et affinitates edocti, . . . Accedit quod, qua ratione haec sunt distincta, quia tamen nulla est multitudo quae non sit una,* discordi quadam concordia ligantur *et multiformibus nexuum quasi catenis devinciuntur* (in de Lubac, *Pic*, 297; emphasis added).

21. See his work *De concordantia catholica* of 1433 and his *De pace fidei* of 1453, a few months after the defeat of Constantinople, although Cusanus falls into a dialectical *coincidentia*. Consider his revealing text: *Omnia enim in tantum sunt in quantum unum sunt. Complectitur autem tam ea quae sunt actu, quam ea quae ossunt fieri. Capacius est igitur unum quam ens, quod non est nisi actu est, licet Aristoteles dicat ens et unum converti (De venatione sapientiae,* 21).

22. E.g., Postel, *Concordia mundi; De orbis terrae concordia;* etc. Erasmus, *Querela pacis; Oratio de pace et discordia; Precatio pro pace Ecclesiae; De amabili Ecclesiae concordia;* Juan Luis Vives, *De concordia et discordia in humano genere* (1529); *De pacificatione* (1529); etc. See also Augusto Gentili, "Problemi del simbolismo armonico nella cultura postelizabettiana," in E. Castelli, ed., *Il Simbolismo del Tiempo* (Rome: Istituto di studi filosofici, 1973), 65.

23. "Introduce unity into diversity, and you create order; order yields harmony, proportion; harmony, where you have perfect integrity, begets beauty. There is beauty in an army when it has order in the ranks, when all the divisions combine to form a single armed force. There is beauty in music when voices, which are true, clear, distinct, blend to produce perfect consonance, perfect harmony, to achieve unity in diversity or diversity in unity—a good description might be *discordant concord;* better still, *concordant discord"* (François de Sales, *Traité de l'amour de Dieu,* I, 1 [1616]; translated by R. C. Zaehner at the beginning of his book cited in the next note).

24. *Concordant Discord: The Interdependence of Faiths,* The Gifford Lectures, 1967–1969 (Oxford: Clarendon Press, 1970).

25. One quotation may suffice: *So wird also die Universalgeschichte, die Geschichtsphilosophie und die Zukunftsgestaltung in Wahrheit zu einem möglichst einheitlichen Selbstverständnis des eigene Gewordenseins und der eigene Entwicklung. Für uns gibt es nur die Universalgeschichte der europäischen Kultur, die natürlich der vergleichenden Blicke auf fremde Kulturen praktisch und theoretisch bedarf, um sich selbst und ihr Verhältnis zu den anderen zu verstehen, die aber mit den andern dadurch nicht et-*

*was in eine allegemeine Menschheitsgeschichte und Menschheitsentwicklung
zusammenfliessen kann.* Unsere *Universalgeschichte ist um so mehr ein
europäisches Selbstverständnis, als nur der Europäer bei seiner Häufung ver-
schiedenster Kulturelemente, seinem niemals ruhenden Intellekt und seiner
unausgesetzt strebenden Selbstbildung eines solchen universalhistorischen
Bewusstseins auf kritischer Forschungsgrundlage für seine Seele bedarf*
(E. Troeltsch, *Der Historismus und seine Probleme* [Tübingen: Mohr, 1922;
reprint, Aalen, 1961], vol. 3 of the *Gesammelte Schriften,* 71). I feel that
most of the efforts at universalizing are still under this post-Hegelian spell.
Der Europäismus is, significantly enough, the title of Troeltsch's chap. 4,
part 2.

26. *Tao Te Ching,* 22; also 40, 51, 62, etc.

27. Plutarch, *Caes.*, 50, 3 (*ēlthon, eizon, enikēsa*) and also *Moralia,* 206
e; quoted also in other sources: Lucius Annaeus Florus (second century),
2, 13, 63; Dio Cassius (second century), 42, 48; up to the twelfth-century
Byzantine historian Johannes Zonaras, 10, 10; etc.

28. See G. Oberhammer, ed., *Inklusivismus: Eine indische Denkform*
(Vienna: Institut für Indologie, 1983).

29. I have now translated my motto differently. *Aphanēs* means literally
"without being *phaneros*" (visible, apparent), from the verb *pháinō,* "to
shine, illumine," and thus "let know, appear, manifest." The root *pha (phn,
phan...)* means "to shine" (cf. fantasy), but immediately related to *phëmn:*
"to say," *phásis,* "the word" *phōnē* (cf. prophet)—cf. voice, symphony,
phenomenology, epiphany, telephone, etc.

30. Heraclitus, Fragm. 8 (cf. also Empedocles, 124, 2). The text refers
probably first to music and from there to the wider reality. Cf. a standard
translation: *Das Widerstrebende vereinigte sich, aus den entgegengeset-
zten (Tönen) entstehe die schönste Harmonie, und alles Geschehen erfolge
auf dem Wege des Streites* (W. Capelle [translation and introductions],
Die Vorsokratiker: Die Fragmente und Quellenberichte [Stuttgart: Kröner;
Taschenausgabe Nr. 119, 1968], 134). W. D. Ross's standard translation
of Aristotle, *Nichomachean Ethics,* VIII (1555 b 4), reads: "and Heraclitus [saying] that 'it is what opposes that helps' and 'from different tones
comes the fairest tune' and 'all things are produced through strife.'" See
the book with which Romano Guardini practically began his intellectual ca-
reer, *Der Gegensatz und Gegensätze: Entwurf eines Systems der Typenlehre*
(Freiburg: Herder, 1917), which had substantial revisions until the 2d edition of 1955 with the title *Der Gegensatz: Versuche zu einer Philosophie
des Lebendig-Konkreten.*

31. The word *eris,* from *erei* or *er* (cf. German *errege, reize*), means
"strife, quarrel, struggle, discord, disputation." *Eris* is also the goddess
of discord in the marriage of Peleus and Thetis. In the *Eumenides* (975)
of Aeschylus, *eris agathōn* appears with a positive meaning. For *eris* see
also Fragm. 80: *polemon eónta xunón kaì dikēn erin kai ginómena panta
kat' erin kai chreōn* ["One should know that] strife is the common thing,

along with the right to struggle, and that all things happen by struggle and necessity."

32. See Fragm. 51, in Diels-Kranz, *Vorsokratiker,* I, 162, and its Platonic commentary in *Symposium,* 187, with the famous metaphor of the arc (bow) and the lyre, quoted in the epigraph of this excursus. We could also translate: "The one conflicting with itself is brought into harmony with itself like the harmony of the bow and the lyre."

33. *Isōs de tōn enantiōn hē phýsis glichetai kaì ek toutōn apoteleï tò symphōnon, ouk ek tōn homoiōn.* See Diels-Kranz, *Vorsokratiker* (Heraklitos, fragm. 10). See also Aristotle, *De mundo* (5, 39 b, 7).

34. "Agonic" contains almost all the elements: it means *assembly, ágora,* gathering. This *gathering,* being a human one, is a *place of speech,* where the *word* is paramount. But persons speak in order to *contest* each other's opinions. *Agòn* is the *struggle,* either in battle or the mental agony (as we still say). It is this *vehemence* that elicits *power,* although, of course, sometimes *anxiety, agony.* A *trial, legal action,* can be *agonizing activities.* All the English words in italics are meanings of this word whose root means precisely "to lead, to carry, to fetch, bring, take," etc. Cf. *agós,* the leader. The root *ago* means to "lead." Cf. Sanskrit *ajah,* to "drive, push."

35. As a single and yet multivalent example I may quote the first lines of the Preface of the Spanish classic *La Celestina* of Fernando de Rojas (first edition, Burgos, 1499): *Todas las cosas ser criadas a manera de contienda o batalla, dice aquel gran sabio Heráclito en este modo:* Omnia secundum litem fiunt. *Sentencia a mi ver digna de perpetua y recordable memoria.... Hallé esta sentencia corroborada por aquel gran orador y poeta laureado Petrarca, diciendo:* Sine lite atque offensione nihil genuit natura parens. *Sin lid y ofensión* [*combate* in modern Spanish] *ninguna casa engendró la natura, madre de todo.* [I note parenthetically that *parens* is here translated *madre.*] In the Roman religion the earth is called *sacra parens;* see J. Ries, *Le sacré comme approche de Dieu et comme ressource de l'homme, Coll. Conferences et Travaux,* no. 1 (Louvaine: la Neuve, 1983).] *Dice más adelante:* Sic est enim, et sic propemodum universa testantur: rapido stellae obviant firmamento; contraria invicem elementa configunt; terrae tremunt; maria fluctuant; aer quatitur; crepant flammae; bellum immortale venti gerunt; tempora temporibus concertant; secum singula, nobiscum omnia. *Que quiere decir; "En verdad así es, y así todas las cosas de esto dan testimonio: Las estrellas se encuentran en el arrebatado firmamento del cielo, los adversos elementos unos con otros rompen pelea, tremen* [in modern Spanish *tiemblan*] *las tierras, ondean los lares, el aire se sacude, suenan las llamas, los vientos entre sí traen perpetua guerra, los tiempos con tiempos contienden y litigan entre si, uno a uno, y todas contra nosotros."... Mayormente pues ella con todas las otras cosas que al mundo son, van debajo de la bandera de esta notable sentencia: "Que aun la misma vida de los hombres, si bien lo miramos, desde la primera edad hasta*

que blanquean las canas, es batalia" edited by Bruno Mario Damiani, *La Celestina* 11th ed. [Madrid: Ediciones Cátedra, 1983], 45–47).

36. See the well-known book by Miguel de Unamuno, *La agonía del cristianismo* (Madrid: Renacimiento, 1931); the French edition dates from 1925 (Paris: F. Rieder).

37. *No es menor la disensión de los filósofos en las escuelas, que la de las ondas del mar* (Rojas, *La Celestina,* 48).

38. *Animus* translates not only the Greek *psychē* but also *thymos* and *pneúma*, although it has its exact Greek counterpart in *anemos*—in Sanskrit *aniti (anilaḥ),* meaning "to breathe."

39. The Latin *sentire* (whence "sense" derives) means to feel (cf. sentiment) and thus also to discern by the senses (sensible, sensibility, etc.); it means also *sentis,* a path (cf. Spanish *sendero*) and thus direction. Cf. Old High German: *sinnen,* to go and also to think (to feel one's way).

40. The etymology of Latin *gratum,* Sanskrit *gurtas,* pleasure, and also joy, is related to *charis,* meaning gracious, grace, joy, gratuitousness, agreeable, favor, charity. Cf. Spanish *agradar,* to please.

41. See KenU, II, 3 (and also RV I, 164, 32), etc.

42. "Knowing others is wisdom. Knowing the self is enlightenment" (*Tao Te Ching,* 33). The reason is apparent. I can know others by shedding the light of my knowledge on them. But I cannot know myself in this way. It needs another light falling upon me from outside me. I need to be illumined in order to be enlightened—i.e., I need to be *known* by somebody else, I need to be *loved.* Cf. *èpignōsomai kathōs kaì epegnōsthen,* "I shall know as I am known"; *cognoscam sicut et cognitus sum,* in the Vulgate (1 Cor. 13:12). Here is the locus of grace—again an openness and movement.

43. RV X, 129, 4 and 190, 1; etc.

44. B G III, 20 and 25.

45. RV X, 90, 16: *dharmani prathamani.* Cf. B G VII, 11.

46. Acts 2:11.

47. This ending is not just a phrase. The core of Western culture is based on the ultimate binomial Being/Thinking, or in theological vocabulary: Father/Son (*Logos*). This basic dyad has often obscured the trinitarian paradigm, which alone overcomes the strictures of science ("the laws of nature are immutable") and makes room for freedom—as I have indicated elsewhere.

Bibliography

Books of Raimon Panikkar are listed in the order of composition, in their latest and, where available, English-language editions.

F. H. Jacobi y la filosofía del sentimiento. Buenos Aires: Sapientia, 1948.

El concepto de naturaleza: Análisis histórico y metafísico de un concepto. Madrid: Consejo Superior de Investigaciones Científicas, 1972 [1951].

La India: Gente, cultura y creencias. Madrid: Ediciones Rialp, 1960.

Patriotismo y cristiandad. Madrid: Ediciones Rialp, 1961.

Ontonomía de la ciencia: Sobre el sentido de la ciencia y sus relaciones con la filosofía. Madrid: Editorial Gredos, 1963.

Humanismo y Cruz. Madrid: Ediciones Rialp, 1963.

L'incontro delle religioni nel mondo contemporaneo: Morfosociologia dell'ecumenismo. Rome: Edizioni Internazionali Sociali, 1963.

Die vielen Götter und der eine Herr: Beiträge zum ökumenischen Gespräch der Weltreligionen. (Munich: O. W. Barth Verlag, 1963.

Religione e Religioni: Concordanza funzionale, essenziale ed esistenziale delle religioni. Brescia, Italy: Editrice Morcelliana, 1964.

The Unknown Christ of Hinduism: Towards an Ecumenical Christophany. Revised and enlarged edition. London: Darton, Longman and Todd; Maryknoll, N.Y.: Orbis Books, 1981 [1964].

Kultmysterium in Hinduismus und Christentum: Ein Beitrag zur vergleichenden Religionstheologie. Freiburg, Munich: Verlag Karl Alber, 1964.

Misterio y revelación: Hinduismo y cristianismo—encuentro de dos culturas. Madrid: Ediciones Marova, 1971 [1966].

Kerygma und Indien: Zur heilsgeschichtlichen Problematik der christlichen Begegnung mit Indien. Hamburg, Germany: Reich, 1967.

Offenbarung und Verkündigung: Indische Briefe. Freiburg, Germany: Verlag Herder, 1967.

Técnica y tiempo. Buenos Aires: Editorial Columba, 1967.

La joia pasqual. Montserrat, Spain: Abadia de Montserrat, 1988 [1968].

L'homme qui devient Dieu: La foi dimension constitutive de l'homme. Paris: Editions Aubier-Montaigne, 1970.

La presenza de Dio. Vicenza, Italy: Editrice La Locusta, 1970.

The Silence of God: The Answer of the Buddha. Maryknoll, N.Y.: Orbis Books, 1989 [1970].

Dimensioni mariane della vita. Vicenza, Italy: Editrice La Locusta, 1972.

Cometas: Fragmentos de un diario espiritual de la postguerra. Madrid: Euramérica, 1972.

Worship and Secular Man: An Essay on the Liturgical Nature of Man, Considering Secularization as a Major Phenomenon of Our Time and Worship as an Apparent Fact of All Times—A Study towards an Integral Anthropology. London: Darton, Longman and Todd; Maryknoll, N.Y.: Orbis Books, 1973.

The Trinity and the Religious Experience of Man: Icon, Person, Mystery. London: Darton, Longman and Todd; Maryknoll, N.Y.: Orbis Books, 1975 [1970].

Spiritualità indù: Lineamenti. Brescia, Italy: Editrice Morcelliana, 1975.

The Vedic Experience: Mantramañjarî: An Anthology of the Vedas for Modern Man and Contemporary Celebration. London: Darton, Longman and Todd; Berkeley, Los Angeles: University of California Press, 1977 (third Indian edition: New Delhi: Motilal Banarsidass, 1994).

The Intrareligious Dialogue. New York: Paulist Press, 1978.

Myth, Faith and Hermeneutics. New York: Paulist Press, 1979.

Blessed Simplicity: The Monk as Universal Archetype. New York: Seabury, 1982.

La torre de Babele: Pace e pluralismo. San Domenico de Florence: Edizioni Cultura della Pace, 1990.

A Dwelling Place for Wisdom. Louisville, Ky.: Westminster/John Knox Press, 1993.

La nueva inocencia. Estella, Spain: Editorial Verbo Divino, 1993.

The Cosmotheandric Experience: Emerging Religious Consciousness. Edited and introduced by Scott Eastham. Maryknoll, N.Y.: Orbis Books, 1993.

Escosofia: la nuova saggezza—per una spiritualità della terra. Assisi, Italy: Cittadella Editrice, 1993.

Paz y desarme cultural. Santander, Spain: Editorial Sal Terrae, 1993.

La experiencia de Dios. Madrid: PPC, 1994.

Cristofania. Bologna, Italy: EDB, 1994

Meinen wir denselben Gott? Ein Streitgesprach. With Pinchas Lapide. Munich: Kösel Verlag, 1994.

Il "daimôn" della politica: agonia e speranza. Bologna, Italy: EDB, 1995.